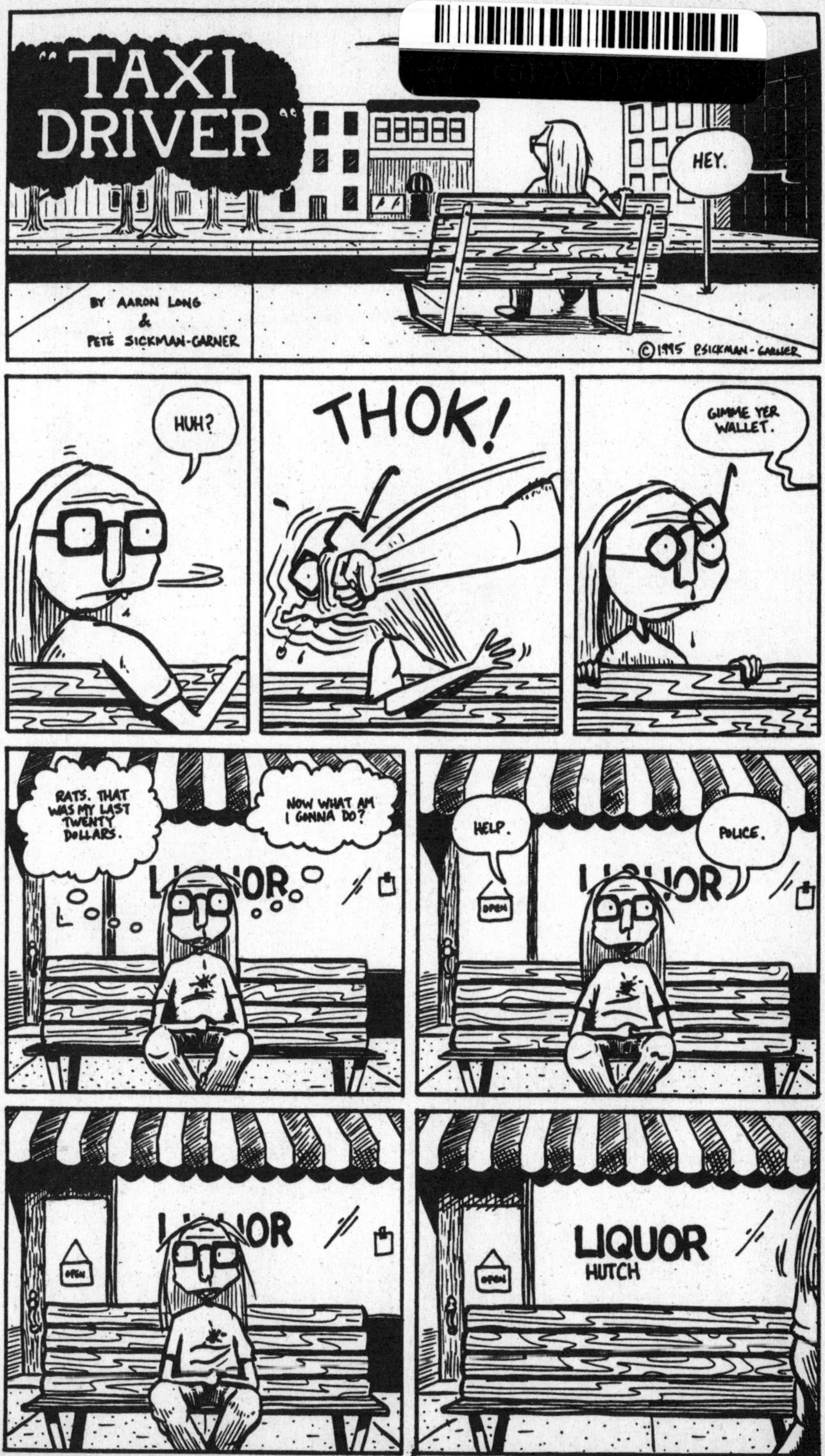
"TAXI DRIVER"
HEY.
BY AARON LONG & PETE SICKMAN-GARNER
©1995 P.SICKMAN-GARNER
HUH?
THOK!
GIMME YER WALLET.
RATS. THAT WAS MY LAST TWENTY DOLLARS.
NOW WHAT AM I GONNA DO?
HELP.
POLICE.
LIQUOR
LIQUOR HUTCH

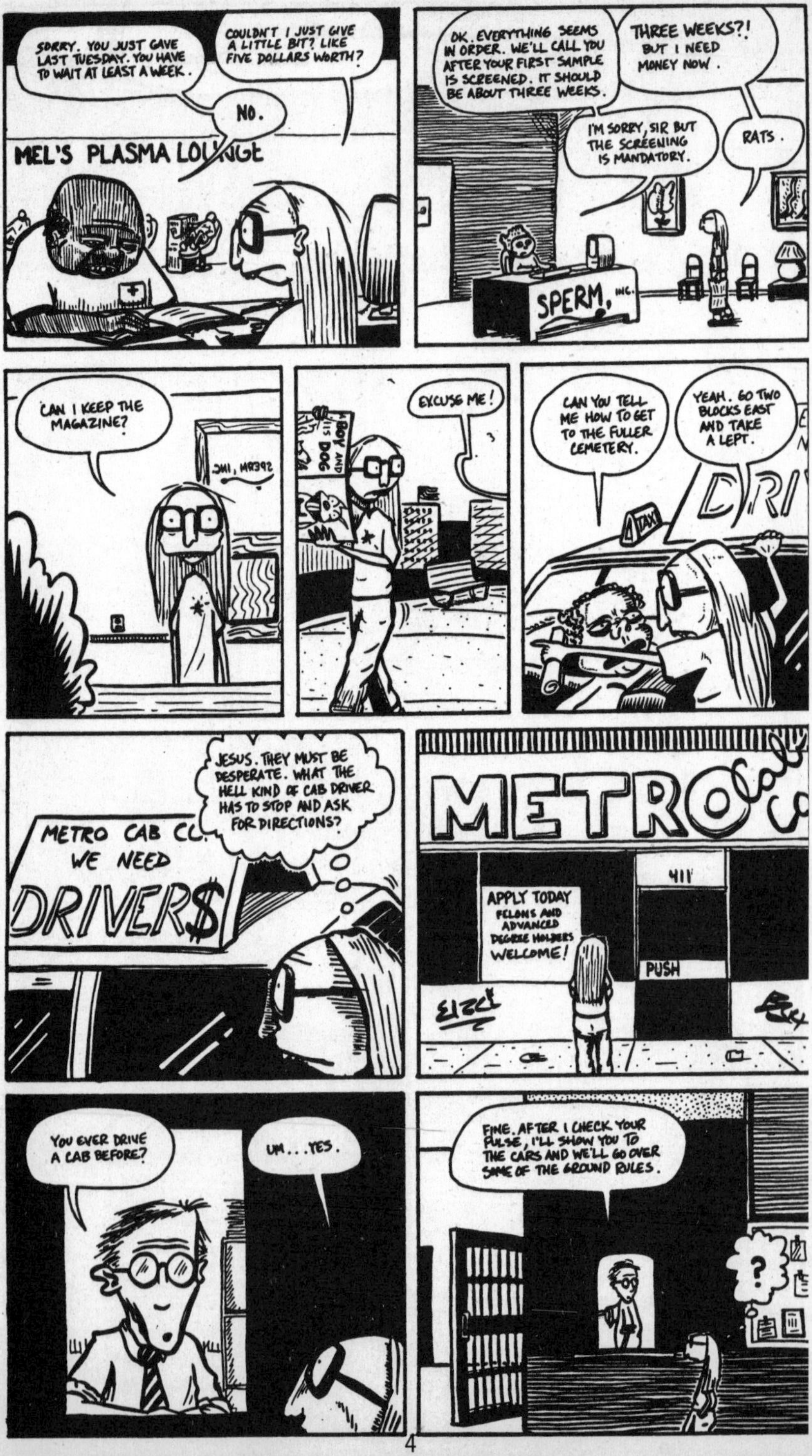
SORRY. YOU JUST GAVE LAST TUESDAY. YOU HAVE TO WAIT AT LEAST A WEEK.
COULDN'T I JUST GIVE A LITTLE BIT? LIKE FIVE DOLLARS WORTH?
NO.
MEL'S PLASMA LOUNGE
OK. EVERYTHING SEEMS IN ORDER. WE'LL CALL YOU AFTER YOUR FIRST SAMPLE IS SCREENED. IT SHOULD BE ABOUT THREE WEEKS.
THREE WEEKS?! BUT I NEED MONEY NOW.
I'M SORRY, SIR BUT THE SCREENING IS MANDATORY.
RATS.
SPERM, INC.
CAN I KEEP THE MAGAZINE?
EXCUSE ME!
A BOY AND HIS DOG
CAN YOU TELL ME HOW TO GET TO THE FULLER CEMETERY.
YEAH. GO TWO BLOCKS EAST AND TAKE A LEFT.
TAXI
JESUS. THEY MUST BE DESPERATE. WHAT THE HELL KIND OF CAB DRIVER HAS TO STOP AND ASK FOR DIRECTIONS?
METRO CAB CO.
WE NEED
DRIVER$
METRO
411
APPLY TODAY
FELONS AND ADVANCED DEGREE HOLDERS
WELCOME!
PUSH
YOU EVER DRIVE A CAB BEFORE?
UM... YES.
FINE. AFTER I CHECK YOUR PULSE, I'LL SHOW YOU TO THE CARS AND WE'LL GO OVER SOME OF THE GROUND RULES.
?

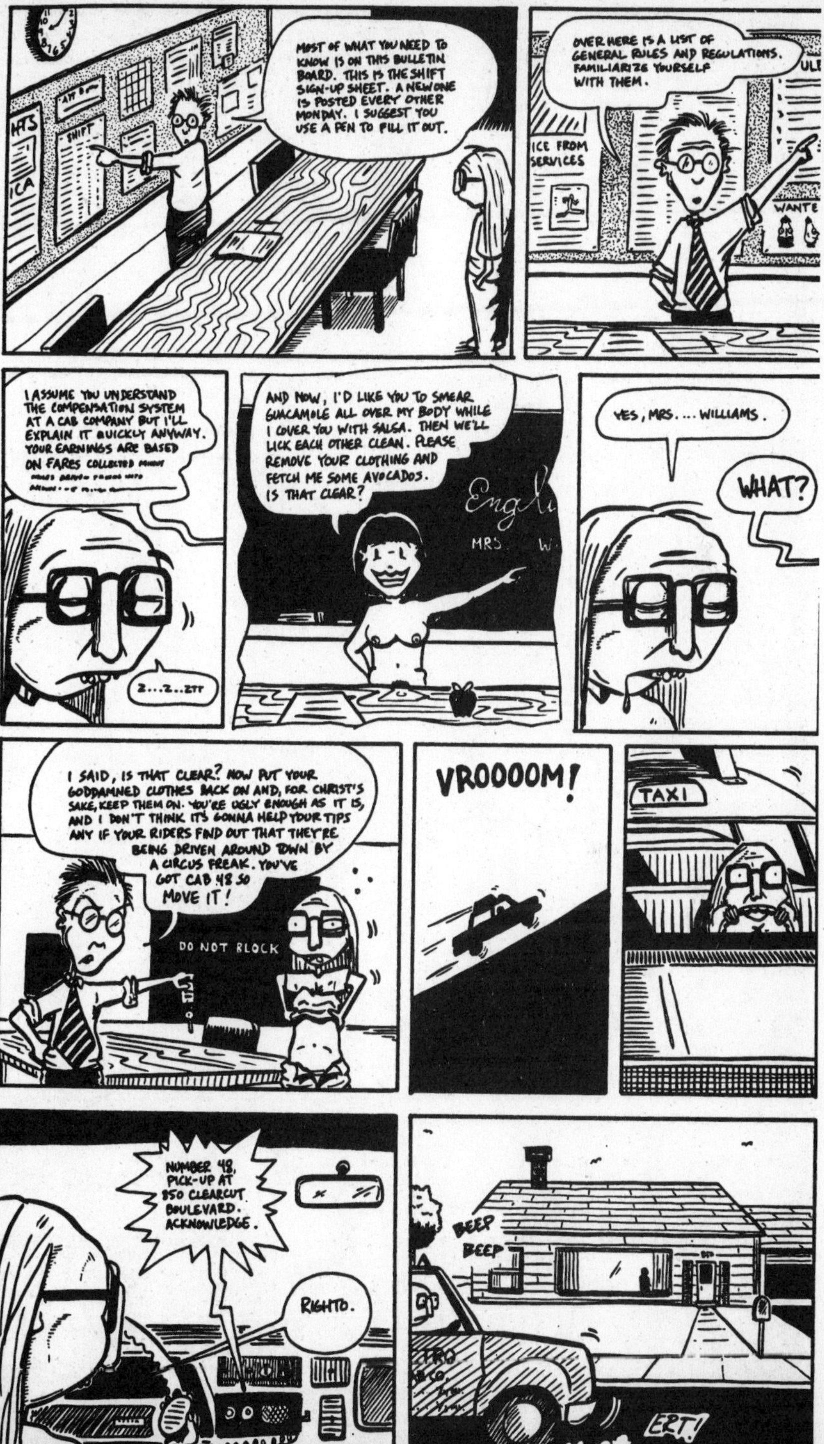
MOST OF WHAT YOU NEED TO KNOW IS ON THIS BULLETIN BOARD. THIS IS THE SHIFT SIGN-UP SHEET. A NEW ONE IS POSTED EVERY OTHER MONDAY. I SUGGEST YOU USE A PEN TO FILL IT OUT.
SHIFT
OVER HERE IS A LIST OF GENERAL RULES AND REGULATIONS. FAMILIARIZE YOURSELF WITH THEM.
ICE FROM SERVICES
WANTE
I ASSUME YOU UNDERSTAND THE COMPENSATION SYSTEM AT A CAB COMPANY BUT I'LL EXPLAIN IT QUICKLY ANYWAY. YOUR EARNINGS ARE BASED ON FARES
Z...Z...ZTT
AND NOW, I'D LIKE YOU TO SMEAR GUACAMOLE ALL OVER MY BODY WHILE I COVER YOU WITH SALSA. THEN WE'LL LICK EACH OTHER CLEAN. PLEASE REMOVE YOUR CLOTHING AND FETCH ME SOME AVOCADOS. IS THAT CLEAR?
MRS.
YES, MRS. ... WILLIAMS.
WHAT?
I SAID, IS THAT CLEAR? NOW PUT YOUR GODDAMNED CLOTHES BACK ON AND, FOR CHRIST'S SAKE, KEEP THEM ON. YOU'RE UGLY ENOUGH AS IT IS, AND I DON'T THINK IT'S GONNA HELP YOUR TIPS ANY IF YOUR RIDERS FIND OUT THAT THEY'RE BEING DRIVEN AROUND TOWN BY A CIRCUS FREAK. YOU'VE GOT CAB 48 SO MOVE IT!
DO NOT BLOCK
VROOOOM!
TAXI
NUMBER 48, PICK-UP AT 850 CLEARCUT BOULEVARD. ACKNOWLEDGE.
RIGHTO.
BEEP
BEEP
ERT!

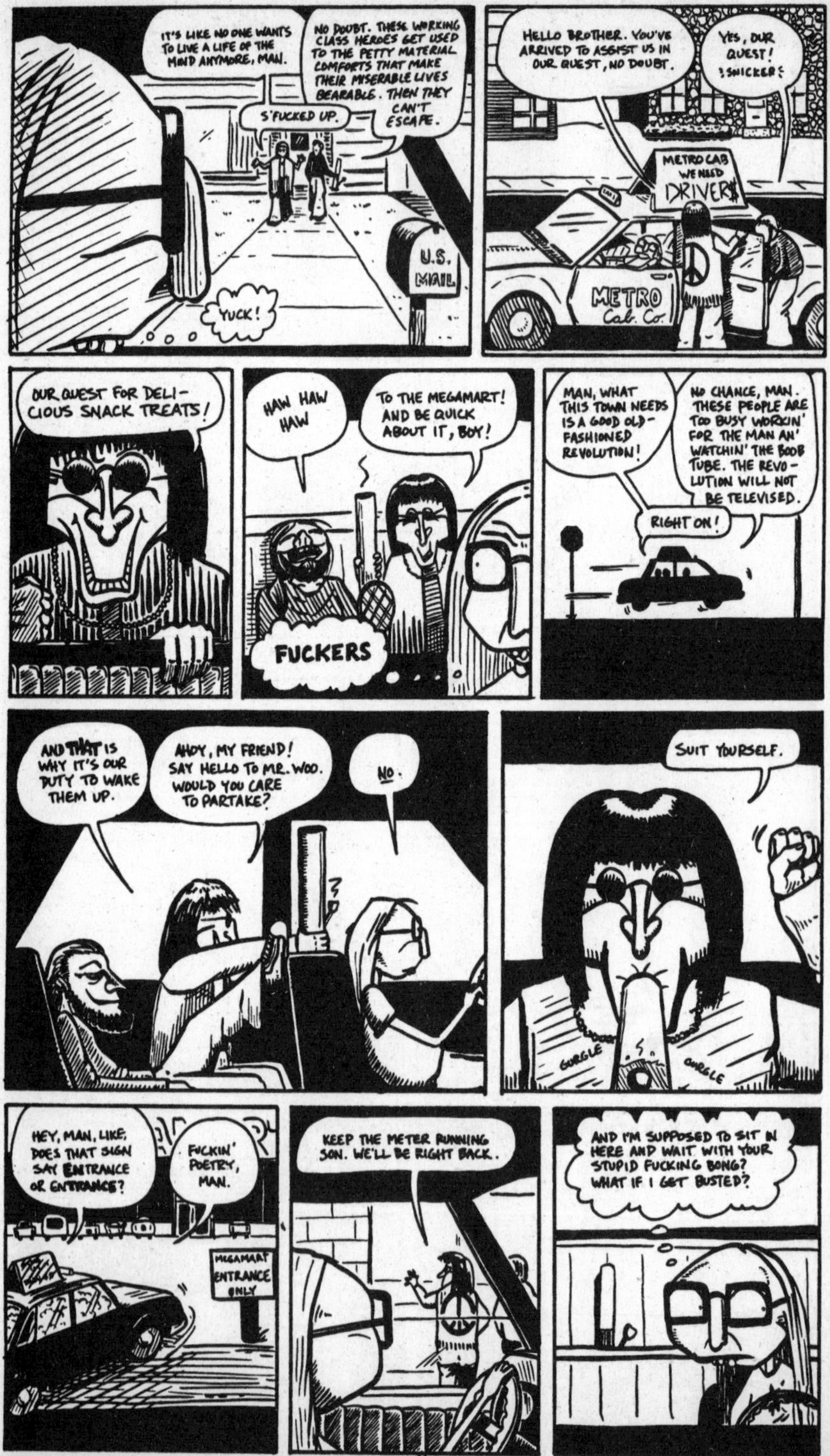
IT'S LIKE NO ONE WANTS TO LIVE A LIFE OF THE MIND ANYMORE, MAN.
NO DOUBT. THESE WORKING CLASS HEROES GET USED TO THE PETTY MATERIAL COMFORTS THAT MAKE THEIR MISERABLE LIVES BEARABLE. THEN THEY CAN'T ESCAPE.
S'FUCKED UP.
U.S. MAIL
YUCK!
HELLO BROTHER. YOU'VE ARRIVED TO ASSIST US IN OUR QUEST, NO DOUBT.
YES, OUR QUEST!
SNICKER
METRO CAB WE NEED DRIVER$
METRO Cab. Co.
OUR QUEST FOR DELI- CIOUS SNACK TREATS!
HAW HAW HAW
TO THE MEGAMART! AND BE QUICK ABOUT IT, BOY!
FUCKERS
MAN, WHAT THIS TOWN NEEDS IS A GOOD OLD-FASHIONED REVOLUTION!
NO CHANCE, MAN. THESE PEOPLE ARE TOO BUSY WORKIN' FOR THE MAN AN' WATCHIN' THE BOOB TUBE. THE REVO- LUTION WILL NOT BE TELEVISED.
RIGHT ON!
AND THAT IS WHY IT'S OUR DUTY TO WAKE THEM UP.
AHOY, MY FRIEND! SAY HELLO TO MR. WOO. WOULD YOU CARE TO PARTAKE?
NO.
SUIT YOURSELF.
GURGLE GURGLE
HEY, MAN, LIKE, DOES THAT SIGN SAY ENTRANCE OR ENTRANCE?
FUCKIN' POETRY, MAN.
MEGAMART ENTRANCE ONLY
KEEP THE METER RUNNING SON. WE'LL BE RIGHT BACK.
AND I'M SUPPOSED TO SIT IN HERE AND WAIT WITH YOUR STUPID FUCKING BONG? WHAT IF I GET BUSTED?

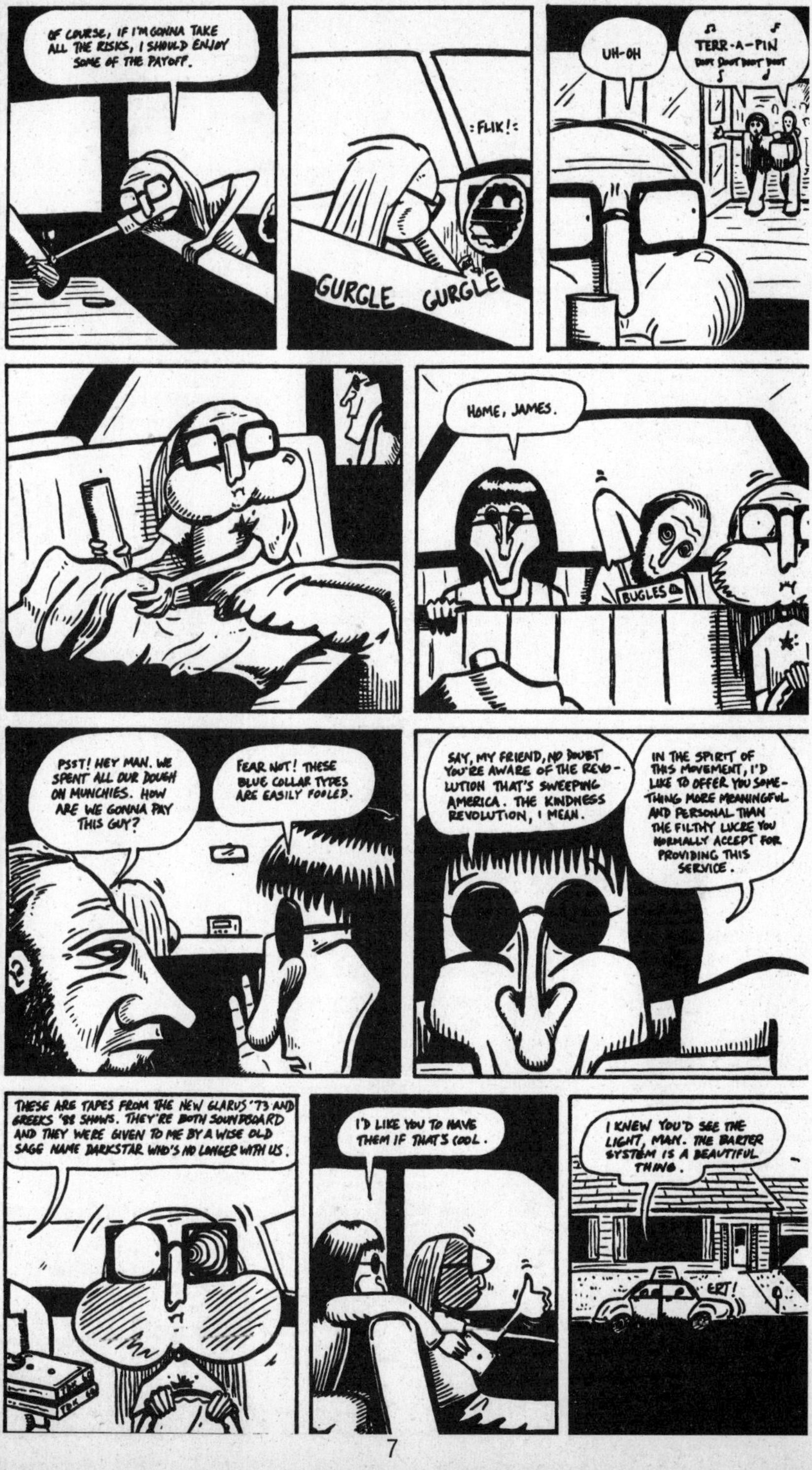
OF COURSE, IF I'M GONNA TAKE ALL THE RISKS, I SHOULD ENJOY SOME OF THE PAYOFF.
:FLIK!:
GURGLE GURGLE
UH-OH
TERR-A-PIN
HOME, JAMES.
BUGLES
PSST! HEY MAN. WE SPENT ALL OUR DOUGH ON MUNCHIES. HOW ARE WE GONNA PAY THIS GUY?
FEAR NOT! THESE BLUE COLLAR TYPES ARE EASILY FOOLED.
SAY, MY FRIEND, NO DOUBT YOU'RE AWARE OF THE REVOLUTION THAT'S SWEEPING AMERICA. THE KINDNESS REVOLUTION, I MEAN.
IN THE SPIRIT OF THIS MOVEMENT, I'D LIKE TO OFFER YOU SOMETHING MORE MEANINGFUL AND PERSONAL THAN THE FILTHY LUCRE YOU NORMALLY ACCEPT FOR PROVIDING THIS SERVICE.
THESE ARE TAPES FROM THE NEW GLARUS '73 AND GREEKS '88 SHOWS. THEY'RE BOTH SOUNDBOARD AND THEY WERE GIVEN TO ME BY A WISE OLD SAGE NAME DARKSTAR WHO'S NO LONGER WITH US.
I'D LIKE YOU TO HAVE THEM IF THAT'S COOL.
I KNEW YOU'D SEE THE LIGHT, MAN. THE BARTER SYSTEM IS A BEAUTIFUL THING.
ERT!

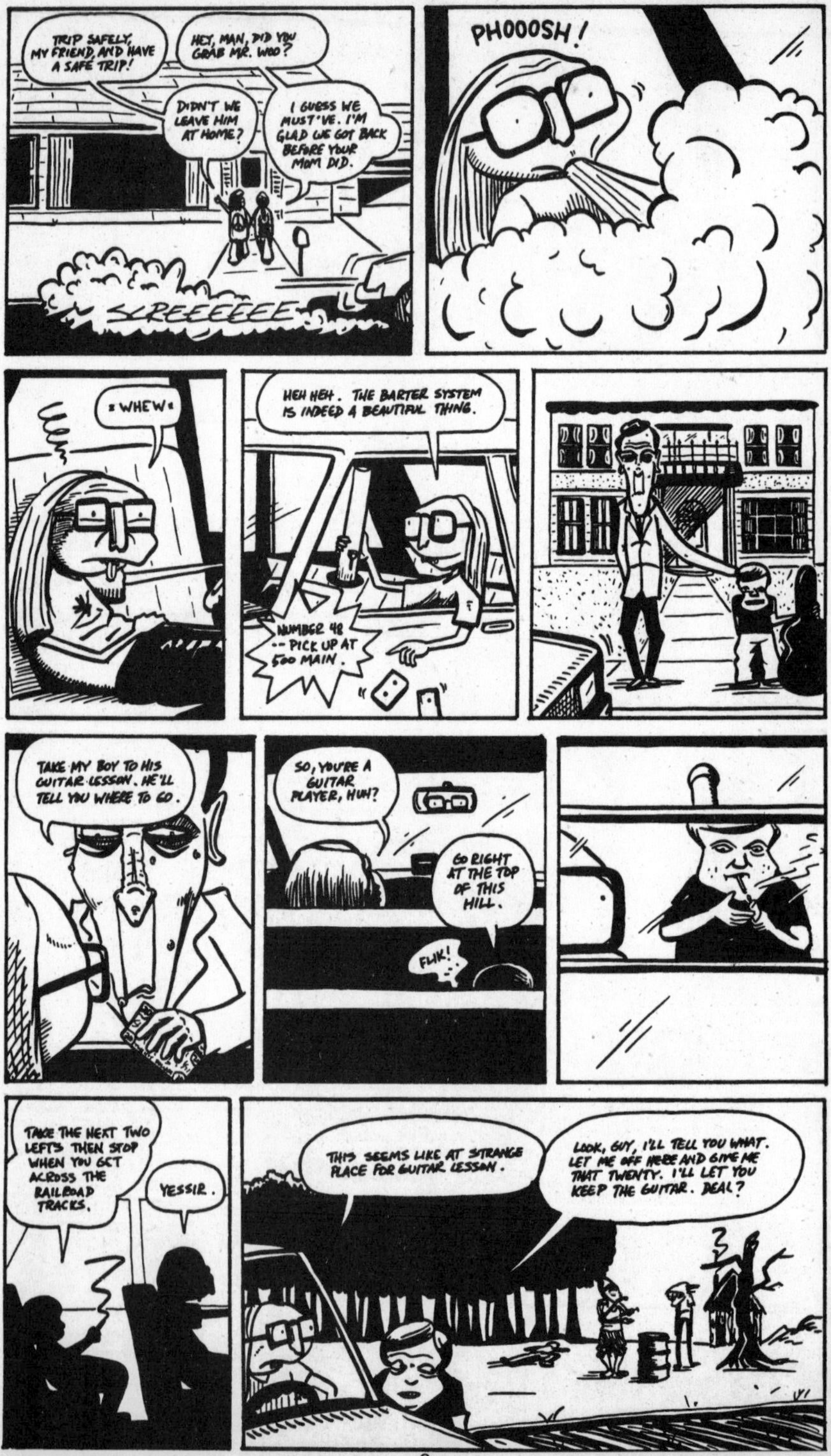
TRIP SAFELY, MY FRIEND, AND HAVE A SAFE TRIP!
HEY, MAN, DID YOU GRAB MR. WOO?
DIDN'T WE LEAVE HIM AT HOME?
I GUESS WE MUST'VE. I'M GLAD WE GOT BACK BEFORE YOUR MOM DID.
SCREEEEEEE
PHOOOSH!
WHEW
HEH HEH. THE BARTER SYSTEM IS INDEED A BEAUTIFUL THING.
NUMBER 48 -- PICK UP AT 500 MAIN.
TAKE MY BOY TO HIS GUITAR LESSON. HE'LL TELL YOU WHERE TO GO.
SO, YOU'RE A GUITAR PLAYER, HUH?
GO RIGHT AT THE TOP OF THIS HILL.
FLIK!
TAKE THE NEXT TWO LEFTS THEN STOP WHEN YOU GET ACROSS THE RAILROAD TRACKS.
YESSIR.
THIS SEEMS LIKE AT STRANGE PLACE FOR GUITAR LESSON.
LOOK, GUY, I'LL TELL YOU WHAT. LET ME OFF HERE AND GIVE ME THAT TWENTY. I'LL LET YOU KEEP THE GUITAR. DEAL?

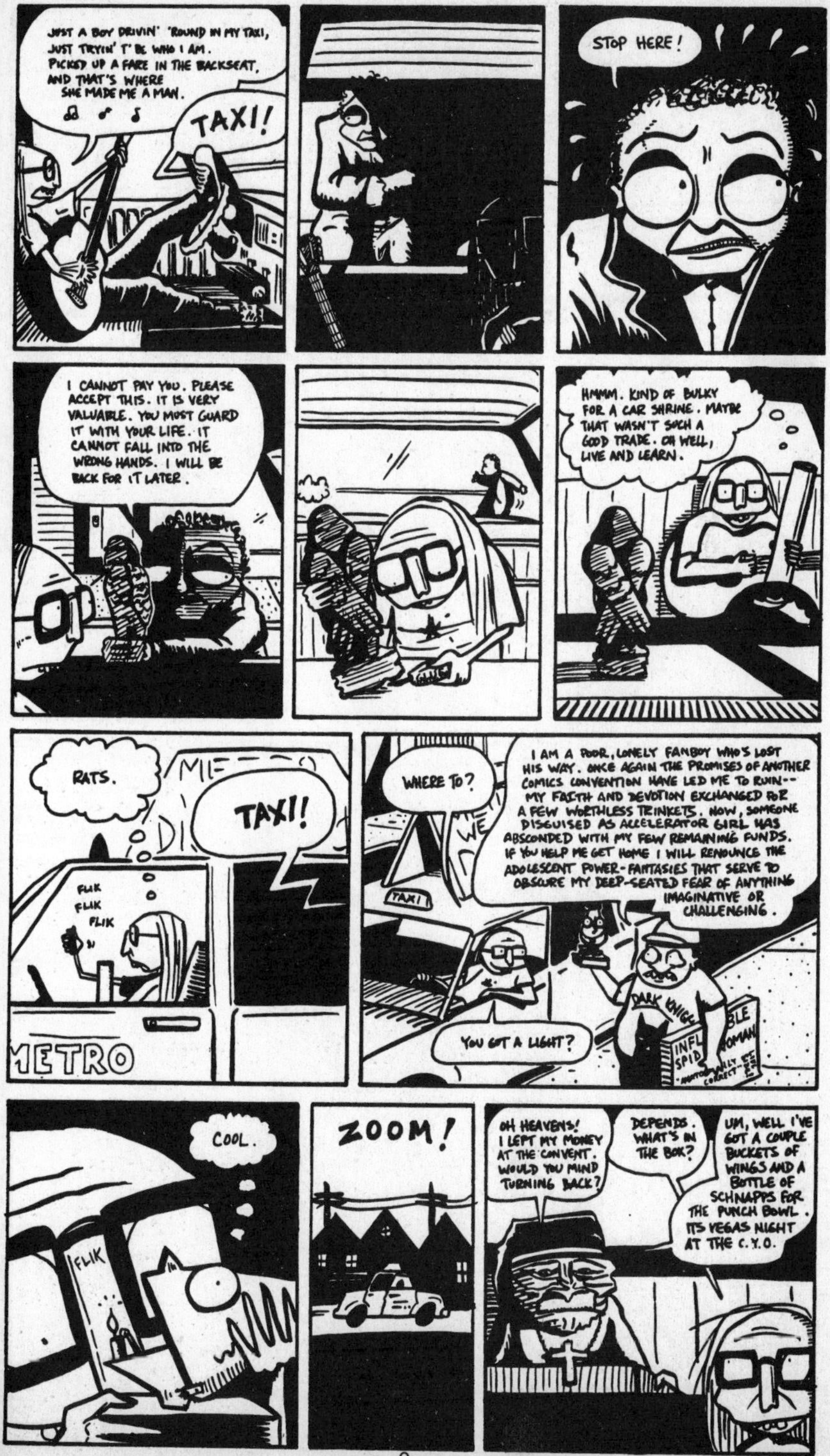
JUST A BOY DRIVIN' 'ROUND IN MY TAXI, JUST TRYIN' T' BE WHO I AM. PICKED UP A FARE IN THE BACKSEAT, AND THAT'S WHERE SHE MADE ME A MAN.
TAXI!
STOP HERE!
I CANNOT PAY YOU. PLEASE ACCEPT THIS. IT IS VERY VALUABLE. YOU MUST GUARD IT WITH YOUR LIFE. IT CANNOT FALL INTO THE WRONG HANDS. I WILL BE BACK FOR IT LATER.
HMMM. KIND OF BULKY FOR A CAR SHRINE. MAYBE THAT WASN'T SUCH A GOOD TRADE. OH WELL, LIVE AND LEARN.
RATS.
TAXI!!
FLIK
FLIK
FLIK
METRO
WHERE TO?
I AM A POOR, LONELY FANBOY WHO'S LOST HIS WAY. ONCE AGAIN THE PROMISES OF ANOTHER COMICS CONVENTION HAVE LED ME TO RUIN-- MY FAITH AND DEVOTION EXCHANGED FOR A FEW WORTHLESS TRINKETS. NOW, SOMEONE DISGUISED AS ACCELERATOR GIRL HAS ABSCONDED WITH MY FEW REMAINING FUNDS. IF YOU HELP ME GET HOME I WILL RENOUNCE THE ADOLESCENT POWER-FANTASIES THAT SERVE TO OBSCURE MY DEEP-SEATED FEAR OF ANYTHING IMAGINATIVE OR CHALLENGING.
TAXI
DARK KNIGHT
YOU GOT A LIGHT?
COOL.
FLIK
ZOOM!
OH HEAVENS! I LEFT MY MONEY AT THE CONVENT. WOULD YOU MIND TURNING BACK?
DEPENDS. WHAT'S IN THE BOX?
UM, WELL I'VE GOT A COUPLE BUCKETS OF WINGS AND A BOTTLE OF SCHNAPPS FOR THE PUNCH BOWL. ITS VEGAS NIGHT AT THE C.Y.O.

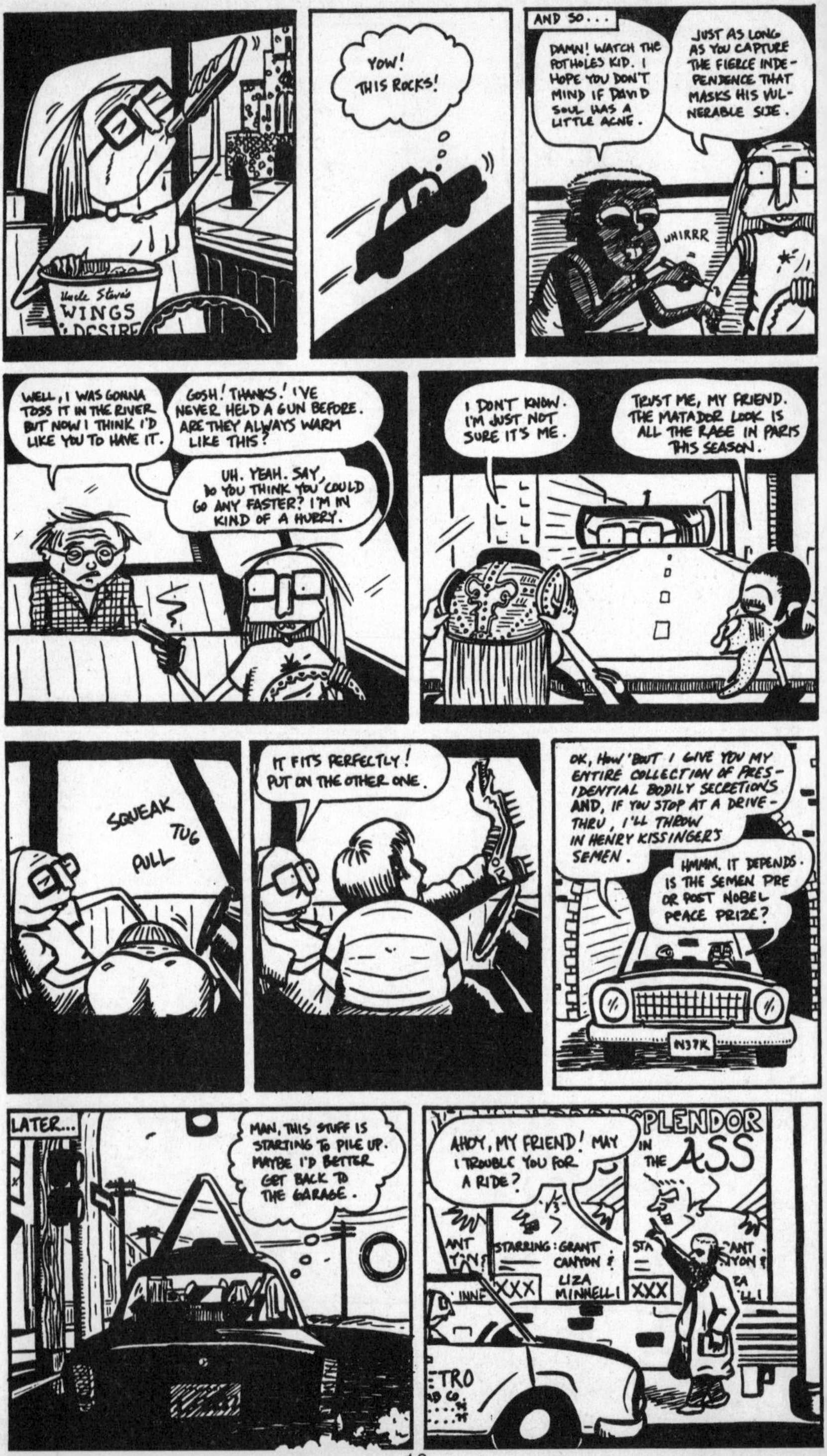
Uncle Steve's WINGS OF DESIRE
YOW! THIS ROCKS!
AND SO...
DAMN! WATCH THE POTHOLES KID. I HOPE YOU DON'T MIND IF DAVID SOUL HAS A LITTLE ACNE.
JUST AS LONG AS YOU CAPTURE THE FIERCE INDEPENDENCE THAT MASKS HIS VULNERABLE SIDE.
WHIRRR
WELL, I WAS GONNA TOSS IT IN THE RIVER BUT NOW I THINK I'D LIKE YOU TO HAVE IT.
GOSH! THANKS! I'VE NEVER HELD A GUN BEFORE. ARE THEY ALWAYS WARM LIKE THIS?
UH. YEAH. SAY, DO YOU THINK YOU COULD GO ANY FASTER? I'M IN KIND OF A HURRY.
I DON'T KNOW. I'M JUST NOT SURE IT'S ME.
TRUST ME, MY FRIEND. THE MATADOR LOOK IS ALL THE RAGE IN PARIS THIS SEASON.
SQUEAK
TUG
PULL
IT FITS PERFECTLY! PUT ON THE OTHER ONE.
OK, HOW 'BOUT I GIVE YOU MY ENTIRE COLLECTION OF PRESIDENTIAL BODILY SECRETIONS AND, IF YOU STOP AT A DRIVE-THRU, I'LL THROW IN HENRY KISSINGER'S SEMEN.
HMMM. IT DEPENDS. IS THE SEMEN PRE OR POST NOBEL PEACE PRIZE?
N37K
LATER...
MAN, THIS STUFF IS STARTING TO PILE UP. MAYBE I'D BETTER GET BACK TO THE GARAGE.
AHOY, MY FRIEND! MAY I TROUBLE YOU FOR A RIDE?
SPLENDOR IN THE ASS
STARRING: GRANT CANYON & LIZA MINNELLI
XXX
XXX

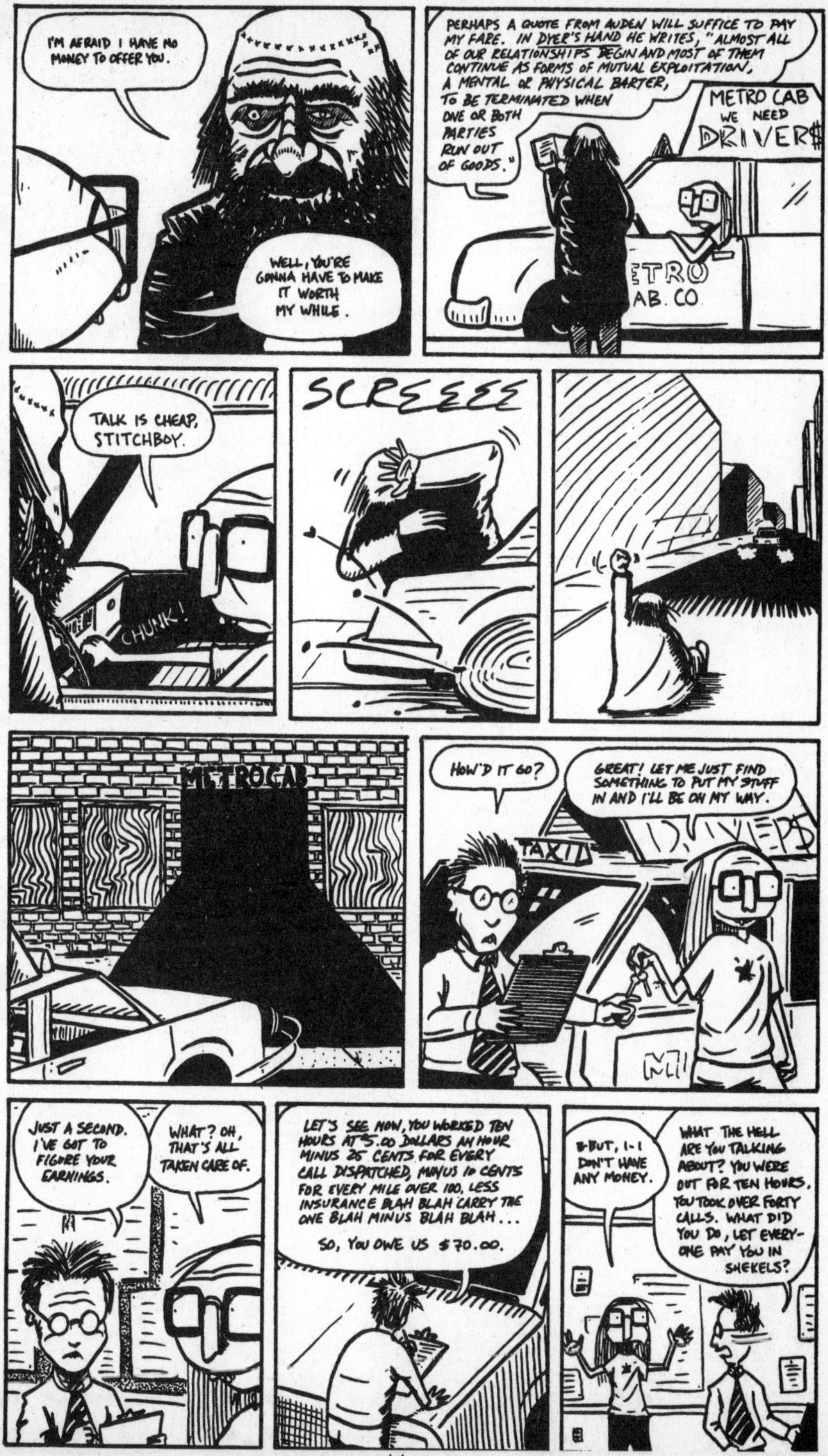
I'M AFRAID I HAVE NO MONEY TO OFFER YOU.
WELL, YOU'RE GONNA HAVE TO MAKE IT WORTH MY WHILE.
PERHAPS A QUOTE FROM AUDEN WILL SUFFICE TO PAY MY FARE. IN DYER'S HAND HE WRITES, "ALMOST ALL OF OUR RELATIONSHIPS BEGIN AND MOST OF THEM CONTINUE AS FORMS OF MUTUAL EXPLOITATION, A MENTAL OR PHYSICAL BARTER, TO BE TERMINATED WHEN ONE OR BOTH PARTIES RUN OUT OF GOODS."
METRO CAB WE NEED DRIVER$
ETRO AB. CO
TALK IS CHEAP, STITCHBOY.
CHUNK!
SCREEEE
METROCAB
HOW'D IT GO?
GREAT! LET ME JUST FIND SOMETHING TO PUT MY STUFF IN AND I'LL BE ON MY WAY.
TAXI
JUST A SECOND. I'VE GOT TO FIGURE YOUR EARNINGS.
WHAT? OH, THAT'S ALL TAKEN CARE OF.
LET'S SEE NOW, YOU WORKED TEN HOURS AT $5.00 DOLLARS AN HOUR MINUS 25 CENTS FOR EVERY CALL DISPATCHED, MINUS 10 CENTS FOR EVERY MILE OVER 100, LESS INSURANCE BLAH BLAH CARRY THE ONE BLAH MINUS BLAH BLAH...
SO, YOU OWE US $70.00.
B-BUT, I-I DON'T HAVE ANY MONEY.
WHAT THE HELL ARE YOU TALKING ABOUT? YOU WERE OUT FOR TEN HOURS. YOU TOOK OVER FORTY CALLS. WHAT DID YOU DO, LET EVERYONE PAY YOU IN SHEKELS?

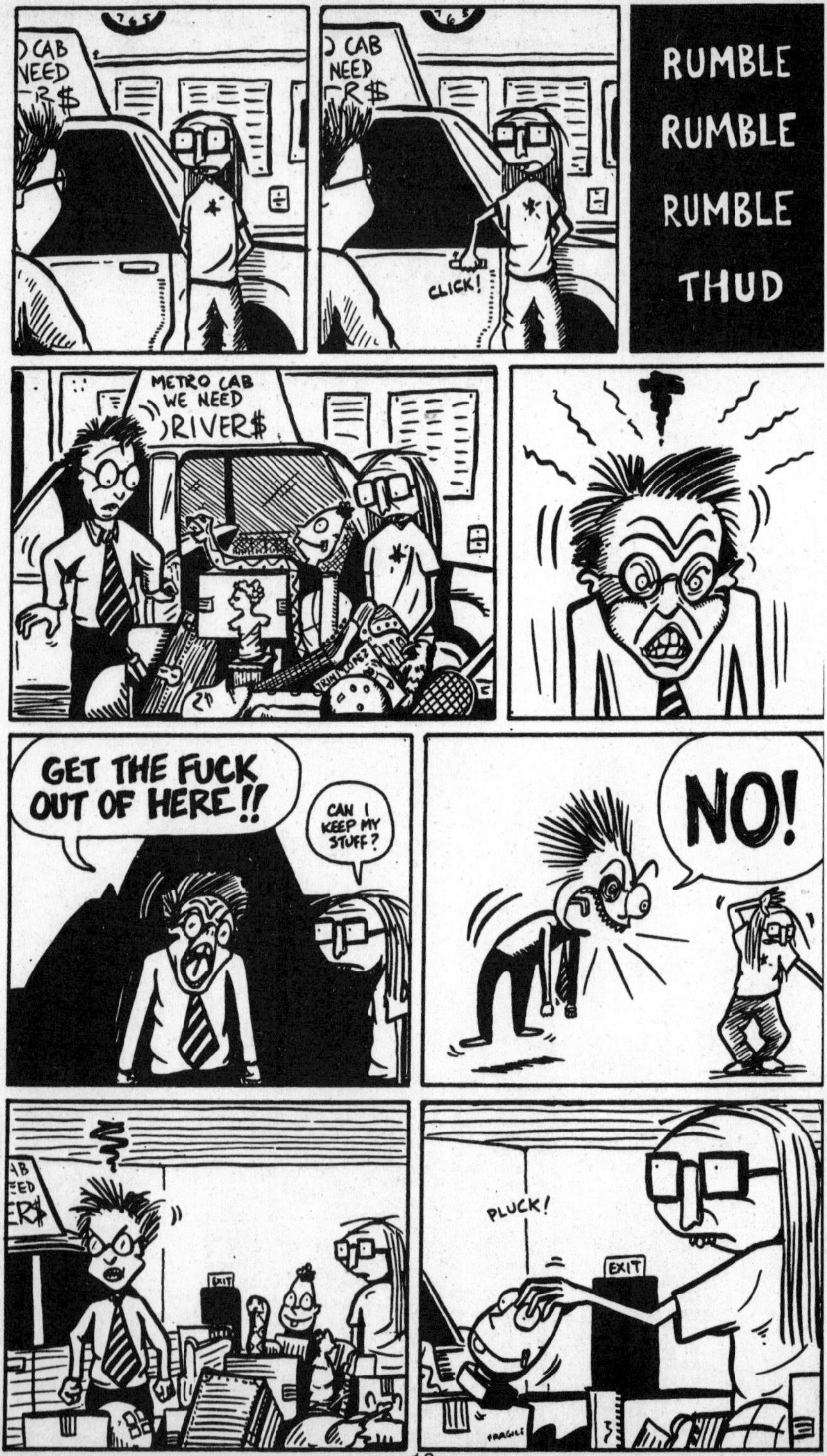

CAB
NEED
R$
CAB
NEED
R$
CLICK!
RUMBLE
RUMBLE
RUMBLE
THUD
METRO CAB
WE NEED
)RIVER$
GET THE FUCK OUT OF HERE!!
CAN I KEEP MY STUFF?
NO!
EXIT
PLUCK!
EXIT

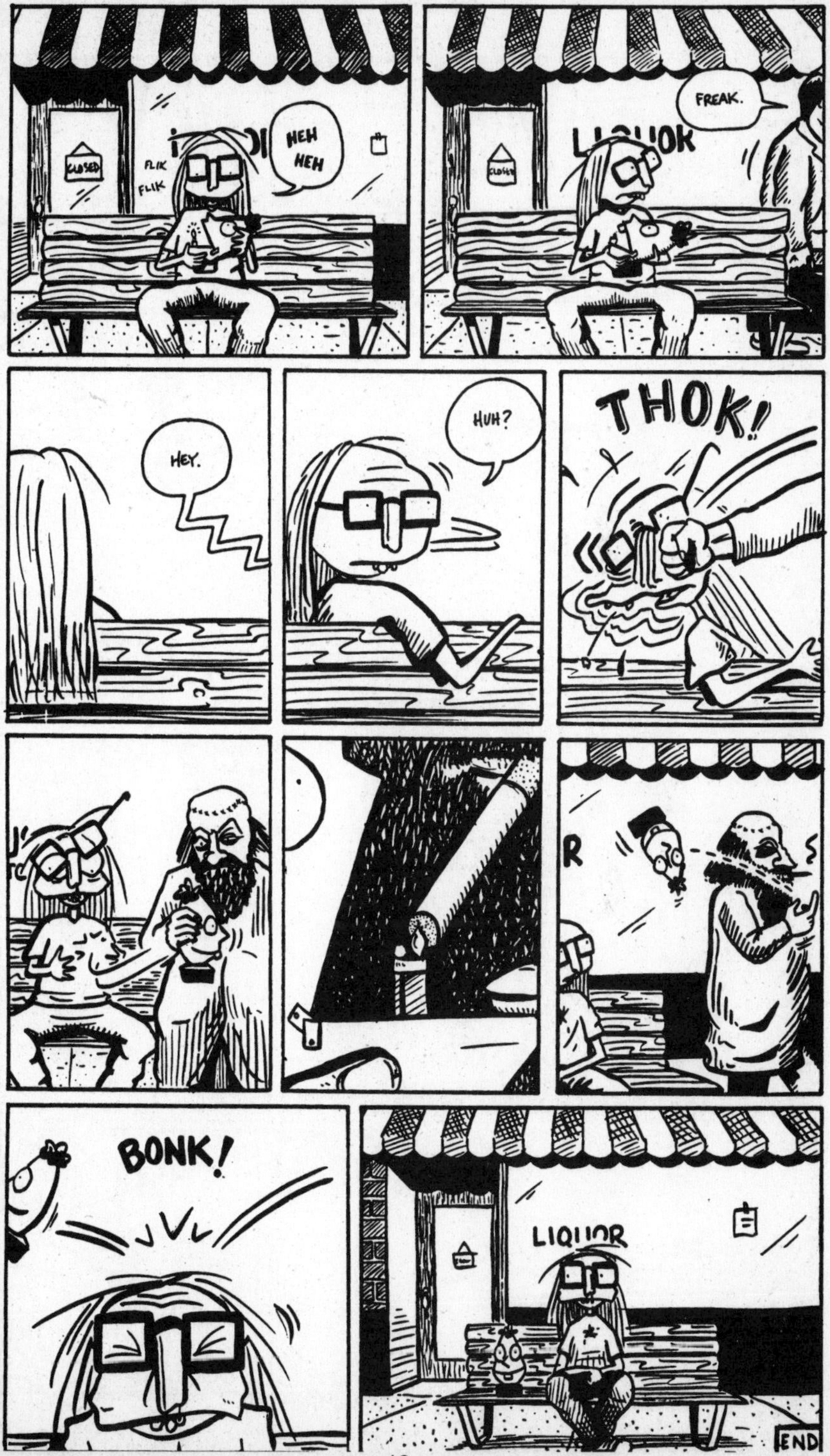
FLIK
FLIK
HEH
HEH
CLOSED
LIQUOR
FREAK.
HEY.
HUH?
THOK!
BONK!
LIQUOR
END

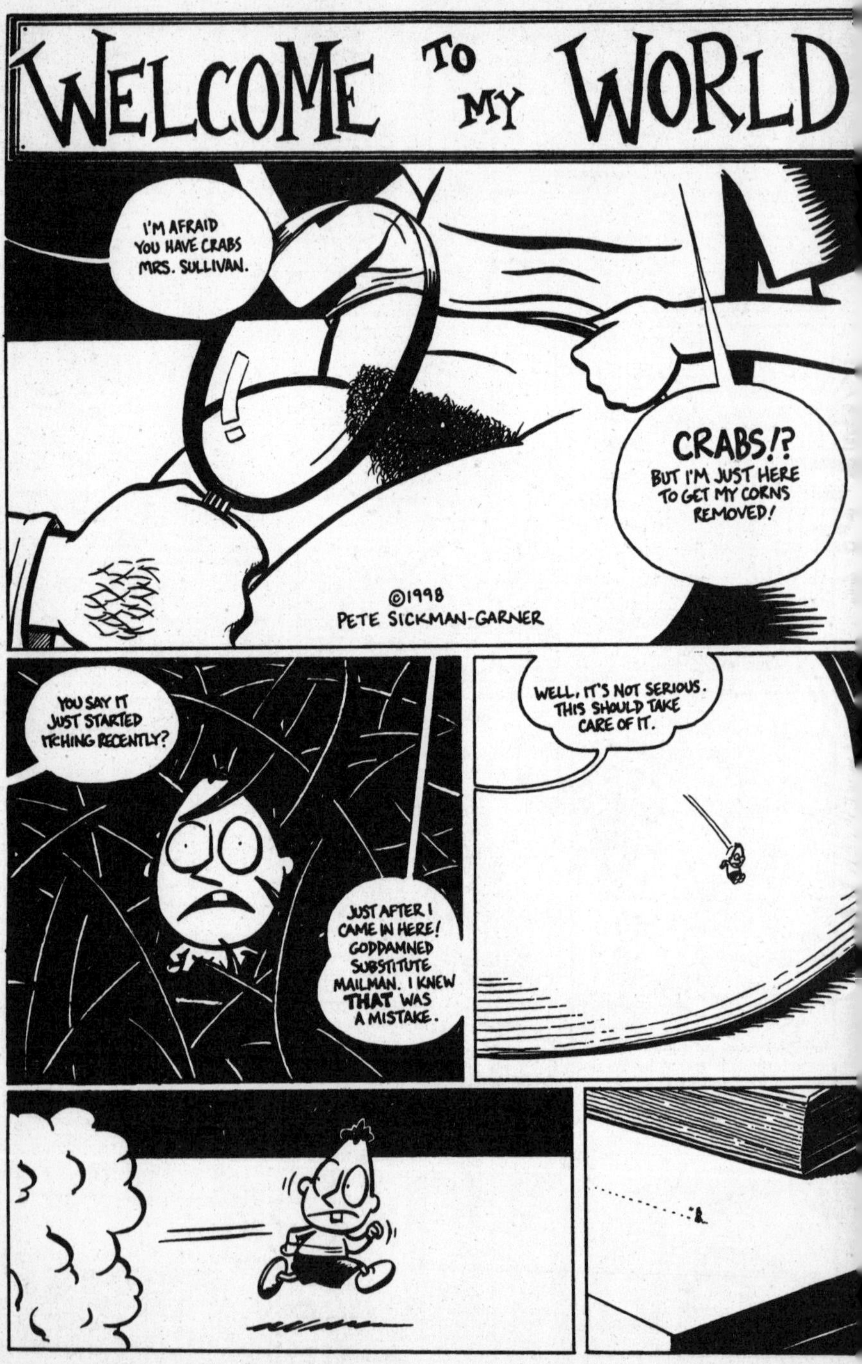
WELCOME TO MY WORLD
I'M AFRAID YOU HAVE CRABS MRS. SULLIVAN.
CRABS!? BUT I'M JUST HERE TO GET MY CORNS REMOVED!
©1998 PETE SICKMAN-GARNER
YOU SAY IT JUST STARTED ITCHING RECENTLY?
JUST AFTER I CAME IN HERE! GODDAMNED SUBSTITUTE MAILMAN. I KNEW THAT WAS A MISTAKE.
WELL, IT'S NOT SERIOUS. THIS SHOULD TAKE CARE OF IT.

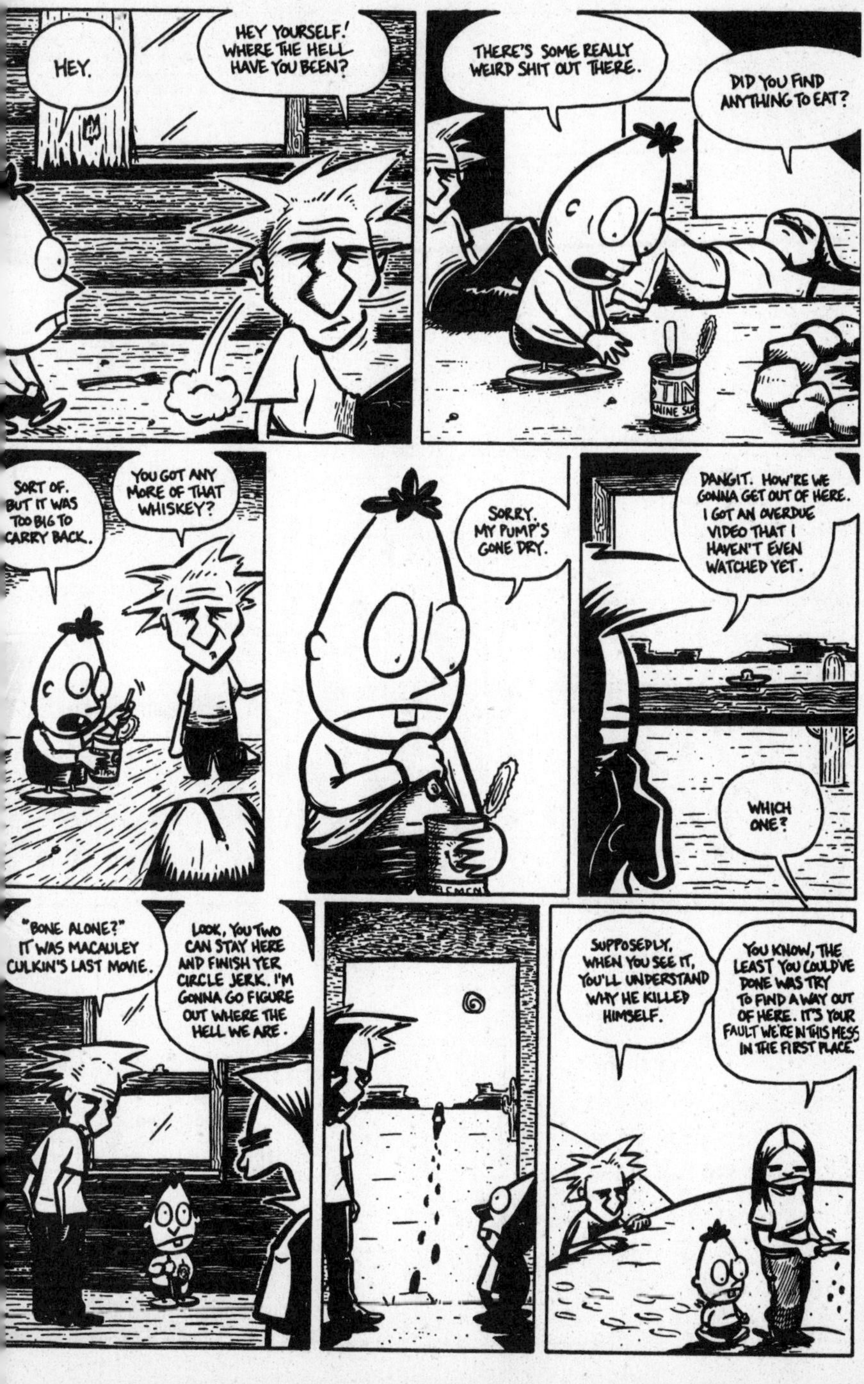
HEY.
HEY YOURSELF! WHERE THE HELL HAVE YOU BEEN?
THERE'S SOME REALLY WEIRD SHIT OUT THERE.
DID YOU FIND ANYTHING TO EAT?
SORT OF. BUT IT WAS TOO BIG TO CARRY BACK.
YOU GOT ANY MORE OF THAT WHISKEY?
SORRY. MY PUMP'S GONE DRY.
DANGIT. HOW'RE WE GONNA GET OUT OF HERE. I GOT AN OVERDUE VIDEO THAT I HAVEN'T EVEN WATCHED YET.
WHICH ONE?
"BONE ALONE?" IT WAS MACAULEY CULKIN'S LAST MOVIE.
LOOK, YOU TWO CAN STAY HERE AND FINISH YER CIRCLE JERK. I'M GONNA GO FIGURE OUT WHERE THE HELL WE ARE.
SUPPOSEDLY, WHEN YOU SEE IT, YOU'LL UNDERSTAND WHY HE KILLED HIMSELF.
YOU KNOW, THE LEAST YOU COULD'VE DONE WAS TRY TO FIND A WAY OUT OF HERE. IT'S YOUR FAULT WE'RE IN THIS MESS IN THE FIRST PLACE.

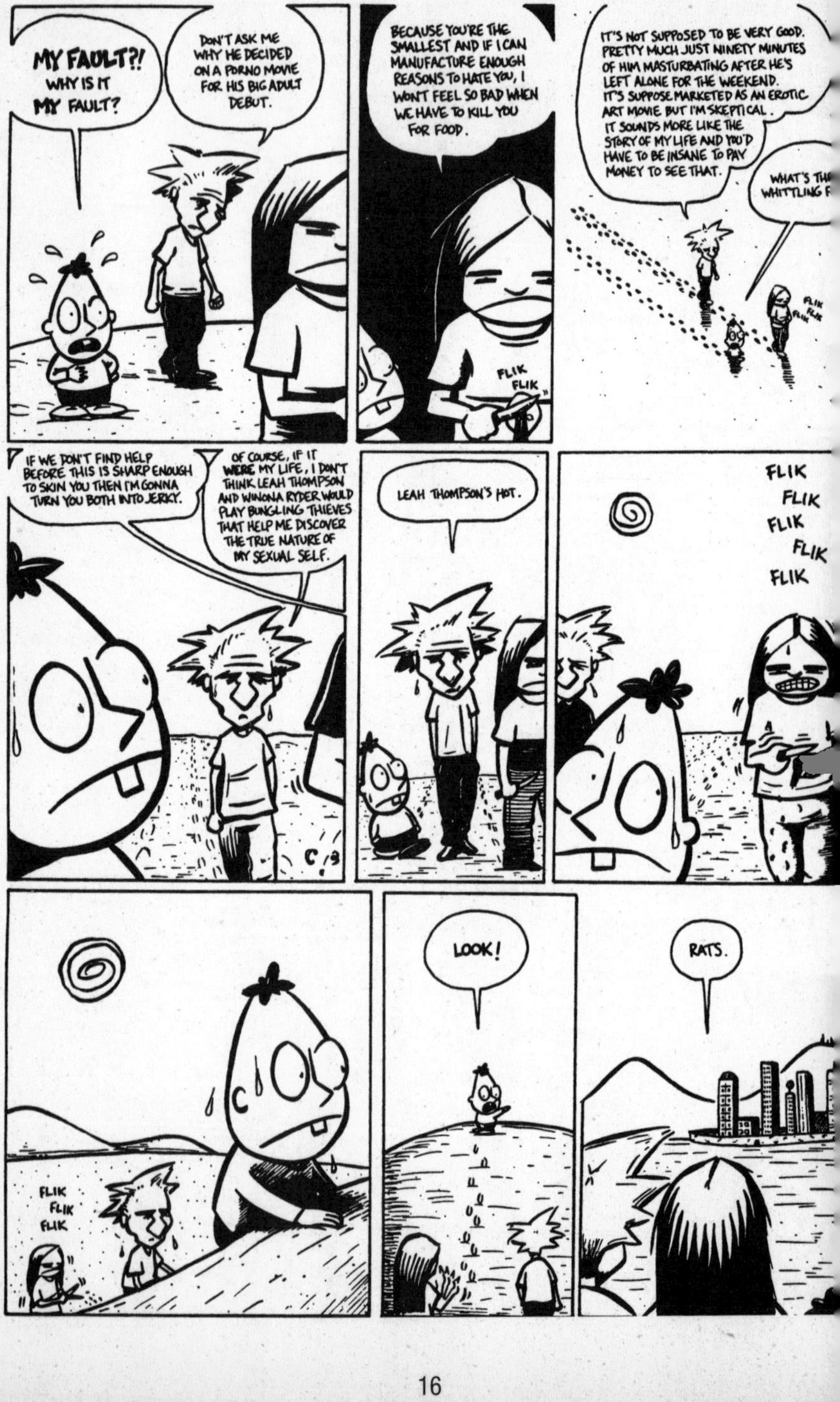

MY FAULT?! WHY IS IT MY FAULT?
DON'T ASK ME WHY HE DECIDED ON A PORNO MOVIE FOR HIS BIG ADULT DEBUT.
BECAUSE YOU'RE THE SMALLEST AND IF I CAN MANUFACTURE ENOUGH REASONS TO HATE YOU, I WON'T FEEL SO BAD WHEN WE HAVE TO KILL YOU FOR FOOD.
FLIK FLIK
IT'S NOT SUPPOSED TO BE VERY GOOD. PRETTY MUCH JUST NINETY MINUTES OF HIM MASTURBATING AFTER HE'S LEFT ALONE FOR THE WEEKEND. IT'S SUPPOSE MARKETED AS AN EROTIC ART MOVIE BUT I'M SKEPTICAL. IT SOUNDS MORE LIKE THE STORY OF MY LIFE AND YOU'D HAVE TO BE INSANE TO PAY MONEY TO SEE THAT.
WHAT'S TH WHITTLING F
FLIK FLIK
IF WE DON'T FIND HELP BEFORE THIS IS SHARP ENOUGH TO SKIN YOU THEN I'M GONNA TURN YOU BOTH INTO JERKY.
OF COURSE, IF IT WERE MY LIFE, I DON'T THINK LEAH THOMPSON AND WINONA RYDER WOULD PLAY BUNGLING THIEVES THAT HELP ME DISCOVER THE TRUE NATURE OF MY SEXUAL SELF.
LEAH THOMPSON'S HOT.
FLIK FLIK FLIK FLIK FLIK
FLIK FLIK FLIK
LOOK!
RATS.

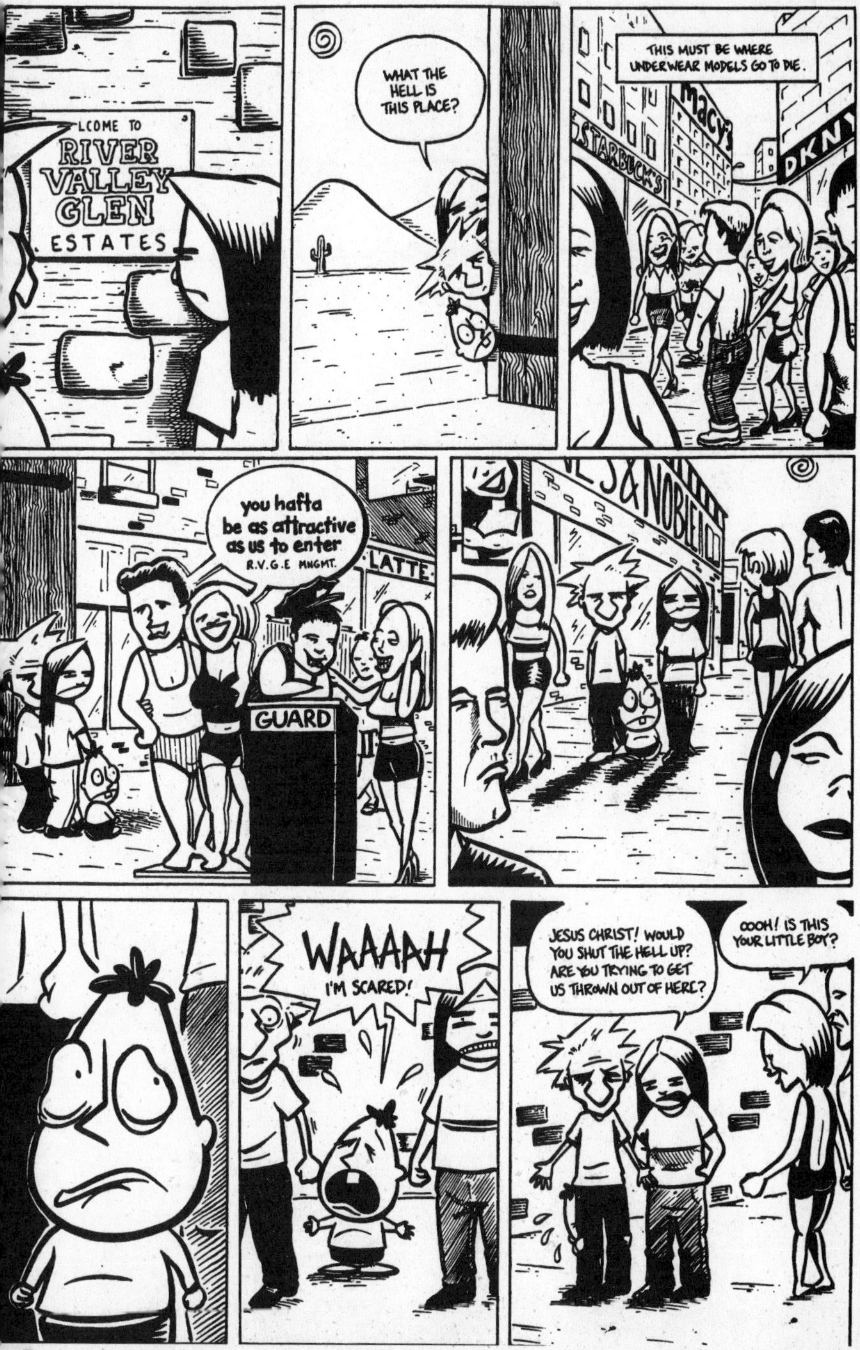
LCOME TO
RIVER VALLEY GLEN ESTATES
WHAT THE HELL IS THIS PLACE?
THIS MUST BE WHERE UNDERWEAR MODELS GO TO DIE.
STARBUCKS
macy's
DKNY
you hafta be as attractive as us to enter
R.V.G.E MNGMT.
LATTE
GUARD
WAAAAH
I'M SCARED!
JESUS CHRIST! WOULD YOU SHUT THE HELL UP? ARE YOU TRYING TO GET US THROWN OUT OF HERE?
OOOH! IS THIS YOUR LITTLE BOY?

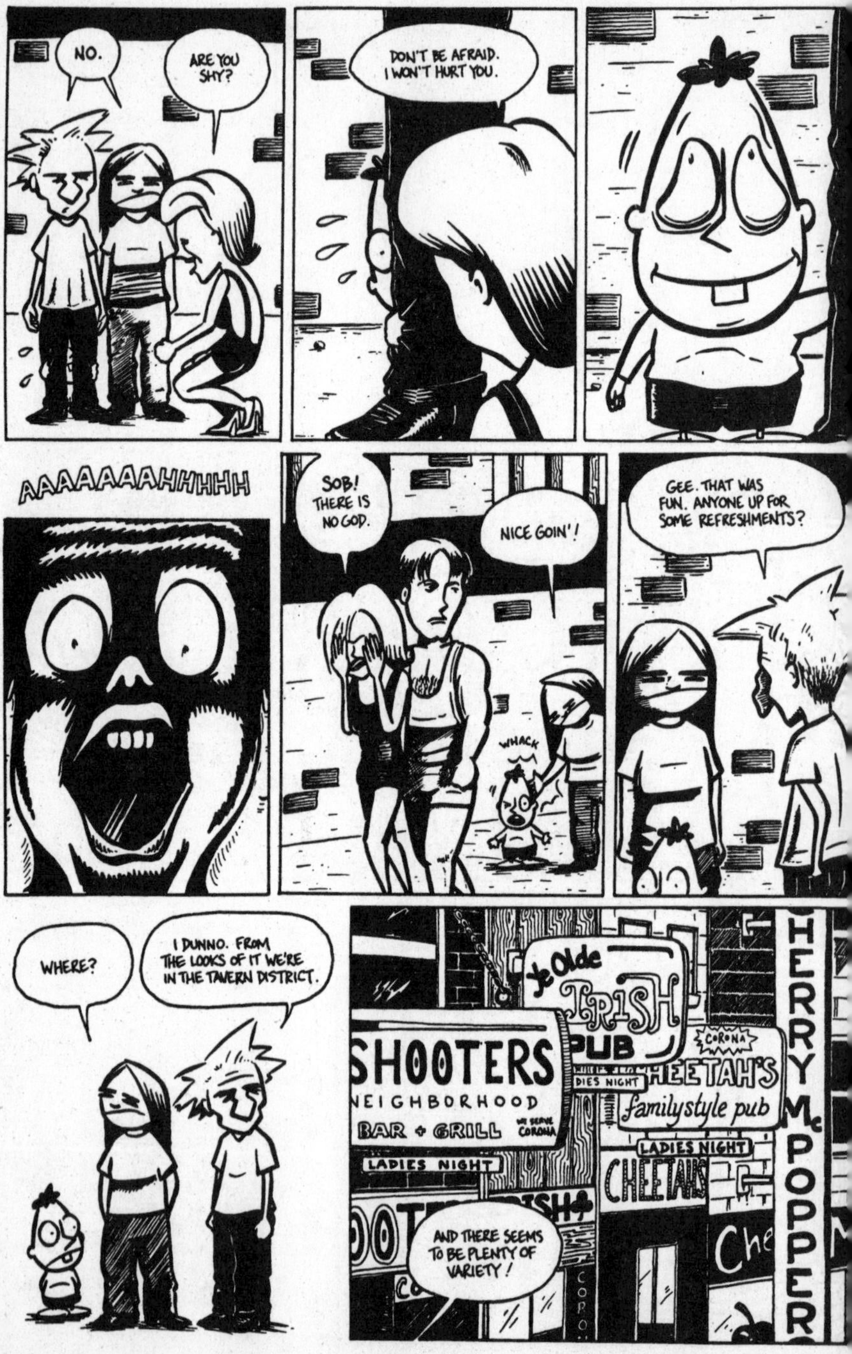
NO.
ARE YOU SHY?
DON'T BE AFRAID. I WON'T HURT YOU.
AAAAAAAHHHHH
SOB! THERE IS NO GOD.
NICE GOIN'!
WHACK
GEE. THAT WAS FUN. ANYONE UP FOR SOME REFRESHMENTS?
WHERE?
I DUNNO. FROM THE LOOKS OF IT WE'RE IN THE TAVERN DISTRICT.
Ye Olde IRISH PUB
SHOOTERS NEIGHBORHOOD BAR + GRILL
WE SERVE CORONA
LADIES NIGHT
CORONA
familystyle pub
LADIES NIGHT
CHEETAHS
AND THERE SEEMS TO BE PLENTY OF VARIETY!

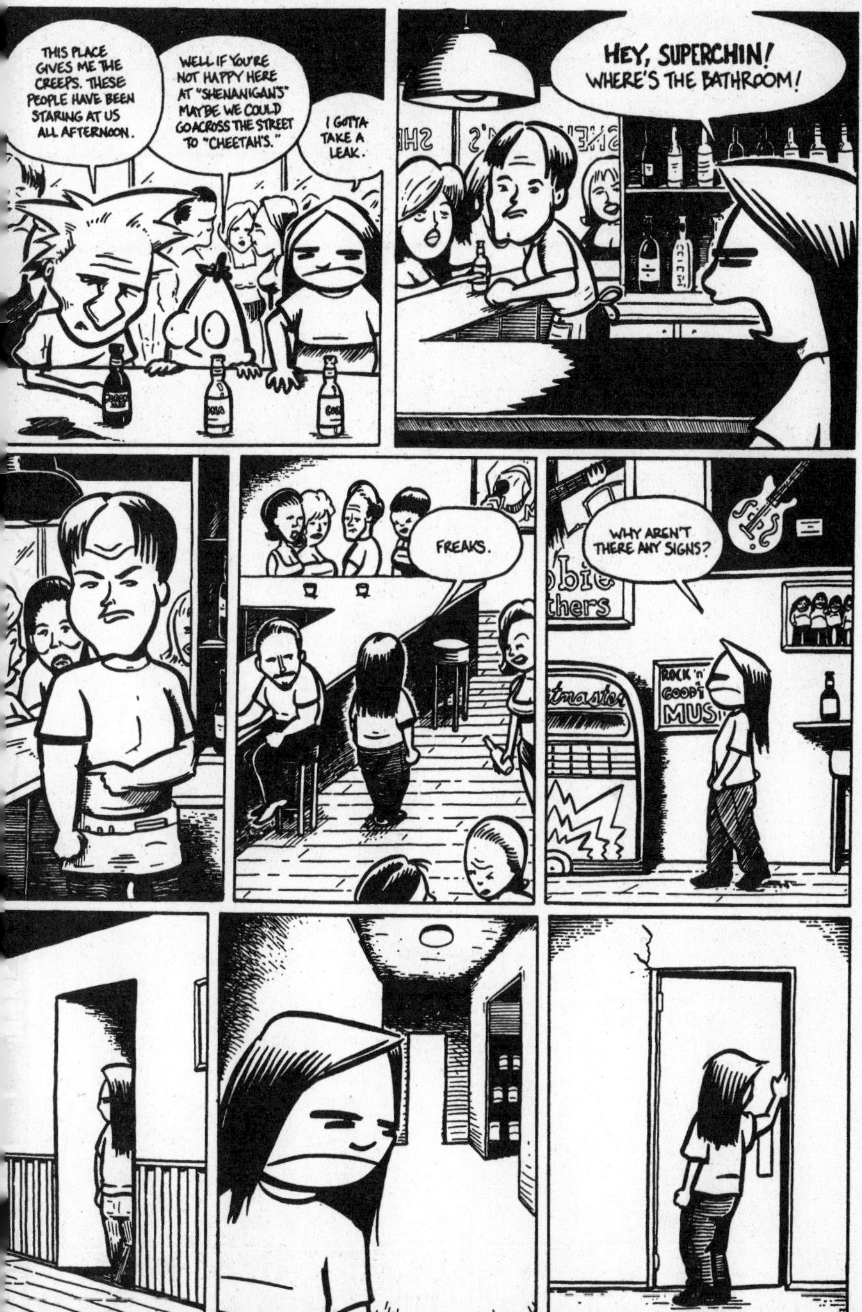
THIS PLACE GIVES ME THE CREEPS. THESE PEOPLE HAVE BEEN STARING AT US ALL AFTERNOON.
WELL IF YOU'RE NOT HAPPY HERE AT "SHENANIGAN'S" MAYBE WE COULD GO ACROSS THE STREET TO "CHEETAH'S."
I GOTTA TAKE A LEAK.
HEY, SUPERCHIN! WHERE'S THE BATHROOM!
FREAKS.
WHY AREN'T THERE ANY SIGNS?
ROCK 'n' GOOD MUS

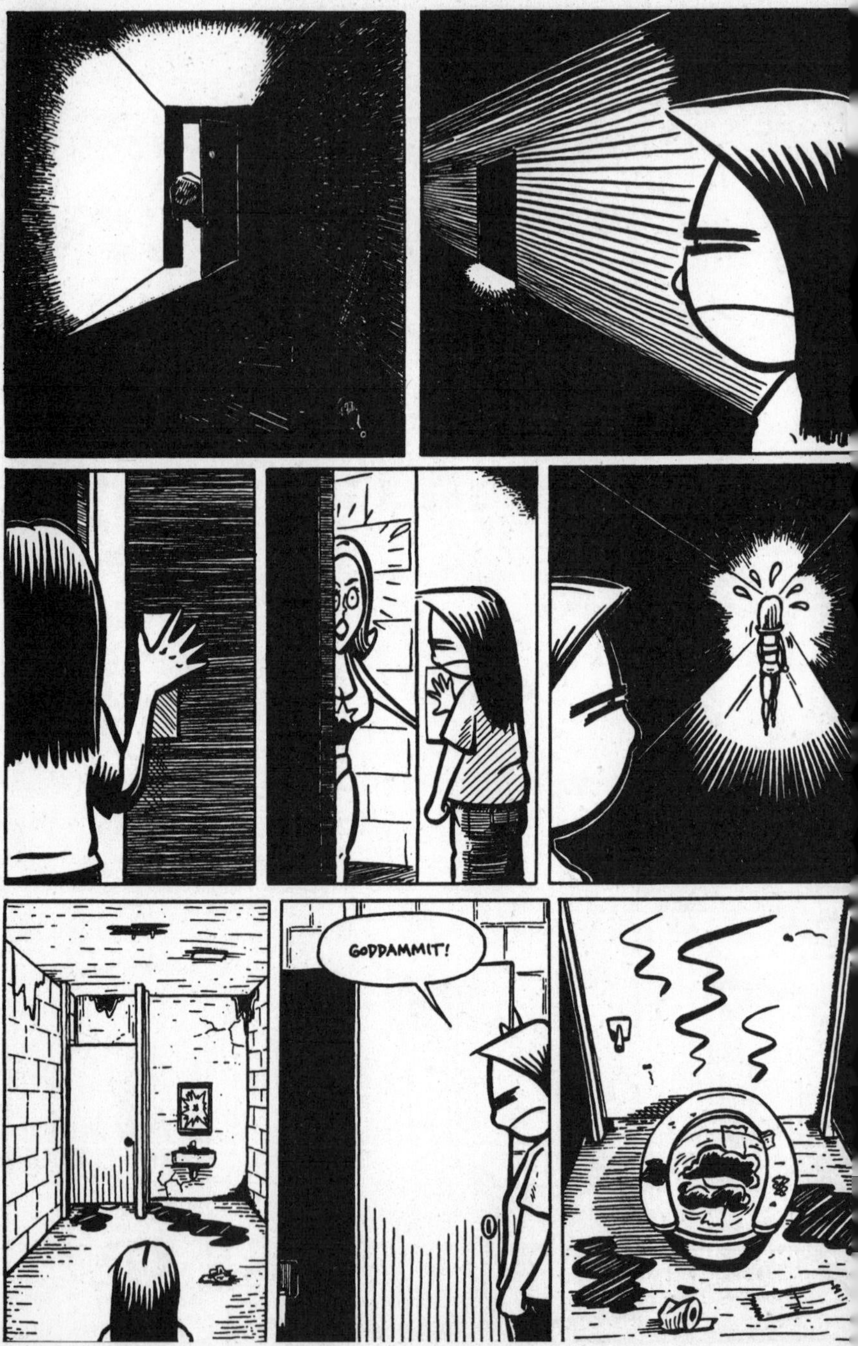
GODDAMMIT!

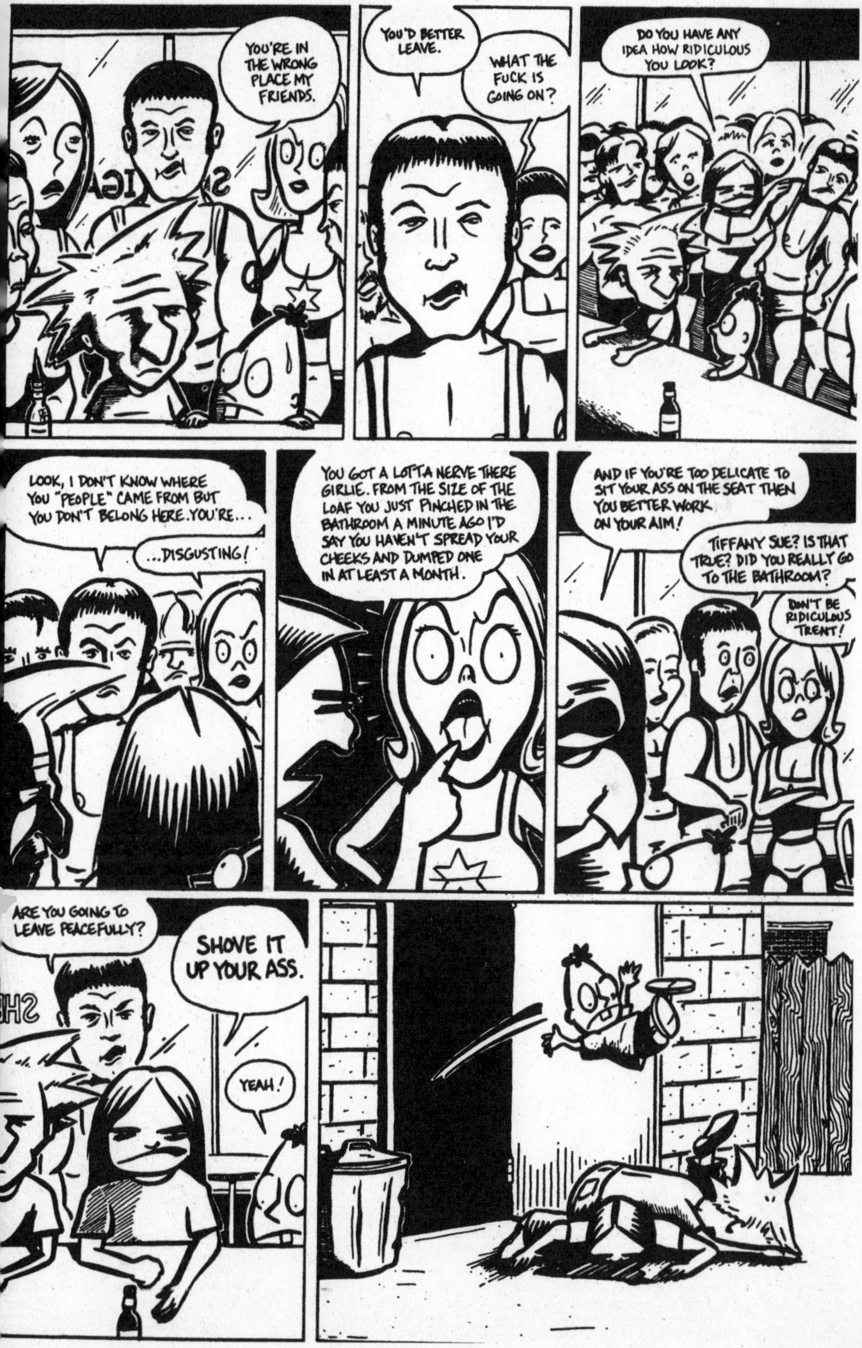
YOU'RE IN THE WRONG PLACE MY FRIENDS.
YOU'D BETTER LEAVE.
WHAT THE FUCK IS GOING ON?
DO YOU HAVE ANY IDEA HOW RIDICULOUS YOU LOOK?
LOOK, I DON'T KNOW WHERE YOU "PEOPLE" CAME FROM BUT YOU DON'T BELONG HERE. YOU'RE...
...DISGUSTING!
YOU GOT A LOTTA NERVE THERE GIRLIE. FROM THE SIZE OF THE LOAF YOU JUST PINCHED IN THE BATHROOM A MINUTE AGO I'D SAY YOU HAVEN'T SPREAD YOUR CHEEKS AND DUMPED ONE IN AT LEAST A MONTH.
AND IF YOU'RE TOO DELICATE TO SIT YOUR ASS ON THE SEAT THEN YOU BETTER WORK ON YOUR AIM!
TIFFANY SUE? IS THAT TRUE? DID YOU REALLY GO TO THE BATHROOM?
DON'T BE RIDICULOUS TRENT!
ARE YOU GOING TO LEAVE PEACEFULLY?
SHOVE IT UP YOUR ASS.
YEAH!

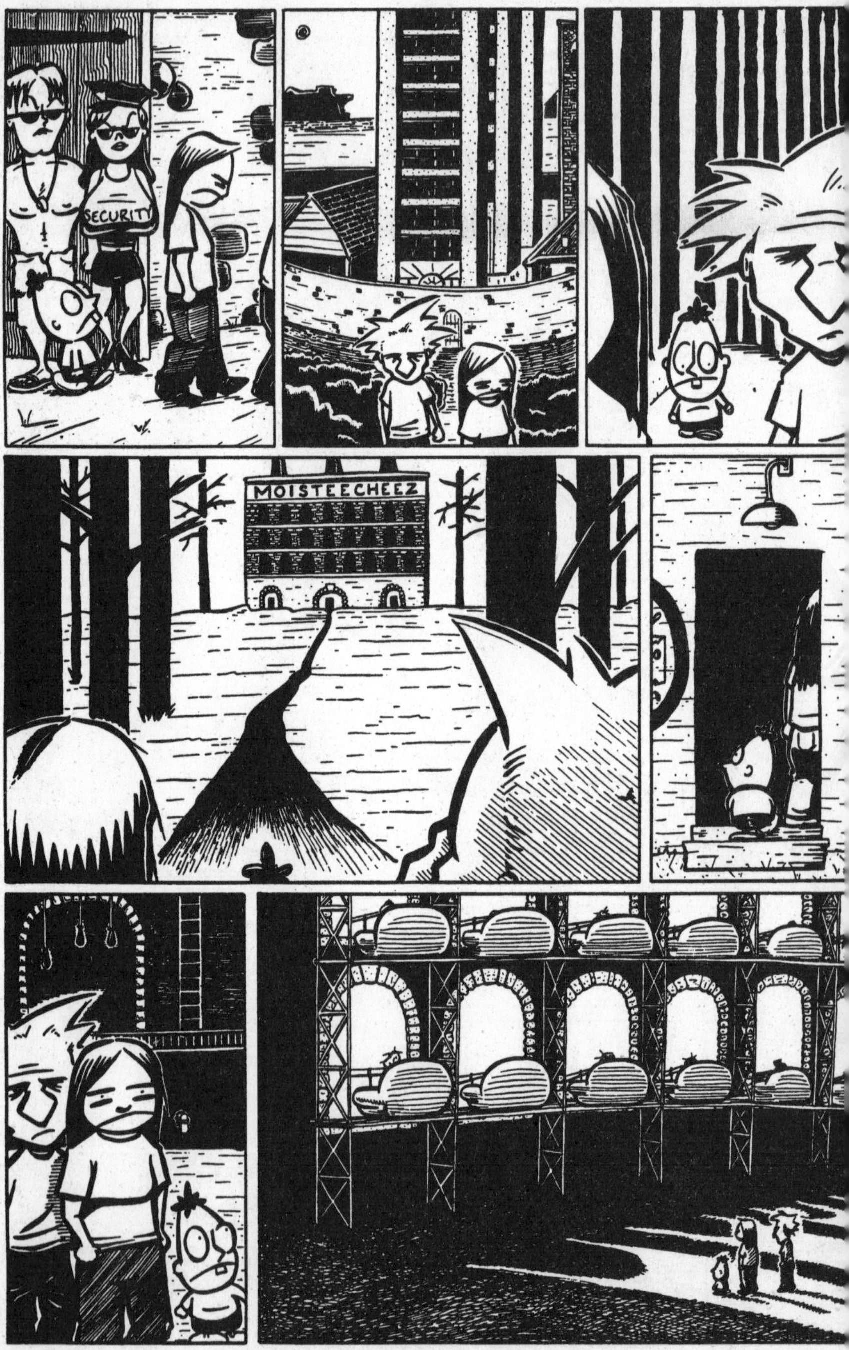
SECURITY
MOISTEECHEEZ

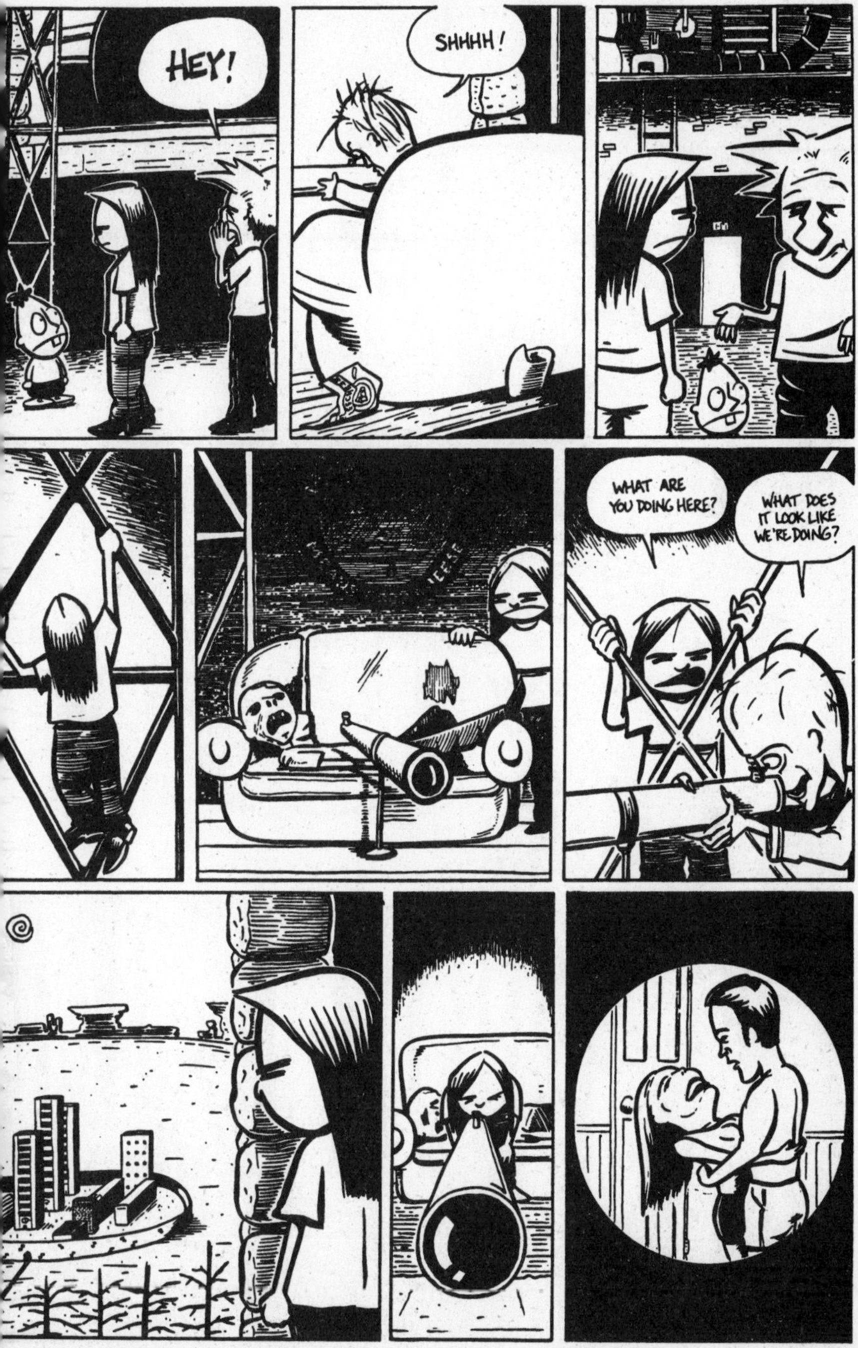
HEY!
SHHHH!
WHAT ARE YOU DOING HERE?
WHAT DOES IT LOOK LIKE WE'RE DOING?

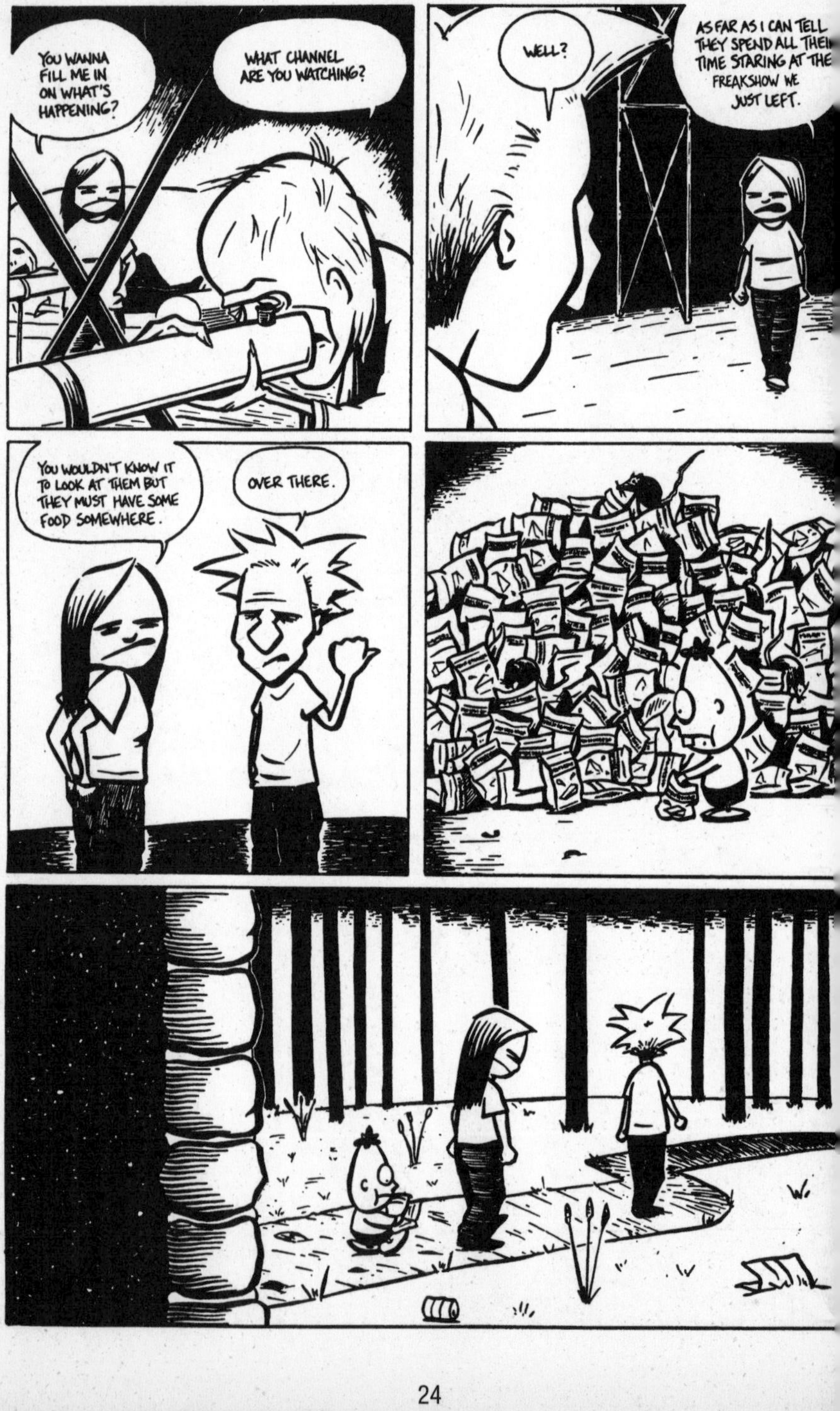
YOU WANNA FILL ME IN ON WHAT'S HAPPENING?
WHAT CHANNEL ARE YOU WATCHING?
WELL?
AS FAR AS I CAN TELL THEY SPEND ALL THEI
TIME STARING AT THE FREAKSHOW WE JUST LEFT.
YOU WOULDN'T KNOW IT TO LOOK AT THEM BUT THEY MUST HAVE SOME FOOD SOMEWHERE.
OVER THERE.

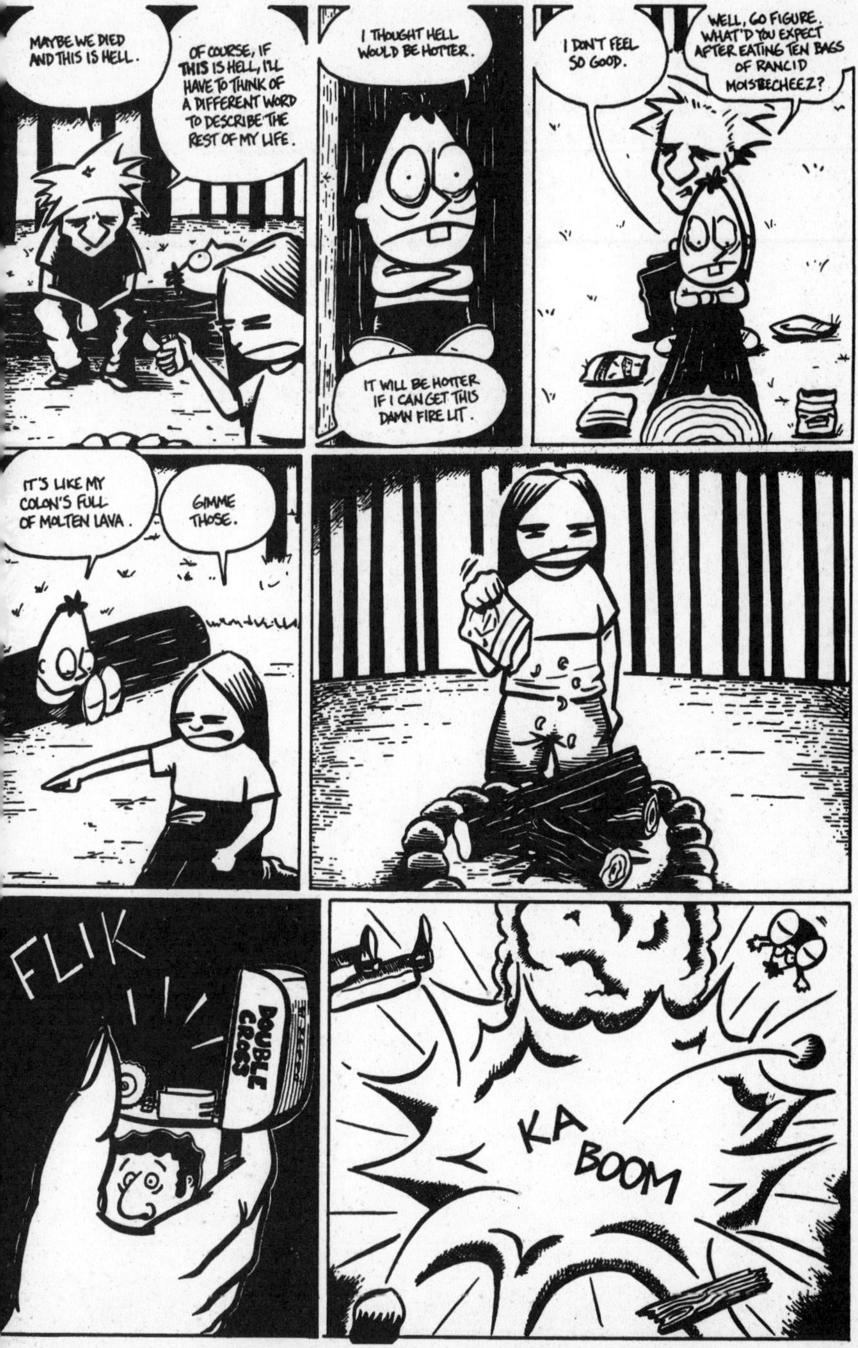
MAYBE WE DIED AND THIS IS HELL.
OF COURSE, IF THIS IS HELL, I'LL HAVE TO THINK OF A DIFFERENT WORD TO DESCRIBE THE REST OF MY LIFE.
I THOUGHT HELL WOULD BE HOTTER.
IT WILL BE HOTTER IF I CAN GET THIS DAMN FIRE LIT.
I DON'T FEEL SO GOOD.
WELL, GO FIGURE. WHAT'D YOU EXPECT AFTER EATING TEN BAGS OF RANCID MOISTEECHEEZ?
IT'S LIKE MY COLON'S FULL OF MOLTEN LAVA.
GIMME THOSE.
FLIK
DOUBLE CROSS
KA BOOM

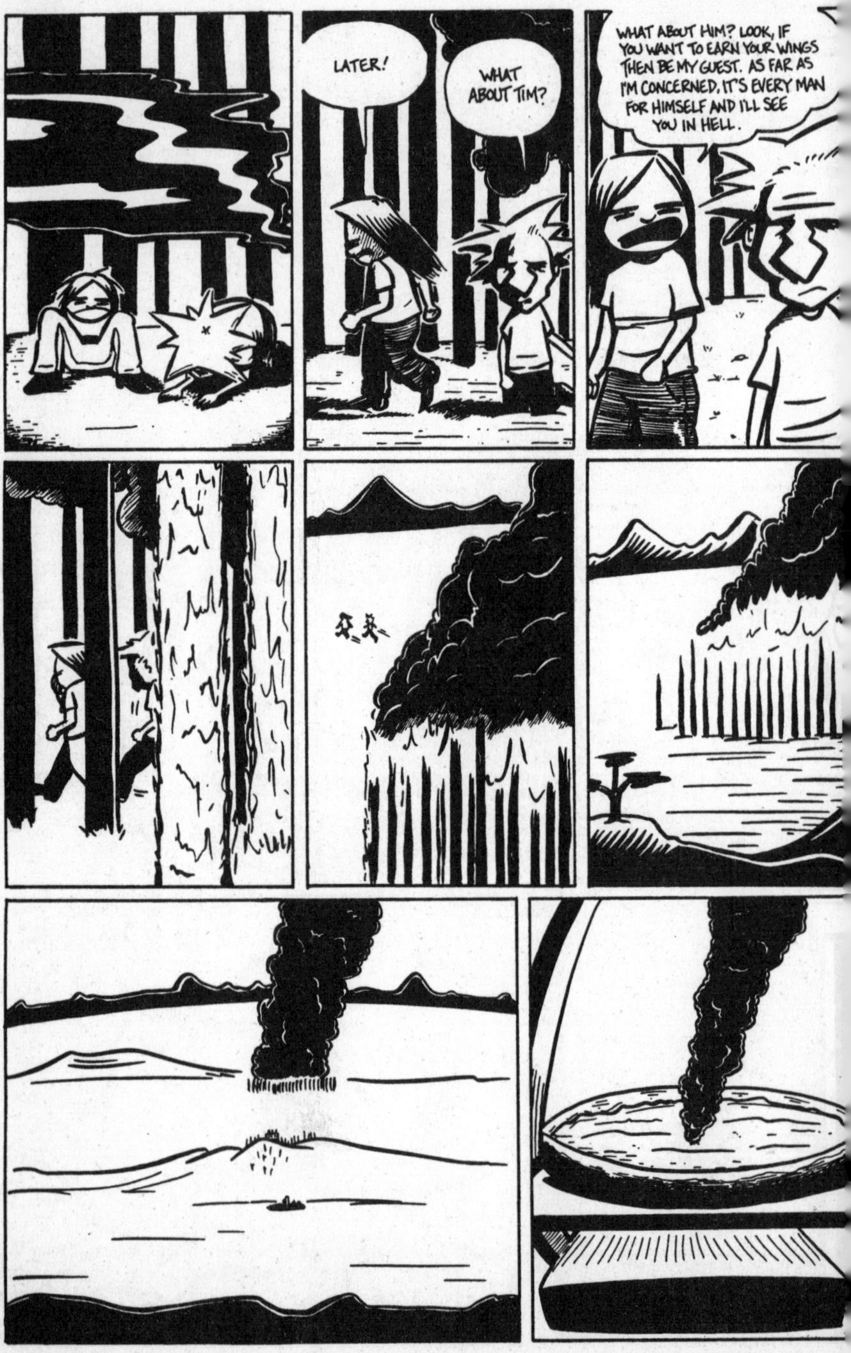
LATER!
WHAT ABOUT TIM?
WHAT ABOUT HIM? LOOK, IF YOU WANT TO EARN YOUR WINGS THEN BE MY GUEST. AS FAR AS I'M CONCERNED, IT'S EVERY MAN FOR HIMSELF AND I'LL SEE YOU IN HELL.

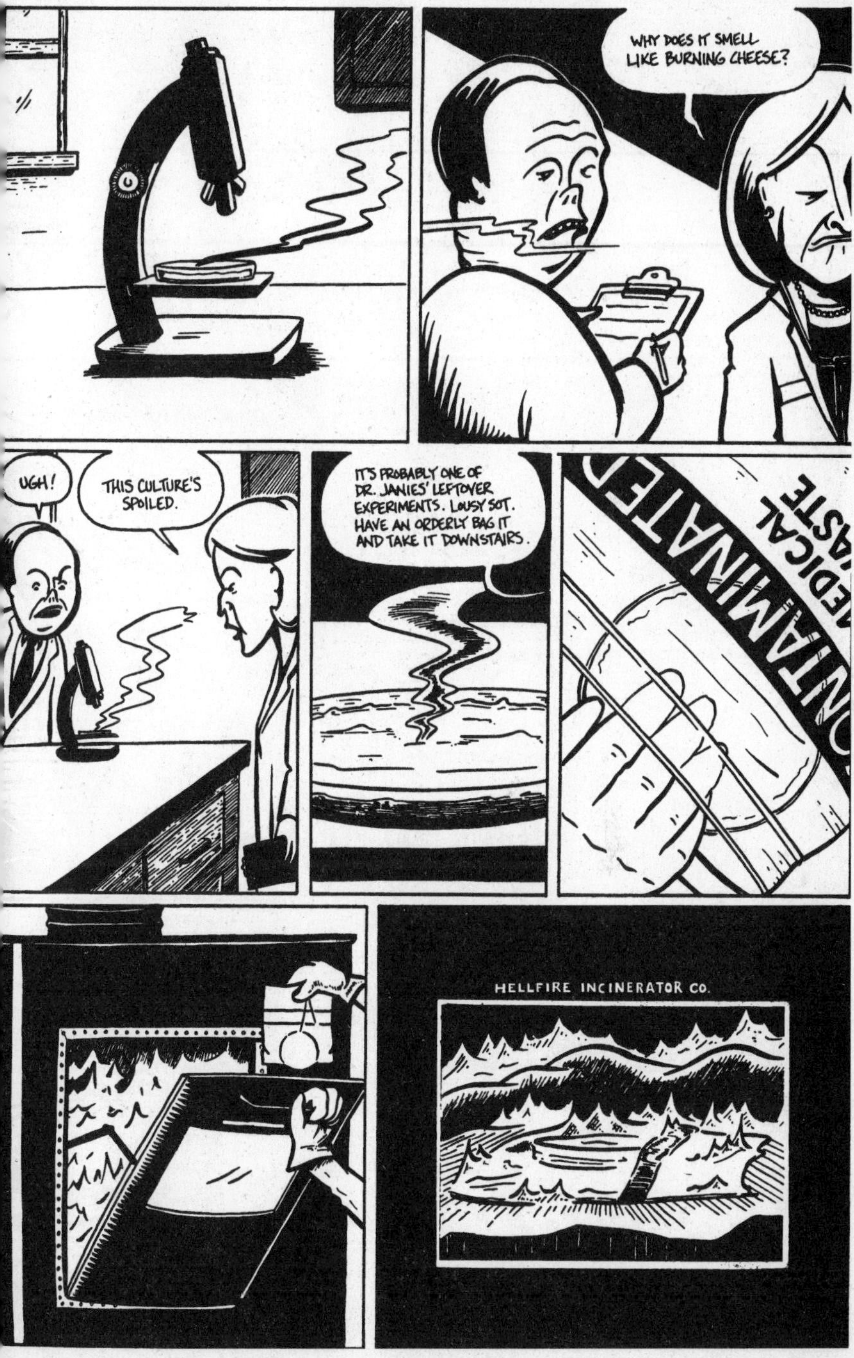
WHY DOES IT SMELL LIKE BURNING CHEESE?
UGH!
THIS CULTURE'S SPOILED.
IT'S PROBABLY ONE OF DR. JANIES' LEFTOVER EXPERIMENTS. LOUSY SOT. HAVE AN ORDERLY BAG IT AND TAKE IT DOWNSTAIRS.
HELLFIRE INCINERATOR CO.

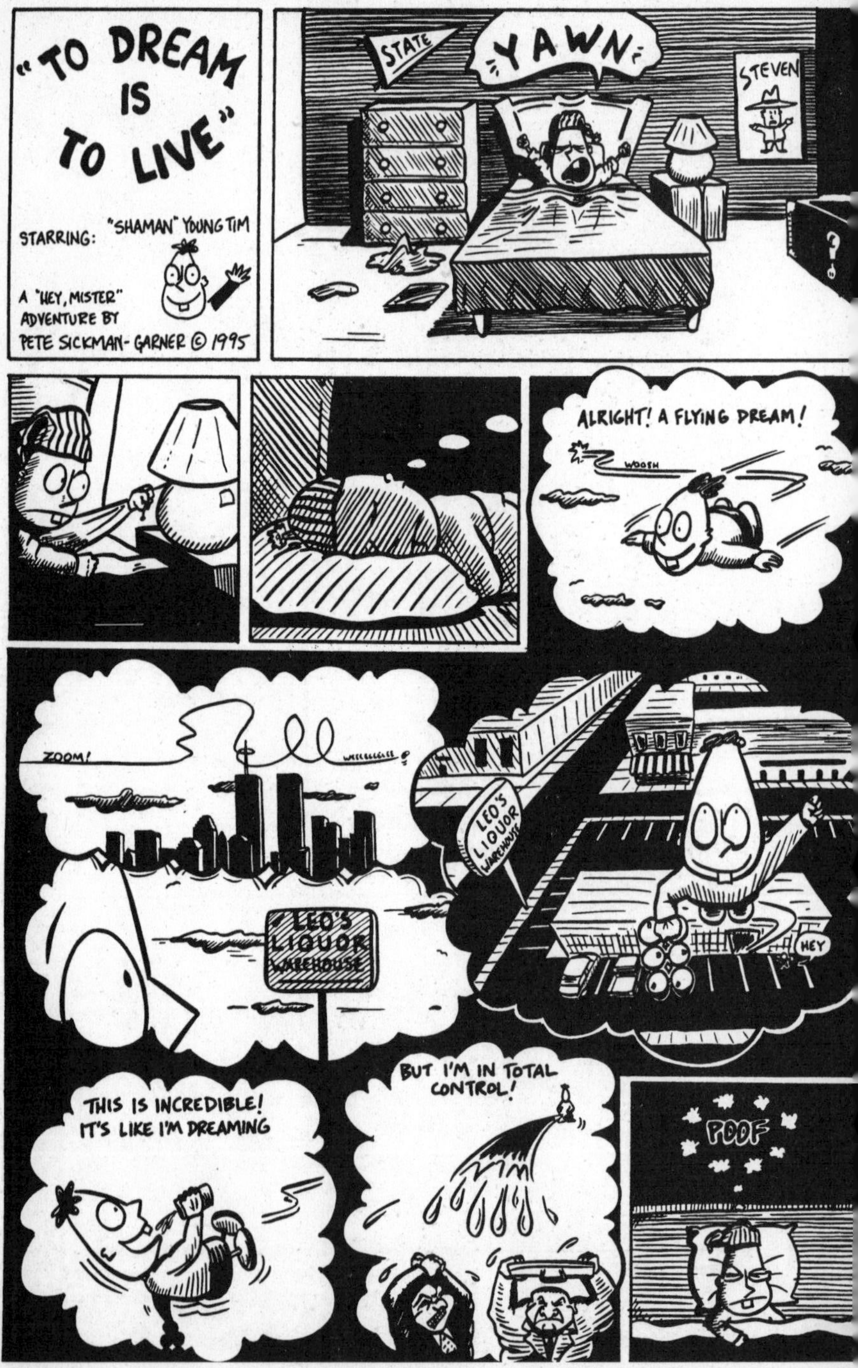
"TO DREAM IS TO LIVE"
STARRING: "SHAMAN" YOUNG TIM
A "HEY, MISTER" ADVENTURE BY PETE SICKMAN-GARNER © 1995
STATE
YAWN
STEVEN
ALRIGHT! A FLYING DREAM!
WOOSH
ZOOM!
LEO'S LIQUOR WAREHOUSE
LEO'S LIQUOR WAREHOUSE
HEY
THIS IS INCREDIBLE! IT'S LIKE I'M DREAMING
BUT I'M IN TOTAL CONTROL!
POOF

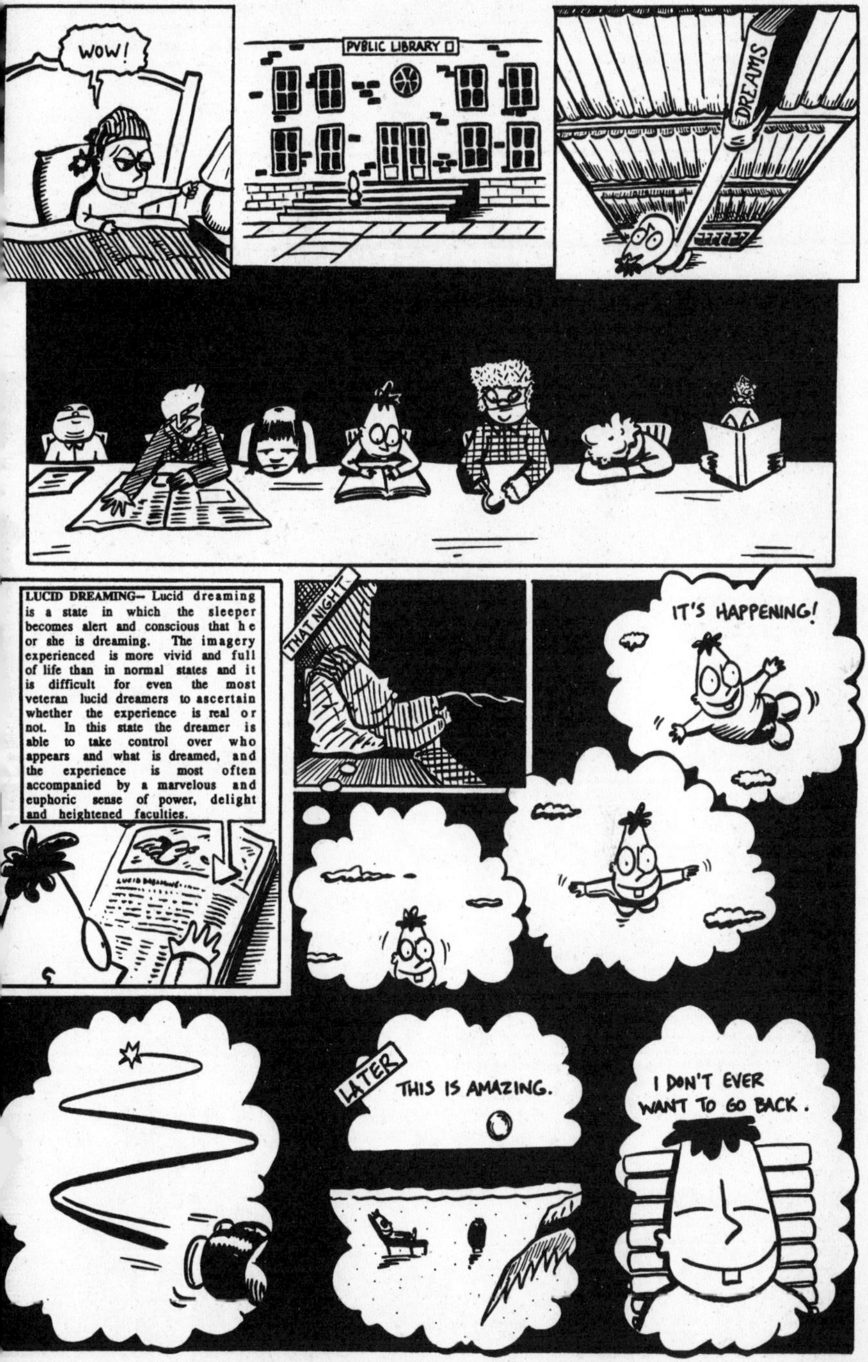
WOW!
PVBLIC LIBRARY
DREAMS
LUCID DREAMING-- Lucid dreaming is a state in which the sleeper becomes alert and conscious that he or she is dreaming. The imagery experienced is more vivid and full of life than in normal states and it is difficult for even the most veteran lucid dreamers to ascertain whether the experience is real or not. In this state the dreamer is able to take control over who appears and what is dreamed, and the experience is most often accompanied by a marvelous and euphoric sense of power, delight and heightened faculties.
THAT NIGHT
IT'S HAPPENING!
LATER
THIS IS AMAZING.
I DON'T EVER WANT TO GO BACK.

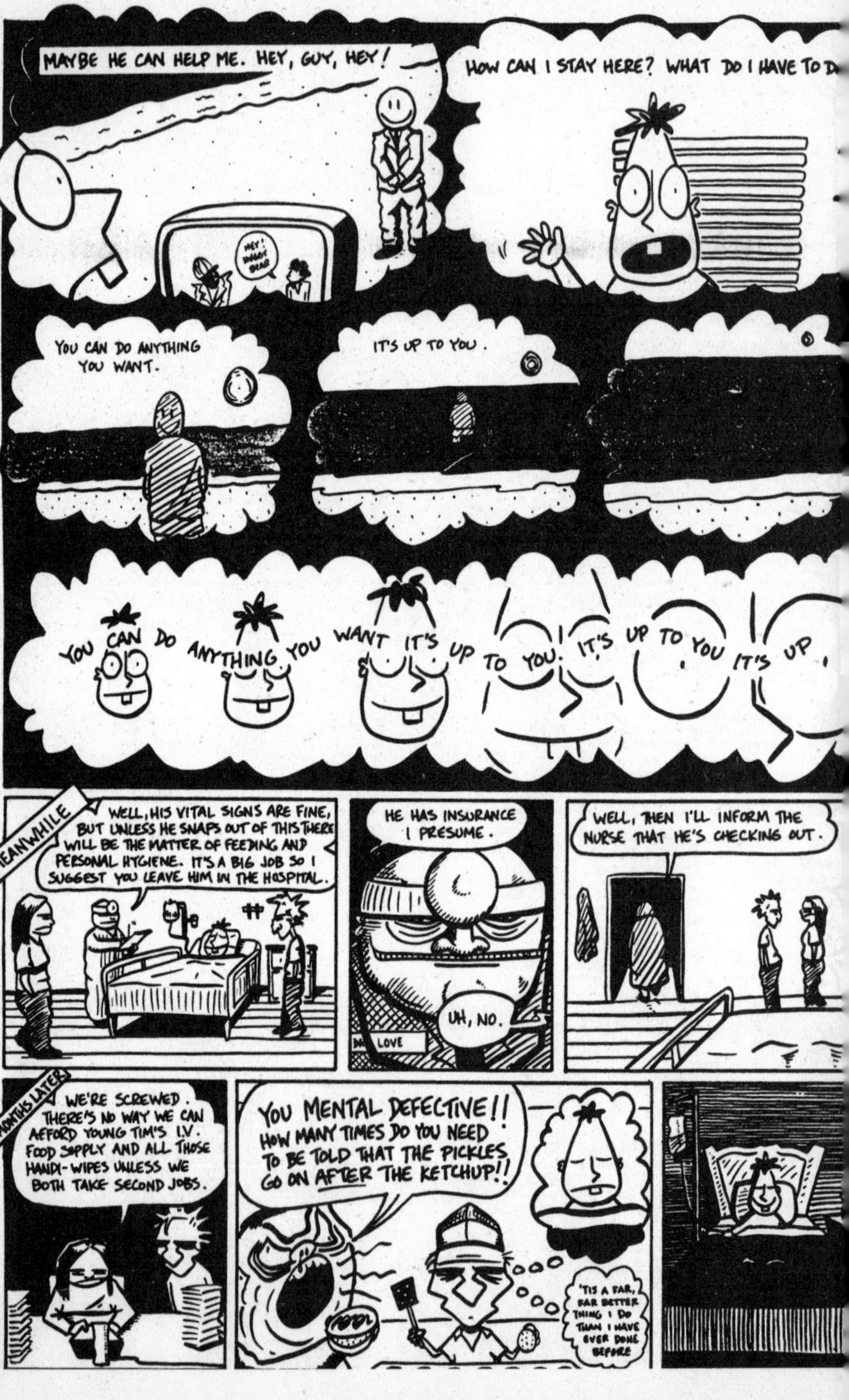
MAYBE HE CAN HELP ME. HEY, GUY, HEY!
HEY! WHAT BEAR
HOW CAN I STAY HERE? WHAT DO I HAVE TO D
YOU CAN DO ANYTHING YOU WANT.
IT'S UP TO YOU.
YOU CAN DO ANYTHING YOU WANT IT'S UP TO YOU. IT'S UP TO YOU IT'S UP.
MEANWHILE
WELL, HIS VITAL SIGNS ARE FINE, BUT UNLESS HE SNAPS OUT OF THIS THERE WILL BE THE MATTER OF FEEDING AND PERSONAL HYGIENE. IT'S A BIG JOB SO I SUGGEST YOU LEAVE HIM IN THE HOSPITAL.
HE HAS INSURANCE I PRESUME.
UH, NO.
LOVE
WELL, THEN I'LL INFORM THE NURSE THAT HE'S CHECKING OUT.
6 MONTHS LATER
WE'RE SCREWED. THERE'S NO WAY WE CAN AFFORD YOUNG TIM'S I.V. FOOD SUPPLY AND ALL THOSE HANDI-WIPES UNLESS WE BOTH TAKE SECOND JOBS.
YOU MENTAL DEFECTIVE!! HOW MANY TIMES DO YOU NEED TO BE TOLD THAT THE PICKLES GO ON AFTER THE KETCHUP!!
'TIS A FAR, FAR BETTER THING I DO THAN I HAVE EVER DONE BEFORE

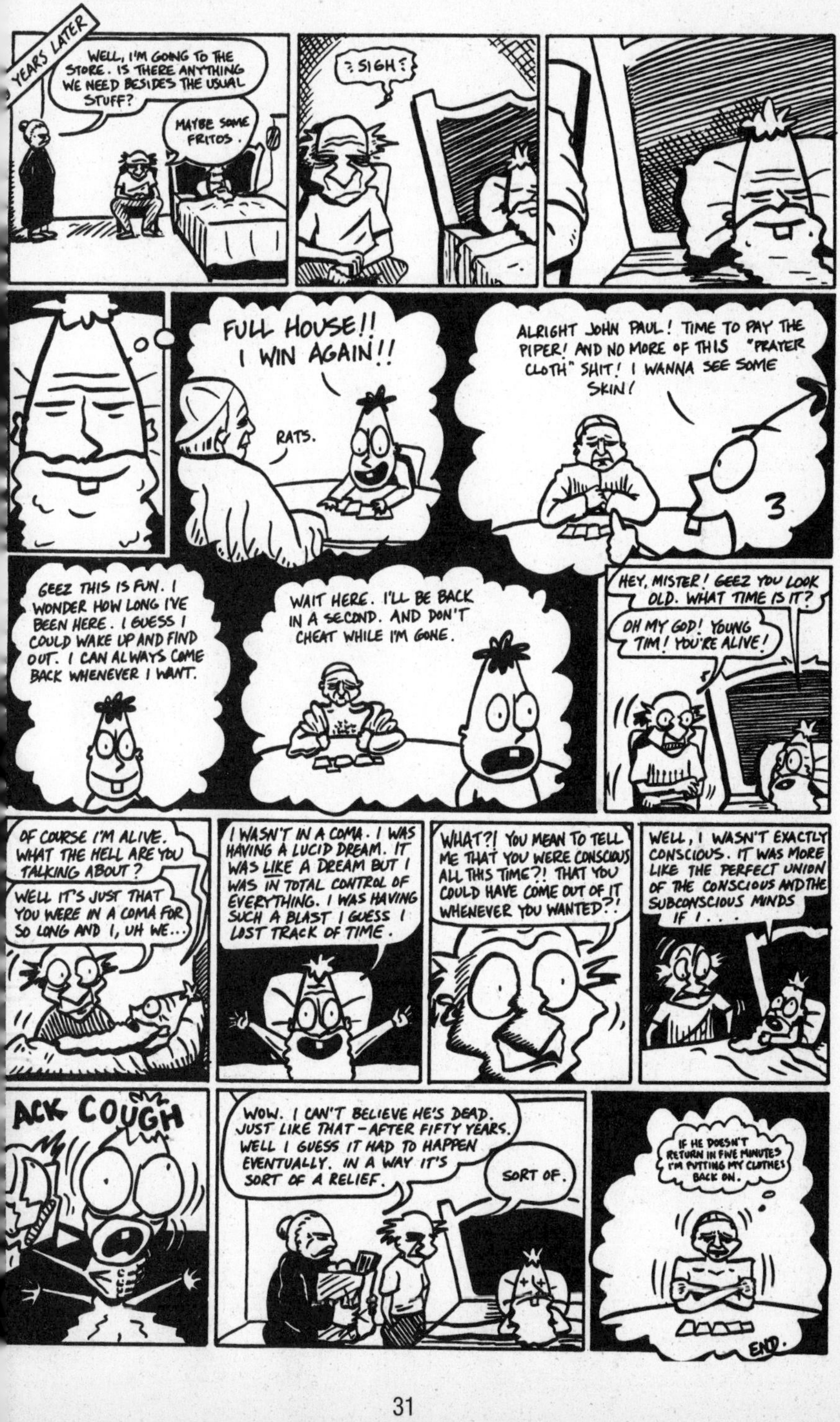
YEARS LATER
WELL, I'M GOING TO THE STORE. IS THERE ANYTHING WE NEED BESIDES THE USUAL STUFF?
MAYBE SOME FRITOS.
SIGH
FULL HOUSE!! I WIN AGAIN!!
RATS.
ALRIGHT JOHN PAUL! TIME TO PAY THE PIPER! AND NO MORE OF THIS "PRAYER CLOTH" SHIT! I WANNA SEE SOME SKIN!
3
GEEZ THIS IS FUN. I WONDER HOW LONG I'VE BEEN HERE. I GUESS I COULD WAKE UP AND FIND OUT. I CAN ALWAYS COME BACK WHENEVER I WANT.
WAIT HERE. I'LL BE BACK IN A SECOND. AND DON'T CHEAT WHILE I'M GONE.
HEY, MISTER! GEEZ YOU LOOK OLD. WHAT TIME IS IT?
OH MY GOD! YOUNG TIM! YOU'RE ALIVE!
OF COURSE I'M ALIVE. WHAT THE HELL ARE YOU TALKING ABOUT?
WELL IT'S JUST THAT YOU WERE IN A COMA FOR SO LONG AND I, UH WE...
I WASN'T IN A COMA. I WAS HAVING A LUCID DREAM. IT WAS LIKE A DREAM BUT I WAS IN TOTAL CONTROL OF EVERYTHING. I WAS HAVING SUCH A BLAST I GUESS I LOST TRACK OF TIME.
WHAT?! YOU MEAN TO TELL ME THAT YOU WERE CONSCIOUS ALL THIS TIME?! THAT YOU COULD HAVE COME OUT OF IT WHENEVER YOU WANTED?!
WELL, I WASN'T EXACTLY CONSCIOUS. IT WAS MORE LIKE THE PERFECT UNION OF THE CONSCIOUS AND THE SUBCONSCIOUS MINDS IF I . . .
ACK COUGH
WOW. I CAN'T BELIEVE HE'S DEAD. JUST LIKE THAT - AFTER FIFTY YEARS. WELL I GUESS IT HAD TO HAPPEN EVENTUALLY. IN A WAY IT'S SORT OF A RELIEF.
SORT OF.
IF HE DOESN'T RETURN IN FIVE MINUTES I'M PUTTING MY CLOTHES BACK ON.
END.

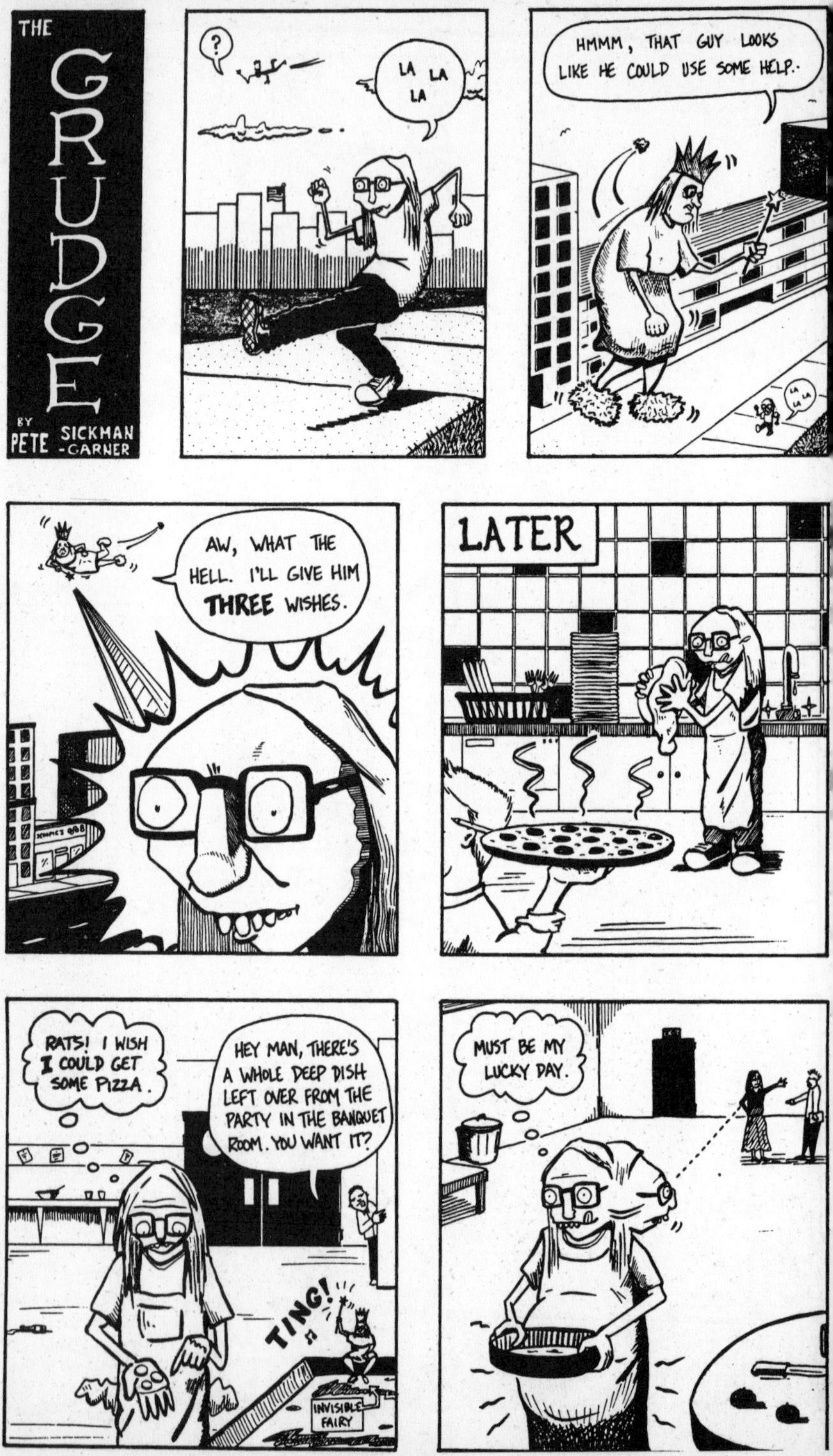
THE GRUDGE
BY PETE SICKMAN-GARNER
?
LA LA LA
HMMM, THAT GUY LOOKS LIKE HE COULD USE SOME HELP.
LA LA LA
AW, WHAT THE HELL. I'LL GIVE HIM THREE WISHES.
LATER
RATS! I WISH I COULD GET SOME PIZZA.
HEY MAN, THERE'S A WHOLE DEEP DISH LEFT OVER FROM THE PARTY IN THE BANQUET ROOM. YOU WANT IT?
TING!
INVISIBLE FAIRY
MUST BE MY LUCKY DAY.

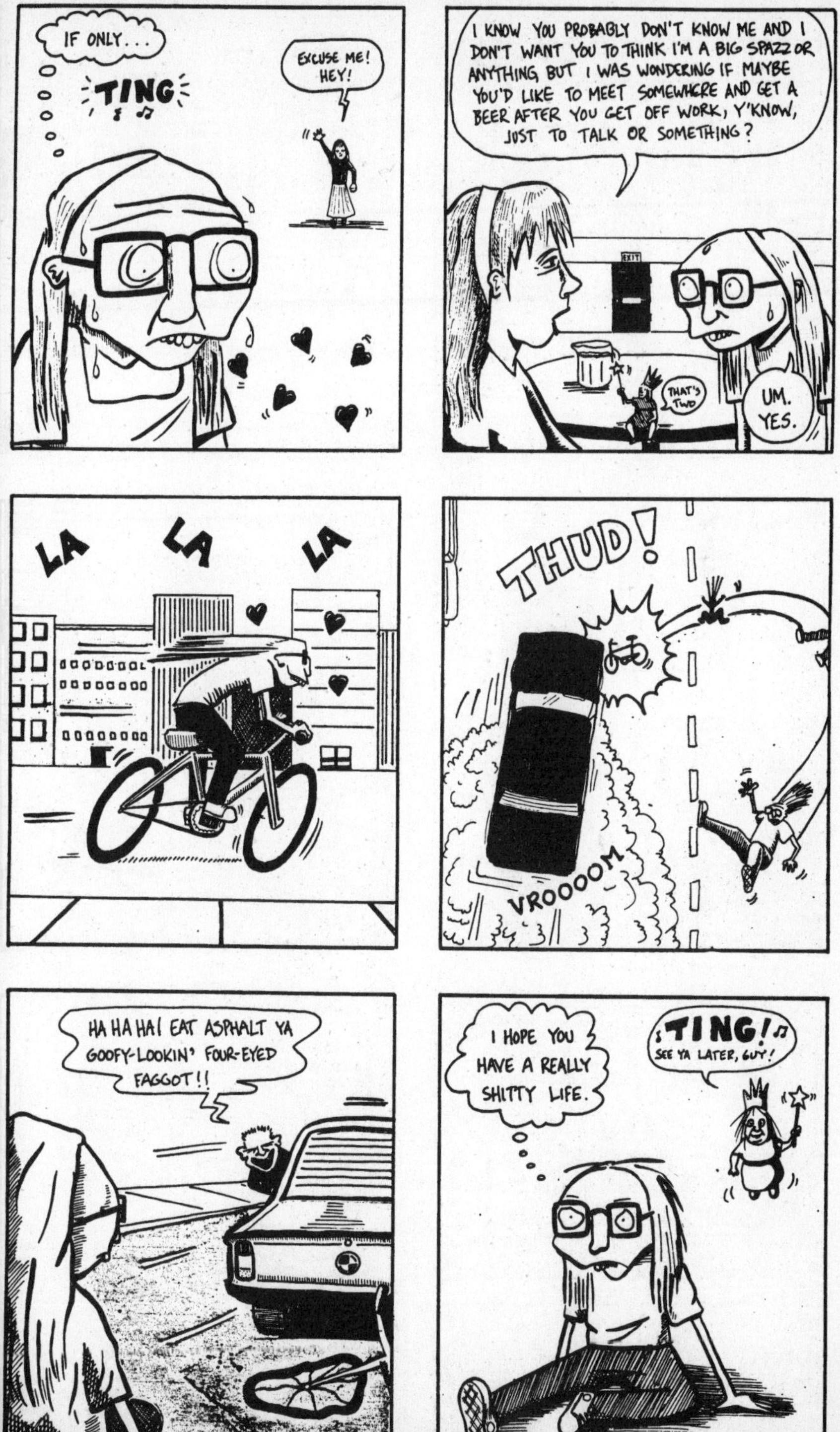
IF ONLY...
TING
EXCUSE ME! HEY!
I KNOW YOU PROBABLY DON'T KNOW ME AND I DON'T WANT YOU TO THINK I'M A BIG SPAZZ OR ANYTHING BUT I WAS WONDERING IF MAYBE YOU'D LIKE TO MEET SOMEWHERE AND GET A BEER AFTER YOU GET OFF WORK, Y'KNOW, JUST TO TALK OR SOMETHING?
EXIT
THAT'S TWO
UM. YES.
LA
LA
LA
THUD!
VROOOOM
HA HA HA! EAT ASPHALT YA GOOFY-LOOKIN' FOUR-EYED FAGGOT!!
I HOPE YOU HAVE A REALLY SHITTY LIFE.
TING!
SEE YA LATER, GUY!

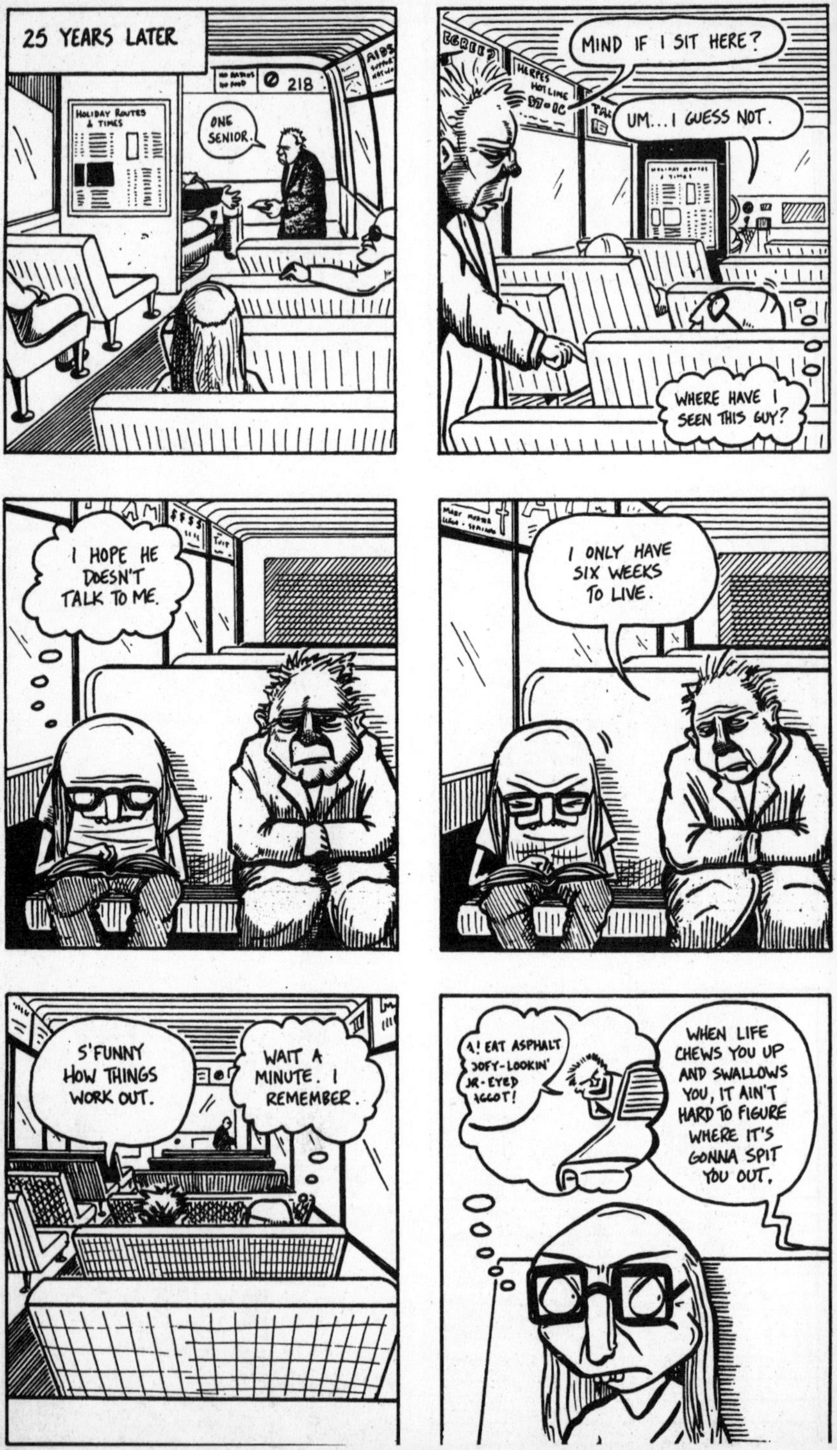
25 YEARS LATER
HOLIDAY ROUTES & TIMES
218
ONE SENIOR.
MIND IF I SIT HERE?
HERPES HOTLINE
UM... I GUESS NOT.
WHERE HAVE I SEEN THIS GUY?
I HOPE HE DOESN'T TALK TO ME.
I ONLY HAVE SIX WEEKS TO LIVE.
S'FUNNY HOW THINGS WORK OUT.
WAIT A MINUTE. I REMEMBER.
EAT ASPHALT
WHEN LIFE CHEWS YOU UP AND SWALLOWS YOU, IT AIN'T HARD TO FIGURE WHERE IT'S GONNA SPIT YOU OUT.

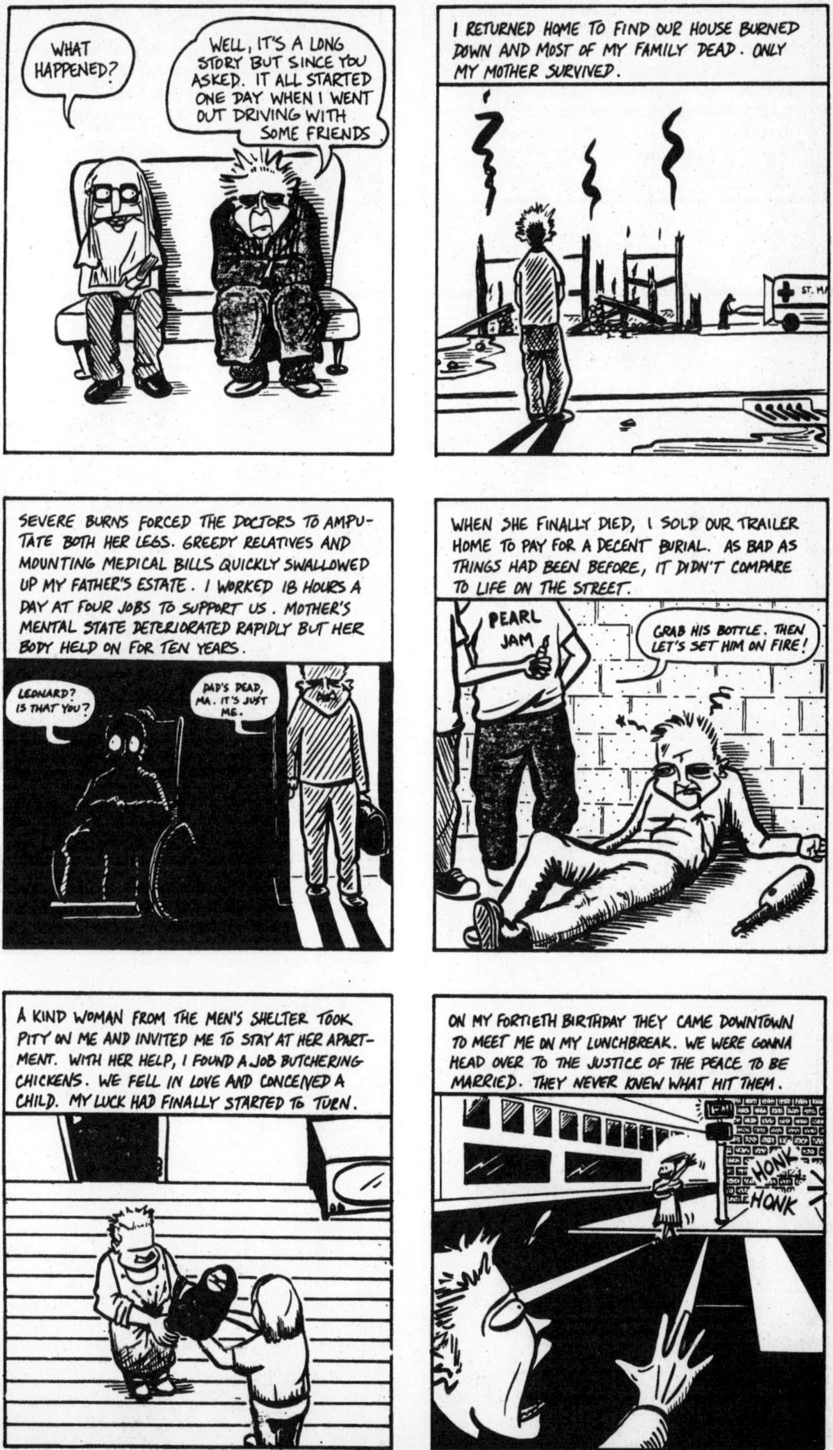
WHAT HAPPENED?
WELL, IT'S A LONG STORY BUT SINCE YOU ASKED. IT ALL STARTED ONE DAY WHEN I WENT OUT DRIVING WITH SOME FRIENDS
I RETURNED HOME TO FIND OUR HOUSE BURNED DOWN AND MOST OF MY FAMILY DEAD. ONLY MY MOTHER SURVIVED.
ST. MA
SEVERE BURNS FORCED THE DOCTORS TO AMPUTATE BOTH HER LEGS. GREEDY RELATIVES AND MOUNTING MEDICAL BILLS QUICKLY SWALLOWED UP MY FATHER'S ESTATE. I WORKED 18 HOURS A DAY AT FOUR JOBS TO SUPPORT US. MOTHER'S MENTAL STATE DETERIORATED RAPIDLY BUT HER BODY HELD ON FOR TEN YEARS.
LEONARD? IS THAT YOU?
DAD'S DEAD, MA. IT'S JUST ME.
WHEN SHE FINALLY DIED, I SOLD OUR TRAILER HOME TO PAY FOR A DECENT BURIAL. AS BAD AS THINGS HAD BEEN BEFORE, IT DIDN'T COMPARE TO LIFE ON THE STREET.
PEARL JAM
GRAB HIS BOTTLE. THEN LET'S SET HIM ON FIRE!
A KIND WOMAN FROM THE MEN'S SHELTER TOOK PITY ON ME AND INVITED ME TO STAY AT HER APARTMENT. WITH HER HELP, I FOUND A JOB BUTCHERING CHICKENS. WE FELL IN LOVE AND CONCEIVED A CHILD. MY LUCK HAD FINALLY STARTED TO TURN.
ON MY FORTIETH BIRTHDAY THEY CAME DOWNTOWN TO MEET ME ON MY LUNCHBREAK. WE WERE GONNA HEAD OVER TO THE JUSTICE OF THE PEACE TO BE MARRIED. THEY NEVER KNEW WHAT HIT THEM.
HONK
HONK

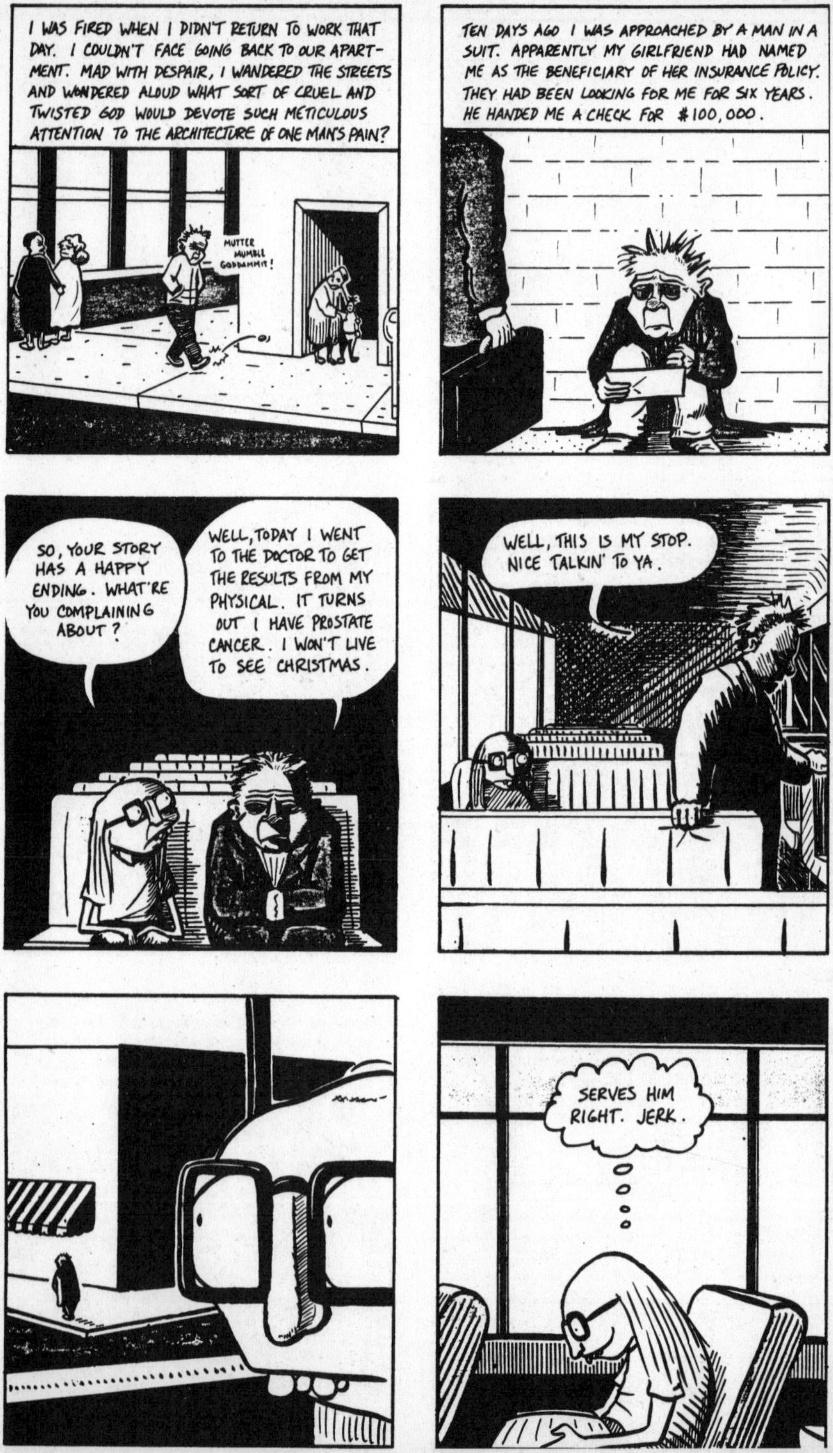
I WAS FIRED WHEN I DIDN'T RETURN TO WORK THAT DAY. I COULDN'T FACE GOING BACK TO OUR APARTMENT. MAD WITH DESPAIR, I WANDERED THE STREETS AND WONDERED ALOUD WHAT SORT OF CRUEL AND TWISTED GOD WOULD DEVOTE SUCH METICULOUS ATTENTION TO THE ARCHITECTURE OF ONE MAN'S PAIN?
MUTTER MUMBLE GODDAMMIT!
TEN DAYS AGO I WAS APPROACHED BY A MAN IN A SUIT. APPARENTLY MY GIRLFRIEND HAD NAMED ME AS THE BENEFICIARY OF HER INSURANCE POLICY. THEY HAD BEEN LOOKING FOR ME FOR SIX YEARS. HE HANDED ME A CHECK FOR $100,000.
SO, YOUR STORY HAS A HAPPY ENDING. WHAT'RE YOU COMPLAINING ABOUT?
WELL, TODAY I WENT TO THE DOCTOR TO GET THE RESULTS FROM MY PHYSICAL. IT TURNS OUT I HAVE PROSTATE CANCER. I WON'T LIVE TO SEE CHRISTMAS.
WELL, THIS IS MY STOP. NICE TALKIN' TO YA.
SERVES HIM RIGHT. JERK.

# Friendship is a Blood Sport

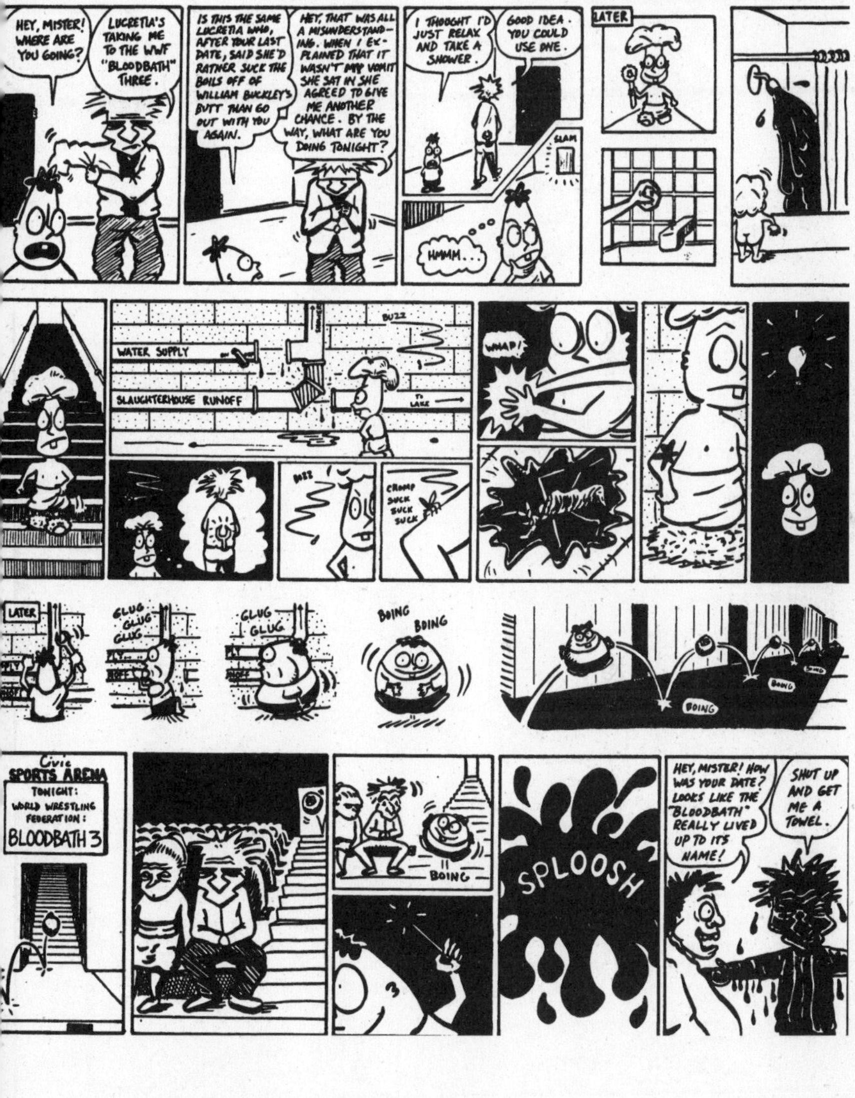
HEY, MISTER! WHERE ARE YOU GOING?
LUCRETIA'S TAKING ME TO THE WWF "BLOODBATH" THREE.
IS THIS THE SAME LUCRETIA WHO, AFTER YOUR LAST DATE, SAID SHE'D RATHER SUCK THE BOILS OFF OF WILLIAM BUCKLEY'S BUTT THAN GO OUT WITH YOU AGAIN.
HEY, THAT WAS ALL A MISUNDERSTANDING. WHEN I EXPLAINED THAT IT WASN'T MY VOMIT SHE SAT IN SHE AGREED TO GIVE ME ANOTHER CHANCE. BY THE WAY, WHAT ARE YOU DOING TONIGHT?
I THOUGHT I'D JUST RELAX AND TAKE A SHOWER.
GOOD IDEA. YOU COULD USE ONE.
SLAM
HMMM...
LATER
WATER SUPPLY
SLAUGHTERHOUSE RUNOFF
BUZZ
TO LAKE
WHAP!
BZZ
CHOMP SUCK SUCK SUCK
LATER
GLUG GLUG GLUG
GLUG GLUG
BOING BOING
BOING
BOING
BOING
CIVIC SPORTS ARENA
TONIGHT: WORLD WRESTLING FEDERATION: BLOODBATH 3
BOING
SPLOOSH
HEY, MISTER! HOW WAS YOUR DATE? LOOKS LIKE THE "BLOODBATH" REALLY LIVED UP TO ITS NAME!
SHUT UP AND GET ME A TOWEL.

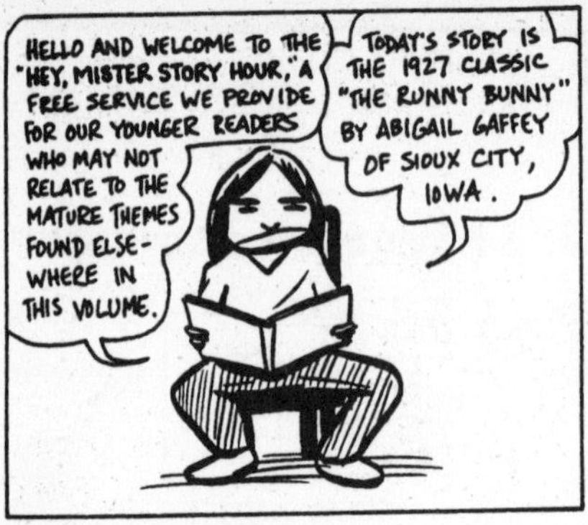
HELLO AND WELCOME TO THE "HEY, MISTER STORY HOUR," A FREE SERVICE WE PROVIDE FOR OUR YOUNGER READERS WHO MAY NOT RELATE TO THE MATURE THEMES FOUND ELSEWHERE IN THIS VOLUME.
TODAY'S STORY IS THE 1927 CLASSIC "THE RUNNY BUNNY" BY ABIGAIL GAFFEY OF SIOUX CITY, IOWA.

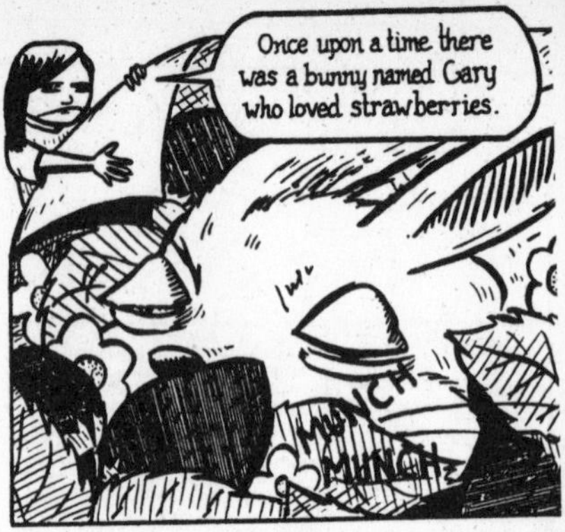
Once upon a time there was a bunny named Gary who loved strawberries.
MUNCH
MUNCH

All day long he would sit in the strawberry patch and eat and eat and eat.

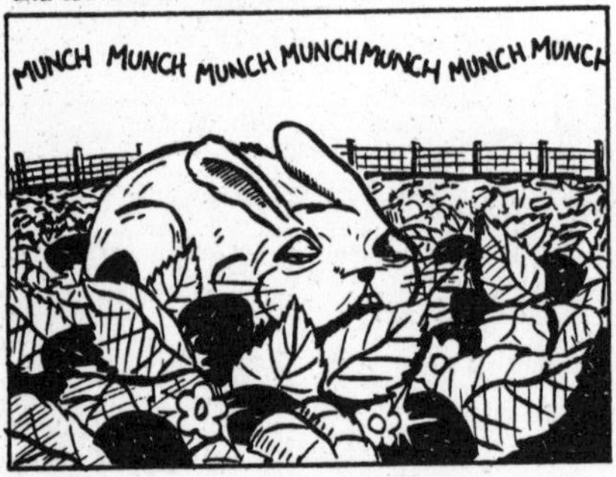
MUNCH MUNCH MUNCH MUNCH MUNCH MUNCH MUNCH

When the other bunnies asked him if he would like to join in their bunny games, he hissed at them. "Stay away from my strawberries!"

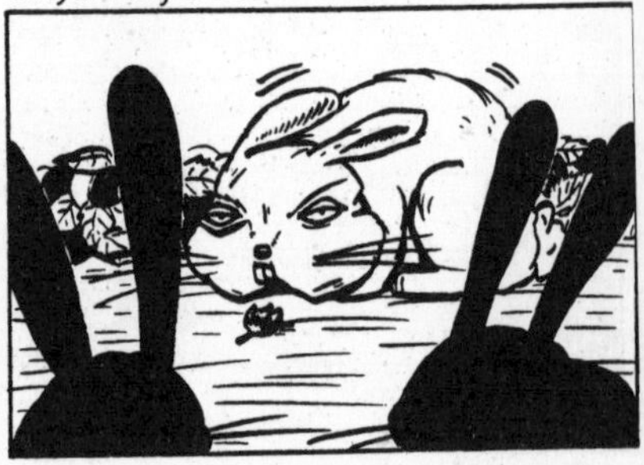

"They're not his strawberries!" complained one bunny to his friends. "He thinks he owns the whole patch," groused a second. "I hate the name Gary," griped a third.

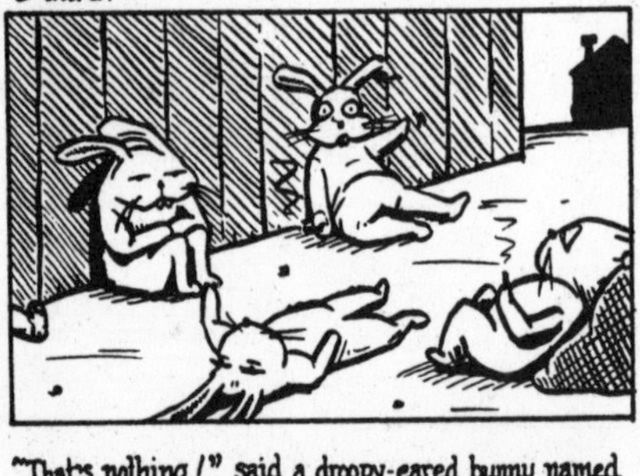

"He was still out there last night when I went to pick some berries for breakfast," said a bunny named Judy. "I thought I had slipped past him but when I woke up today my berries had been eaten."

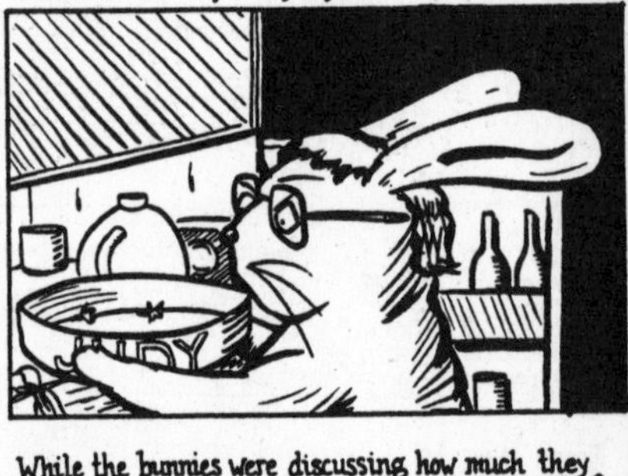

"That's nothing!" said a droopy-eared bunny named Lisa. "Yesterday I went to tell him that his mom was looking for him and he turned around and bit me!" she announced while holding up a bandaged paw. "That freak probably gave me rabies!"

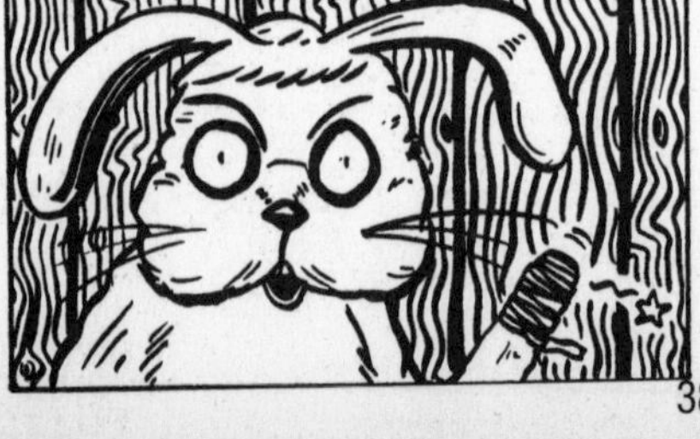

While the bunnies were discussing how much they hated Gary, they saw Farmer John coming out of the shed with a shotgun. "Quick! Everyone hide!" they shouted as they hopped away to the bushes at the edge of the garden.

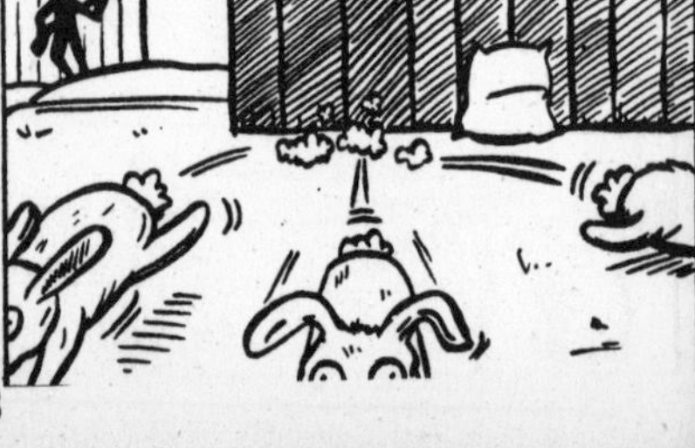

Gary tried to hop away, too, but all the strawberries had made him feel a little sick. The best he could manage was a slow crawl towards the bushes.

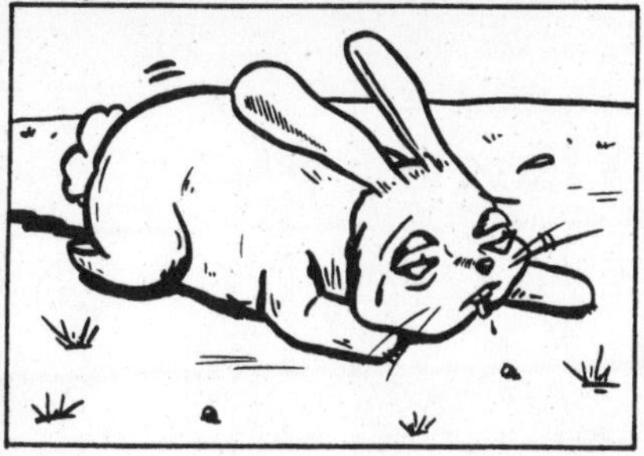

When Farmer John reached the strawberry patch, he noticed a trail of slick, brown liquid leading away from it. "One of these bunnies has been eating too many strawberries," he thought to himself.

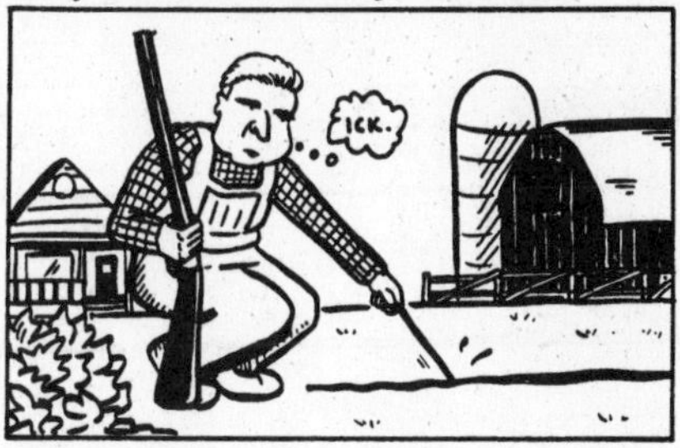
ICK.

He followed the trail which led toward the bushes at the edge of the garden. After about twenty yards, he came upon Gary who was struggling to reach cover.

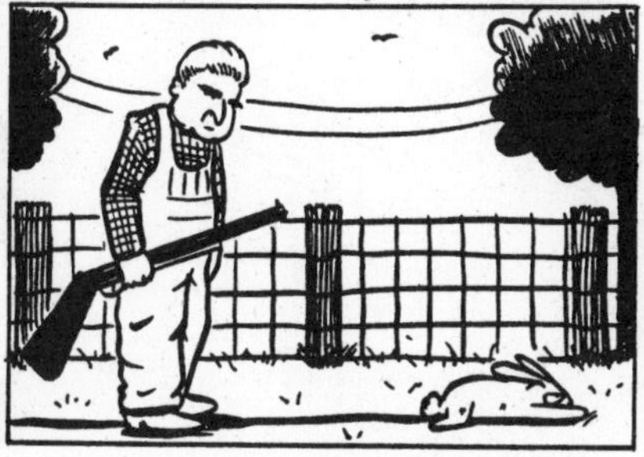

"I've never known a bunny who liked strawberries as much as you do," said Farmer John. "Ooooogh," moaned Gary.

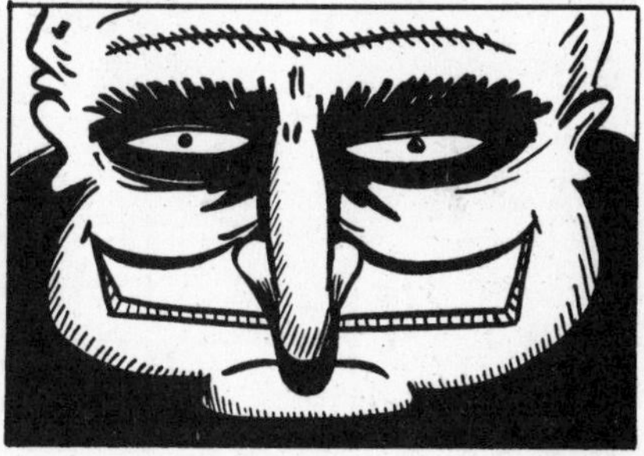

"You sure are a funny little bunny," said Farmer John as he raised his gun and fired.

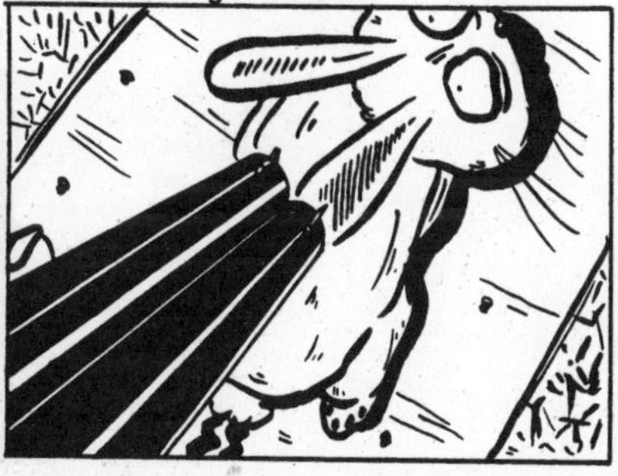

When the other bunnies saw what happened, they were overcome with fits of laughter and glee. "Hooray!" cried one bunny. "No more Scary Gary!" screamed another.

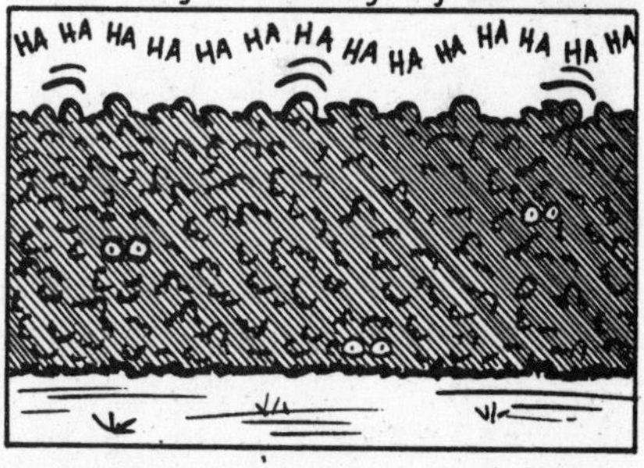
HA HA HA HA HA HA HA HA HA HA HA HA HA HA

Farmer John heard the noise from the bushes and wondered what the commotion was all about. When he found the other bunnies there he shot them, too.

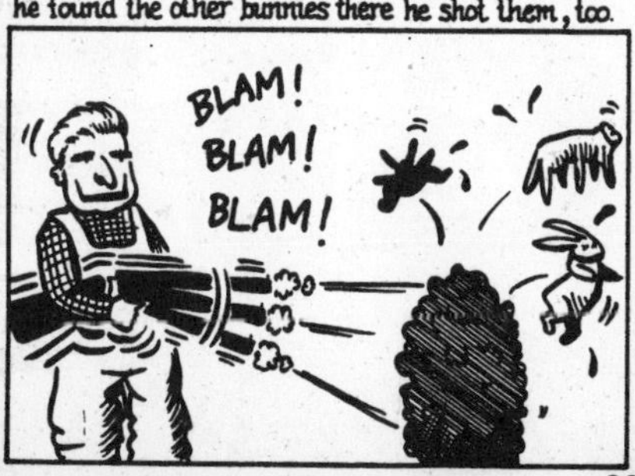
BLAM!
BLAM!
BLAM!

That night, everyone in the village came over to Farmer John's and feasted on his wife Mary's world famous hasenpfeffer.

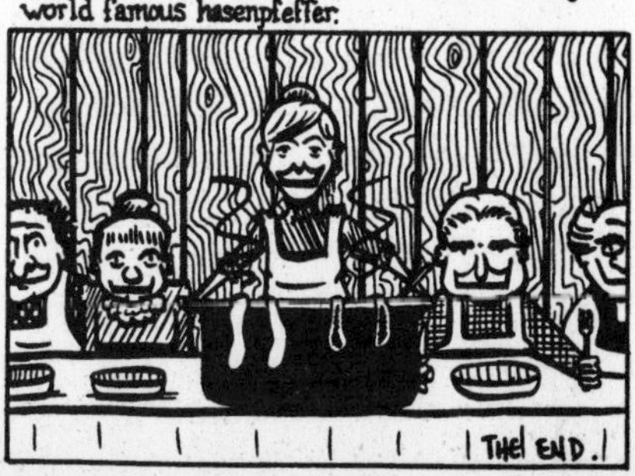
THE END.

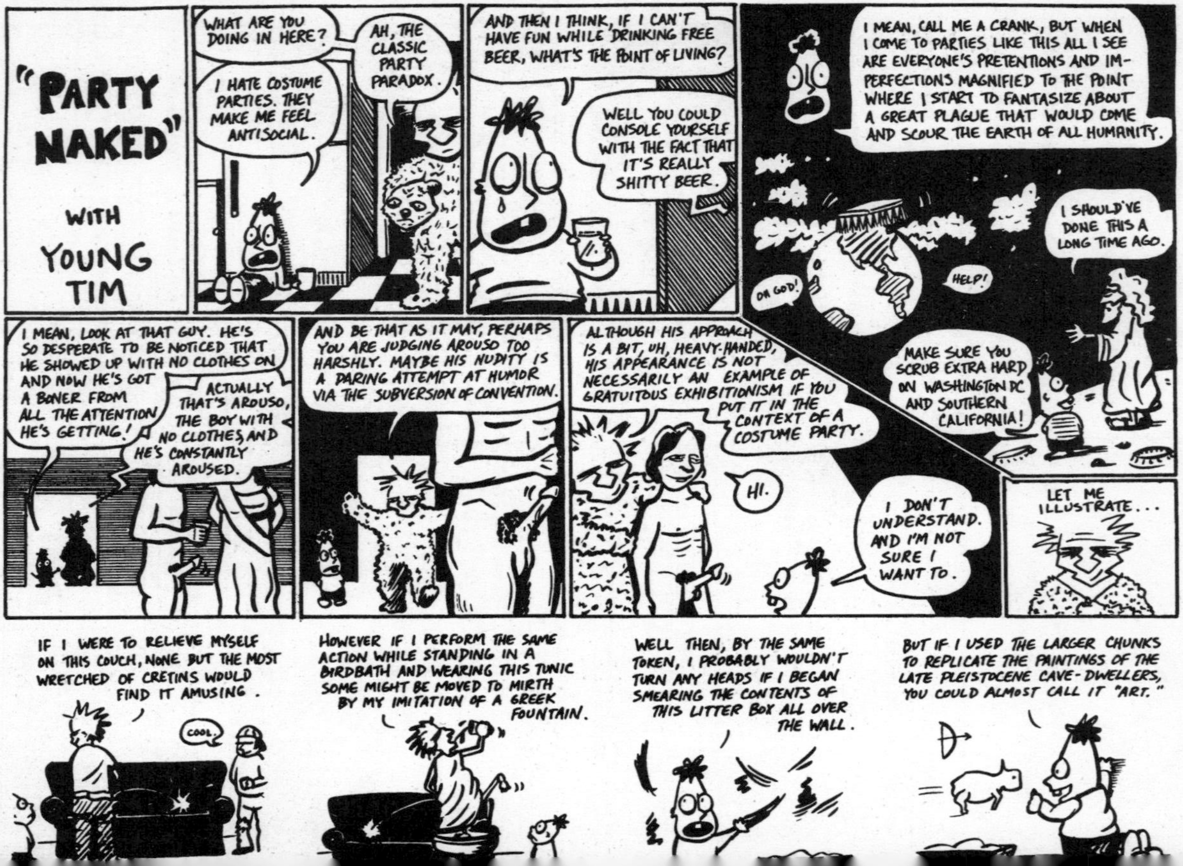

"PARTY NAKED" WITH YOUNG TIM
WHAT ARE YOU DOING IN HERE?
I HATE COSTUME PARTIES. THEY MAKE ME FEEL ANTISOCIAL.
AH, THE CLASSIC PARTY PARADOX.
AND THEN I THINK, IF I CAN'T HAVE FUN WHILE DRINKING FREE BEER, WHAT'S THE POINT OF LIVING?
WELL YOU COULD CONSOLE YOURSELF WITH THE FACT THAT IT'S REALLY SHITTY BEER.
I MEAN, CALL ME A CRANK, BUT WHEN I COME TO PARTIES LIKE THIS ALL I SEE ARE EVERYONE'S PRETENTIONS AND IMPERFECTIONS MAGNIFIED TO THE POINT WHERE I START TO FANTASIZE ABOUT A GREAT PLAGUE THAT WOULD COME AND SCOUR THE EARTH OF ALL HUMANITY.
OH GOD!
HELP!
I SHOULD'VE DONE THIS A LONG TIME AGO.
MAKE SURE YOU SCRUB EXTRA HARD ON WASHINGTON DC AND SOUTHERN CALIFORNIA!
I MEAN, LOOK AT THAT GUY. HE'S SO DESPERATE TO BE NOTICED THAT HE SHOWED UP WITH NO CLOTHES ON AND NOW HE'S GOT A BONER FROM ALL THE ATTENTION HE'S GETTING!
ACTUALLY THAT'S AROUSO, THE BOY WITH NO CLOTHES, AND HE'S CONSTANTLY AROUSED.
AND BE THAT AS IT MAY, PERHAPS YOU ARE JUDGING AROUSO TOO HARSHLY. MAYBE HIS NUDITY IS A DARING ATTEMPT AT HUMOR VIA THE SUBVERSION OF CONVENTION.
ALTHOUGH HIS APPROACH IS A BIT, UH, HEAVY-HANDED, HIS APPEARANCE IS NOT NECESSARILY AN EXAMPLE OF GRATUITOUS EXHIBITIONISM IF YOU PUT IT IN THE CONTEXT OF A COSTUME PARTY.
HI.
I DON'T UNDERSTAND. AND I'M NOT SURE I WANT TO.
LET ME ILLUSTRATE...
IF I WERE TO RELIEVE MYSELF ON THIS COUCH, NONE BUT THE MOST WRETCHED OF CRETINS WOULD FIND IT AMUSING.
COOL.
HOWEVER IF I PERFORM THE SAME ACTION WHILE STANDING IN A BIRDBATH AND WEARING THIS TUNIC SOME MIGHT BE MOVED TO MIRTH BY MY IMITATION OF A GREEK FOUNTAIN.
WELL THEN, BY THE SAME TOKEN, I PROBABLY WOULDN'T TURN ANY HEADS IF I BEGAN SMEARING THE CONTENTS OF THIS LITTER BOX ALL OVER THE WALL.
BUT IF I USED THE LARGER CHUNKS TO REPLICATE THE PAINTINGS OF THE LATE PLEISTOCENE CAVE-DWELLERS, YOU COULD ALMOST CALL IT "ART."

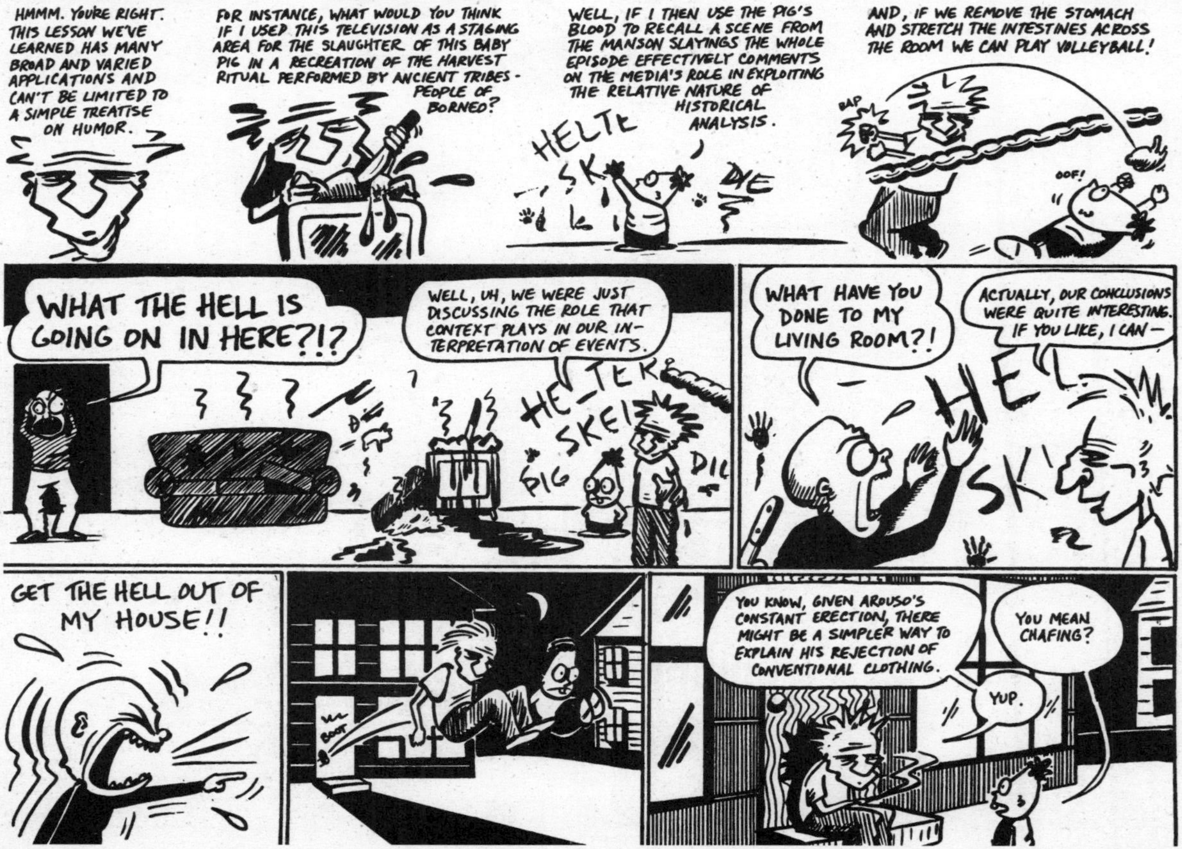
HMMM. YOU'RE RIGHT. THIS LESSON WE'VE LEARNED HAS MANY BROAD AND VARIED APPLICATIONS AND CAN'T BE LIMITED TO A SIMPLE TREATISE ON HUMOR.
FOR INSTANCE, WHAT WOULD YOU THINK IF I USED THIS TELEVISION AS A STAGING AREA FOR THE SLAUGHTER OF THIS BABY PIG IN A RECREATION OF THE HARVEST RITUAL PERFORMED BY ANCIENT TRIBES - PEOPLE OF BORNEO?
WELL, IF I THEN USE THE PIG'S BLOOD TO RECALL A SCENE FROM THE MANSON SLAYINGS THE WHOLE EPISODE EFFECTIVELY COMMENTS ON THE MEDIA'S ROLE IN EXPLOITING THE RELATIVE NATURE OF HISTORICAL ANALYSIS.
HELTE
SK
DIE
AND, IF WE REMOVE THE STOMACH AND STRETCH THE INTESTINES ACROSS THE ROOM WE CAN PLAY VOLLEYBALL!
BAP
OOF!
WHAT THE HELL IS GOING ON IN HERE?!?
WELL, UH, WE WERE JUST DISCUSSING THE ROLE THAT CONTEXT PLAYS IN OUR INTERPRETATION OF EVENTS.
HELTER
SKE
PIG
WHAT HAVE YOU DONE TO MY LIVING ROOM?!
ACTUALLY, OUR CONCLUSIONS WERE QUITE INTERESTING. IF YOU LIKE, I CAN—
GET THE HELL OUT OF MY HOUSE!!
BOOT
YOU KNOW, GIVEN AROUSO'S CONSTANT ERECTION, THERE MIGHT BE A SIMPLER WAY TO EXPLAIN HIS REJECTION OF CONVENTIONAL CLOTHING.
YOU MEAN CHAFING?
YUP.

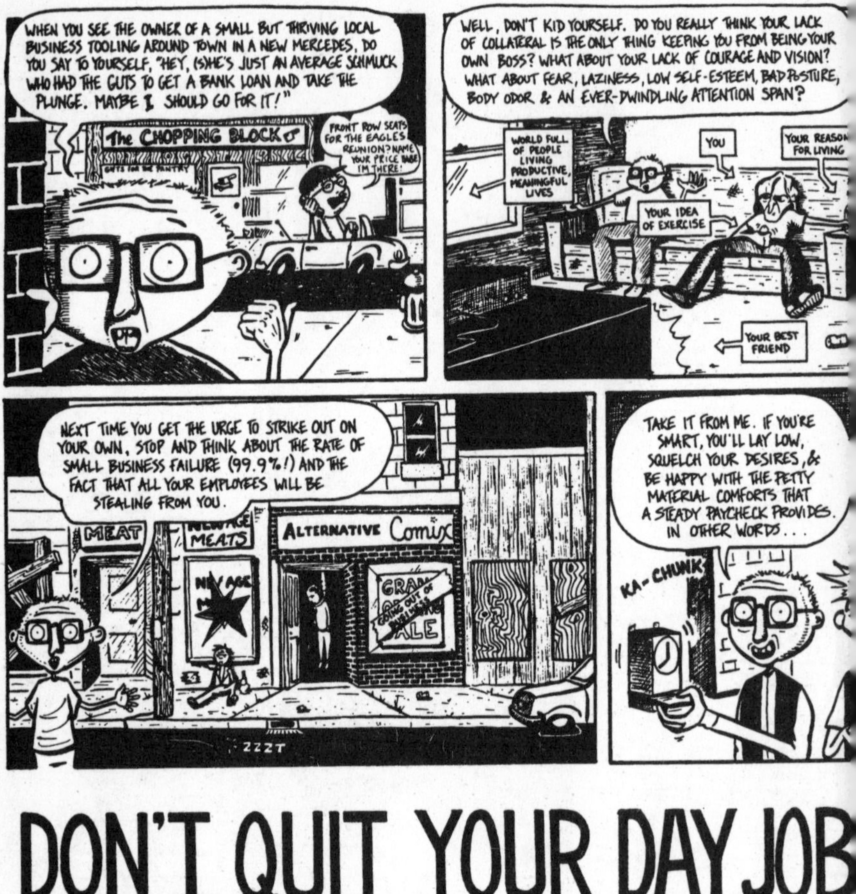
WHEN YOU SEE THE OWNER OF A SMALL BUT THRIVING LOCAL BUSINESS TOOLING AROUND TOWN IN A NEW MERCEDES, DO YOU SAY TO YOURSELF, "HEY, (S)HE'S JUST AN AVERAGE SCHMUCK WHO HAD THE GUTS TO GET A BANK LOAN AND TAKE THE PLUNGE. MAYBE I SHOULD GO FOR IT!"
The CHOPPING BLOCK
FRONT ROW SEATS FOR THE EAGLES REUNION? NAME YOUR PRICE BABE I'M THERE!
WELL, DON'T KID YOURSELF. DO YOU REALLY THINK YOUR LACK OF COLLATERAL IS THE ONLY THING KEEPING YOU FROM BEING YOUR OWN BOSS? WHAT ABOUT YOUR LACK OF COURAGE AND VISION? WHAT ABOUT FEAR, LAZINESS, LOW SELF-ESTEEM, BAD POSTURE, BODY ODOR & AN EVER-DWINDLING ATTENTION SPAN?
WORLD FULL OF PEOPLE LIVING PRODUCTIVE, MEANINGFUL LIVES
YOU
YOUR REASON FOR LIVING
YOUR IDEA OF EXERCISE
YOUR BEST FRIEND
NEXT TIME YOU GET THE URGE TO STRIKE OUT ON YOUR OWN, STOP AND THINK ABOUT THE RATE OF SMALL BUSINESS FAILURE (99.9%!) AND THE FACT THAT ALL YOUR EMPLOYEES WILL BE STEALING FROM YOU.
MEAT
MEATS
ALTERNATIVE Comix
GOING OUT OF BUSINESS
ZZZT
TAKE IT FROM ME. IF YOU'RE SMART, YOU'LL LAY LOW, SQUELCH YOUR DESIRES, & BE HAPPY WITH THE PETTY MATERIAL COMFORTS THAT A STEADY PAYCHECK PROVIDES. IN OTHER WORDS...
KA-CHUNK

# DON'T QUIT YOUR DAY JOB

©1995 BY P. SICKMAN-GARNER

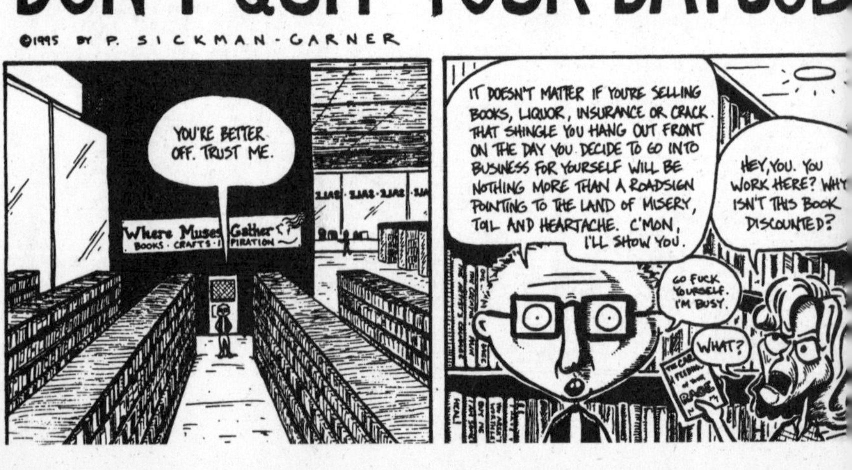
YOU'RE BETTER OFF. TRUST ME.
Where Muses Gather
BOOKS · CRAFTS · I PIRATION
IT DOESN'T MATTER IF YOU'RE SELLING BOOKS, LIQUOR, INSURANCE OR CRACK. THAT SHINGLE YOU HANG OUT FRONT ON THE DAY YOU DECIDE TO GO INTO BUSINESS FOR YOURSELF WILL BE NOTHING MORE THAN A ROADSIGN POINTING TO THE LAND OF MISERY, TOIL AND HEARTACHE. C'MON, I'LL SHOW YOU.
HEY, YOU. YOU WORK HERE? WHY ISN'T THIS BOOK DISCOUNTED?
GO FUCK YOURSELF. I'M BUSY.
WHAT?

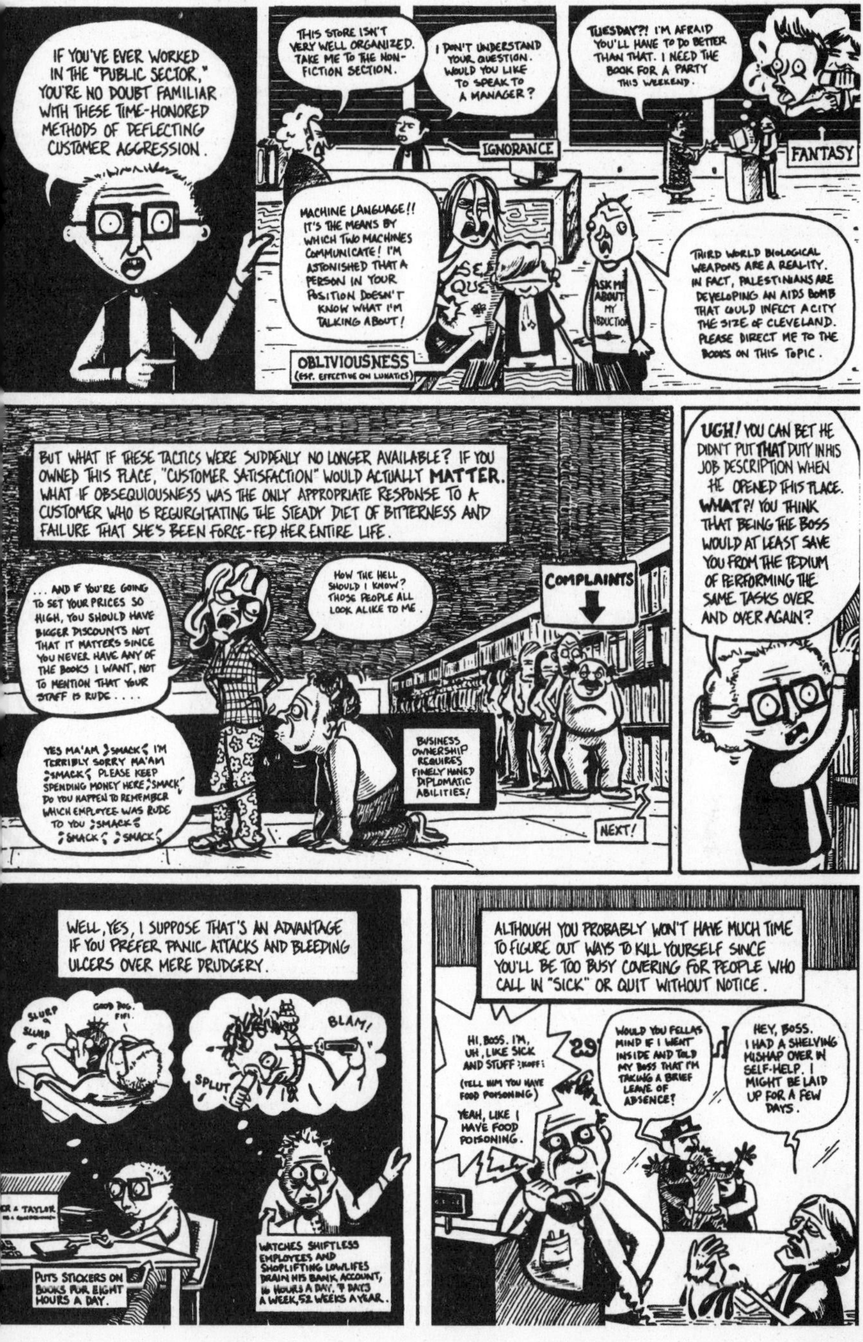
IF YOU'VE EVER WORKED IN THE "PUBLIC SECTOR," YOU'RE NO DOUBT FAMILIAR WITH THESE TIME-HONORED METHODS OF DEFLECTING CUSTOMER AGGRESSION.
THIS STORE ISN'T VERY WELL ORGANIZED. TAKE ME TO THE NON-FICTION SECTION.
I DON'T UNDERSTAND YOUR QUESTION. WOULD YOU LIKE TO SPEAK TO A MANAGER?
IGNORANCE
TUESDAY?! I'M AFRAID YOU'LL HAVE TO DO BETTER THAN THAT. I NEED THE BOOK FOR A PARTY THIS WEEKEND.
FANTASY
MACHINE LANGUAGE!! IT'S THE MEANS BY WHICH TWO MACHINES COMMUNICATE! I'M ASTONISHED THAT A PERSON IN YOUR POSITION DOESN'T KNOW WHAT I'M TALKING ABOUT!
ASK ME ABOUT MY ABDUCTION
THIRD WORLD BIOLOGICAL WEAPONS ARE A REALITY. IN FACT, PALESTINIANS ARE DEVELOPING AN AIDS BOMB THAT COULD INFECT A CITY THE SIZE OF CLEVELAND. PLEASE DIRECT ME TO THE BOOKS ON THIS TOPIC.
OBLIVIOUSNESS
(ESP. EFFECTIVE ON LUNATICS)
BUT WHAT IF THESE TACTICS WERE SUDDENLY NO LONGER AVAILABLE? IF YOU OWNED THIS PLACE, "CUSTOMER SATISFACTION" WOULD ACTUALLY MATTER. WHAT IF OBSEQUIOUSNESS WAS THE ONLY APPROPRIATE RESPONSE TO A CUSTOMER WHO IS REGURGITATING THE STEADY DIET OF BITTERNESS AND FAILURE THAT SHE'S BEEN FORCE-FED HER ENTIRE LIFE.
... AND IF YOU'RE GOING TO SET YOUR PRICES SO HIGH, YOU SHOULD HAVE BIGGER DISCOUNTS NOT THAT IT MATTERS SINCE YOU NEVER HAVE ANY OF THE BOOKS I WANT, NOT TO MENTION THAT YOUR STAFF IS RUDE....
HOW THE HELL SHOULD I KNOW? THOSE PEOPLE ALL LOOK ALIKE TO ME.
COMPLAINTS
YES MA'AM *SMACK* I'M TERRIBLY SORRY MA'AM *SMACK* PLEASE KEEP SPENDING MONEY HERE *SMACK* DO YOU HAPPEN TO REMEMBER WHICH EMPLOYEE WAS RUDE TO YOU *SMACK* *SMACK* *SMACK*
BUSINESS OWNERSHIP REQUIRES FINELY HONED DIPLOMATIC ABILITIES!
NEXT!
UGH! YOU CAN BET HE DIDN'T PUT THAT DUTY IN HIS JOB DESCRIPTION WHEN HE OPENED THIS PLACE. WHAT?! YOU THINK THAT BEING THE BOSS WOULD AT LEAST SAVE YOU FROM THE TEDIUM OF PERFORMING THE SAME TASKS OVER AND OVER AGAIN?
WELL, YES, I SUPPOSE THAT'S AN ADVANTAGE IF YOU PREFER PANIC ATTACKS AND BLEEDING ULCERS OVER MERE DRUDGERY.
SLURP SLURP
GOOD DOG, FIFI.
BLAM!
SPLUT
PUTS STICKERS ON BOOKS FOR EIGHT HOURS A DAY.
WATCHES SHIFTLESS EMPLOYEES AND SHOPLIFTING LOWLIFES DRAIN HIS BANK ACCOUNT, 16 HOURS A DAY, 7 DAYS A WEEK, 52 WEEKS A YEAR.
ALTHOUGH YOU PROBABLY WON'T HAVE MUCH TIME TO FIGURE OUT WAYS TO KILL YOURSELF SINCE YOU'LL BE TOO BUSY COVERING FOR PEOPLE WHO CALL IN "SICK" OR QUIT WITHOUT NOTICE.
HI, BOSS. I'M, UH, LIKE SICK AND STUFF *KOFF*
(TELL HIM YOU HAVE FOOD POISONING)
YEAH, LIKE I HAVE FOOD POISONING.
WOULD YOU FELLAS MIND IF I WENT INSIDE AND TOLD MY BOSS THAT I'M TAKING A BRIEF LEAVE OF ABSENCE?
HEY, BOSS. I HAD A SHELVING MISHAP OVER IN SELF-HELP. I MIGHT BE LAID UP FOR A FEW DAYS.

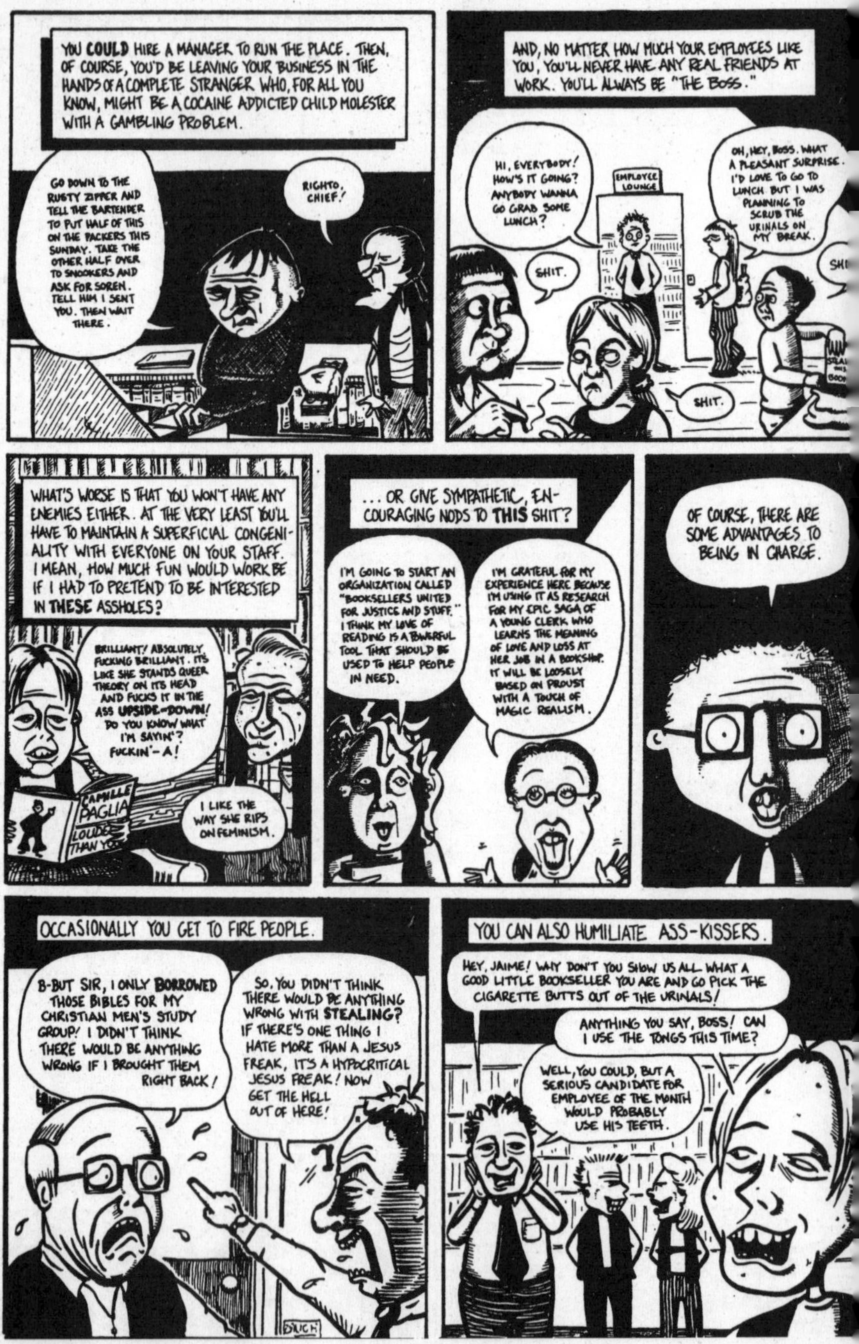

YOU COULD HIRE A MANAGER TO RUN THE PLACE. THEN, OF COURSE, YOU'D BE LEAVING YOUR BUSINESS IN THE HANDS OF A COMPLETE STRANGER WHO, FOR ALL YOU KNOW, MIGHT BE A COCAINE ADDICTED CHILD MOLESTER WITH A GAMBLING PROBLEM.
GO DOWN TO THE RUSTY ZIPPER AND TELL THE BARTENDER TO PUT HALF OF THIS ON THE PACKERS THIS SUNDAY. TAKE THE OTHER HALF OVER TO SNOOKERS AND ASK FOR SOREN. TELL HIM I SENT YOU. THEN WAIT THERE.
RIGHTO, CHIEF!
AND, NO MATTER HOW MUCH YOUR EMPLOYEES LIKE YOU, YOU'LL NEVER HAVE ANY REAL FRIENDS AT WORK. YOU'LL ALWAYS BE "THE BOSS."
HI, EVERYBODY! HOW'S IT GOING? ANYBODY WANNA GO GRAB SOME LUNCH?
EMPLOYEE LOUNGE
OH, HEY, BOSS. WHAT A PLEASANT SURPRISE. I'D LOVE TO GO TO LUNCH BUT I WAS PLANNING TO SCRUB THE URINALS ON MY BREAK.
SHIT.
SHIT.
WHAT'S WORSE IS THAT YOU WON'T HAVE ANY ENEMIES EITHER. AT THE VERY LEAST YOU'LL HAVE TO MAINTAIN A SUPERFICIAL CONGENIALITY WITH EVERYONE ON YOUR STAFF. I MEAN, HOW MUCH FUN WOULD WORK BE IF I HAD TO PRETEND TO BE INTERESTED IN THESE ASSHOLES?
BRILLIANT! ABSOLUTELY FUCKING BRILLIANT. IT'S LIKE SHE STANDS QUEER THEORY ON ITS HEAD AND FUCKS IT IN THE ASS UPSIDE-DOWN! DO YOU KNOW WHAT I'M SAYIN'? FUCKIN'-A!
CAMILLE PAGLIA
I LIKE THE WAY SHE RIPS ON FEMINISM.
... OR GIVE SYMPATHETIC, ENCOURAGING NODS TO THIS SHIT?
I'M GOING TO START AN ORGANIZATION CALLED "BOOKSELLERS UNITED FOR JUSTICE AND STUFF." I THINK MY LOVE OF READING IS A POWERFUL TOOL THAT SHOULD BE USED TO HELP PEOPLE IN NEED.
I'M GRATEFUL FOR MY EXPERIENCE HERE BECAUSE I'M USING IT AS RESEARCH FOR MY EPIC SAGA OF A YOUNG CLERK WHO LEARNS THE MEANING OF LOVE AND LOSS AT HER JOB IN A BOOKSHOP. IT WILL BE LOOSELY BASED ON PROUST WITH A TOUCH OF MAGIC REALISM.
OF COURSE, THERE ARE SOME ADVANTAGES TO BEING IN CHARGE.
OCCASIONALLY YOU GET TO FIRE PEOPLE.
B-BUT SIR, I ONLY BORROWED THOSE BIBLES FOR MY CHRISTIAN MEN'S STUDY GROUP! I DIDN'T THINK THERE WOULD BE ANYTHING WRONG IF I BROUGHT THEM RIGHT BACK!
SO, YOU DIDN'T THINK THERE WOULD BE ANYTHING WRONG WITH STEALING? IF THERE'S ONE THING I HATE MORE THAN A JESUS FREAK, IT'S A HYPOCRITICAL JESUS FREAK! NOW GET THE HELL OUT OF HERE!
YOU CAN ALSO HUMILIATE ASS-KISSERS.
HEY, JAIME! WHY DON'T YOU SHOW US ALL WHAT A GOOD LITTLE BOOKSELLER YOU ARE AND GO PICK THE CIGARETTE BUTTS OUT OF THE URINALS!
ANYTHING YOU SAY, BOSS! CAN I USE THE TONGS THIS TIME?
WELL, YOU COULD, BUT A SERIOUS CANDIDATE FOR EMPLOYEE OF THE MONTH WOULD PROBABLY USE HIS TEETH.

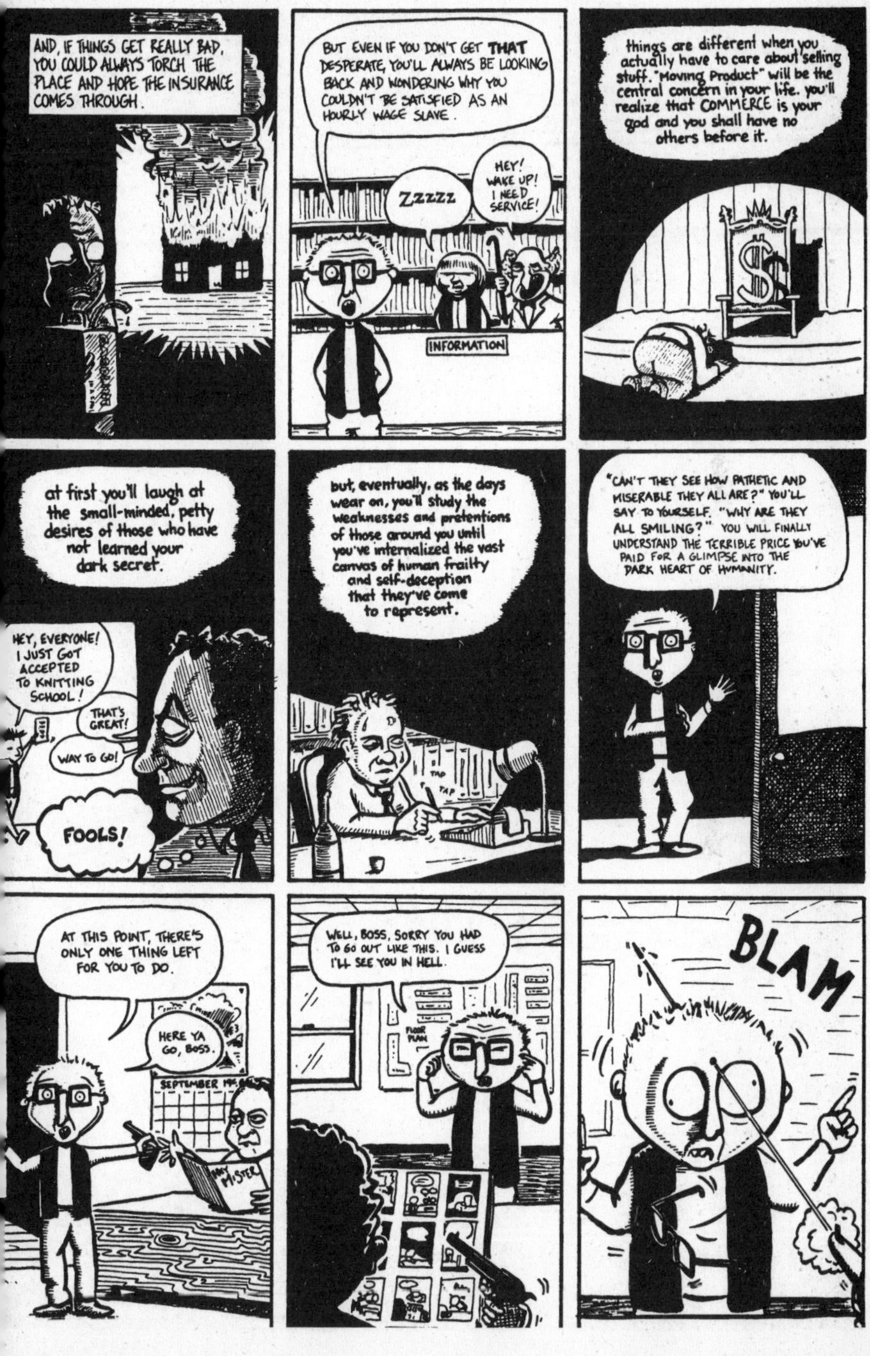
AND, IF THINGS GET REALLY BAD, YOU COULD ALWAYS TORCH THE PLACE AND HOPE THE INSURANCE COMES THROUGH.
BUT EVEN IF YOU DON'T GET THAT DESPERATE, YOU'LL ALWAYS BE LOOKING BACK AND WONDERING WHY YOU COULDN'T BE SATISFIED AS AN HOURLY WAGE SLAVE.
ZZZZZ
HEY! WAKE UP! I NEED SERVICE!
INFORMATION
things are different when you actually have to care about selling stuff. "Moving Product" will be the central concern in your life. you'll realize that COMMERCE is your god and you shall have no others before it.
at first you'll laugh at the small-minded, petty desires of those who have not learned your dark secret.
HEY, EVERYONE! I JUST GOT ACCEPTED TO KNITTING SCHOOL!
THAT'S GREAT!
WAY TO GO!
FOOLS!
but, eventually, as the days wear on, you'll study the weaknesses and pretentions of those around you until you've internalized the vast canvas of human frailty and self-deception that they've come to represent.
TAP
TAP
"CAN'T THEY SEE HOW PATHETIC AND MISERABLE THEY ALL ARE?" YOU'LL SAY TO YOURSELF. "WHY ARE THEY ALL SMILING?" YOU WILL FINALLY UNDERSTAND THE TERRIBLE PRICE YOU'VE PAID FOR A GLIMPSE INTO THE DARK HEART OF HUMANITY.
AT THIS POINT, THERE'S ONLY ONE THING LEFT FOR YOU TO DO.
HERE YA GO, BOSS.
SEPTEMBER
MISTER
WELL, BOSS, SORRY YOU HAD TO GO OUT LIKE THIS. I GUESS I'LL SEE YOU IN HELL.
FLOOR PLAN
BLAM

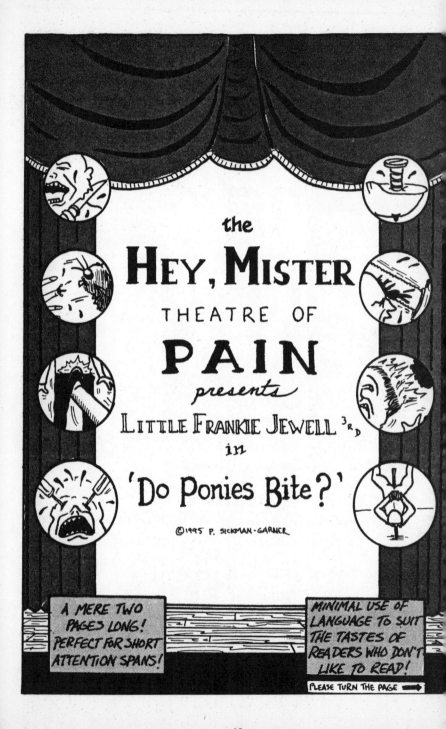

the
# HEY, MISTER
## THEATRE OF
# PAIN
*presents*
LITTLE FRANKIE JEWELL 3RD
*in*
'Do Ponies Bite?'

© 1995 P. SICKMAN-GARNER

A MERE TWO PAGES LONG! PERFECT FOR SHORT ATTENTION SPANS!

MINIMAL USE OF LANGUAGE TO SUIT THE TASTES OF READERS WHO DON'T LIKE TO READ!

PLEASE TURN THE PAGE ➡

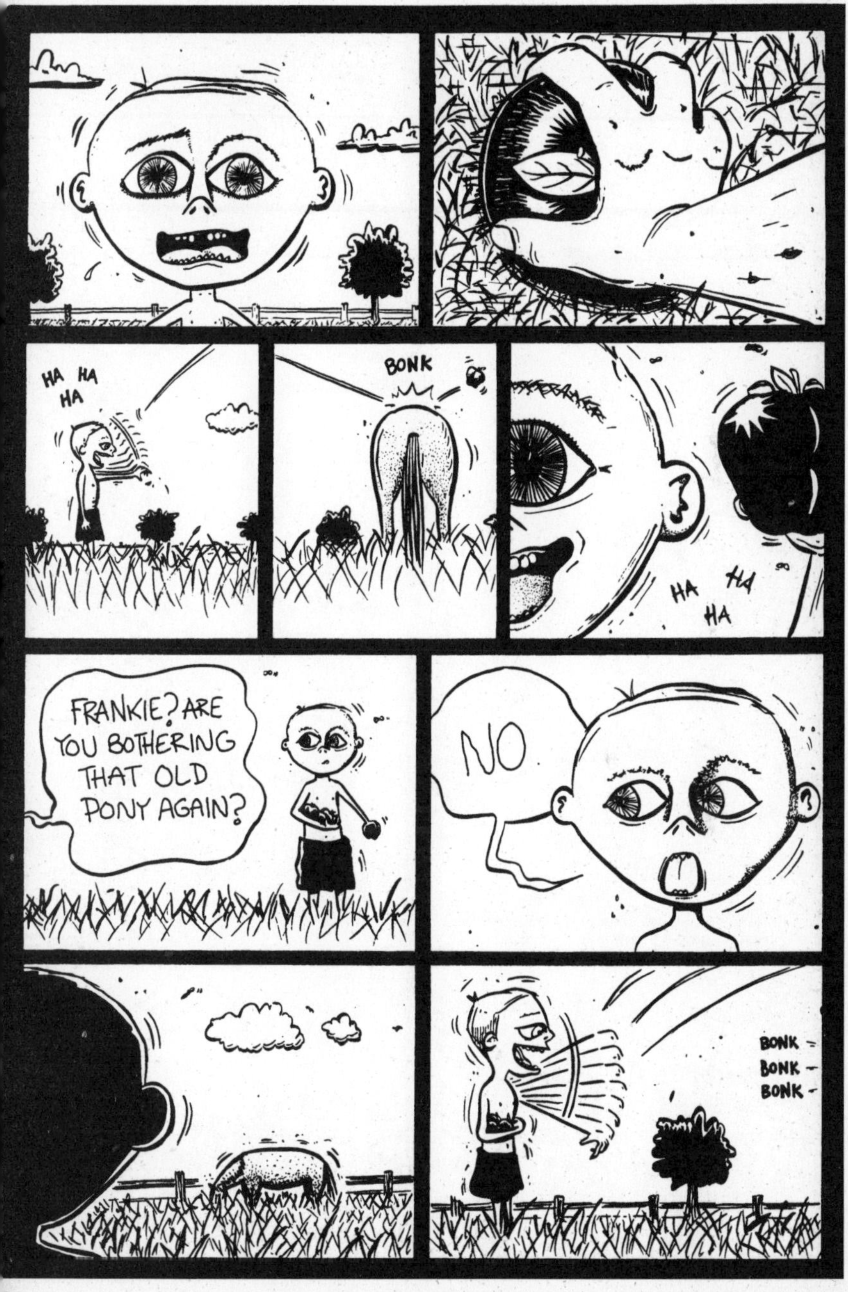
HA HA
HA
BONK
HA HA
HA
FRANKIE? ARE YOU BOTHERING THAT OLD PONY AGAIN?
NO
BONK
BONK
BONK

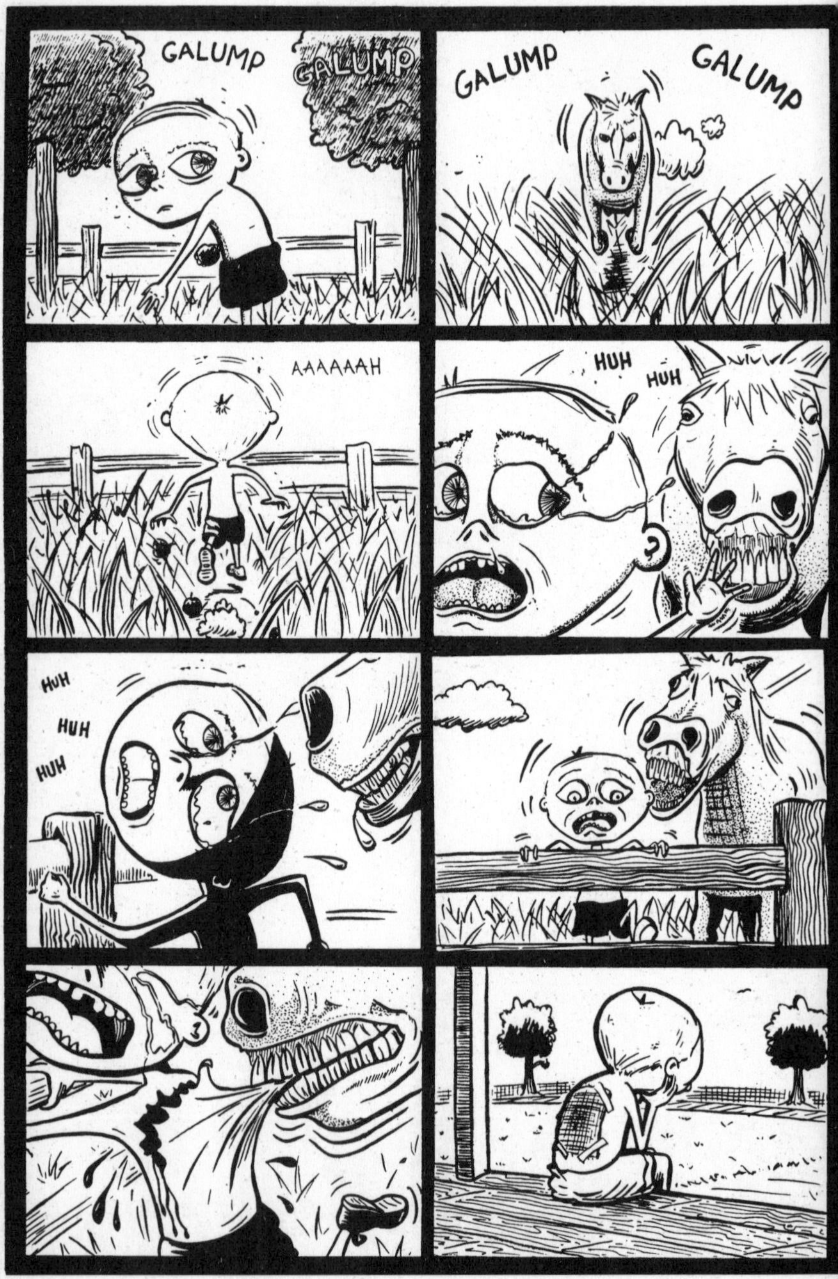
GALUMP
GALUMP
GALUMP
GALUMP
AAAAAAH
HUH
HUH
HUH
HUH
HUH

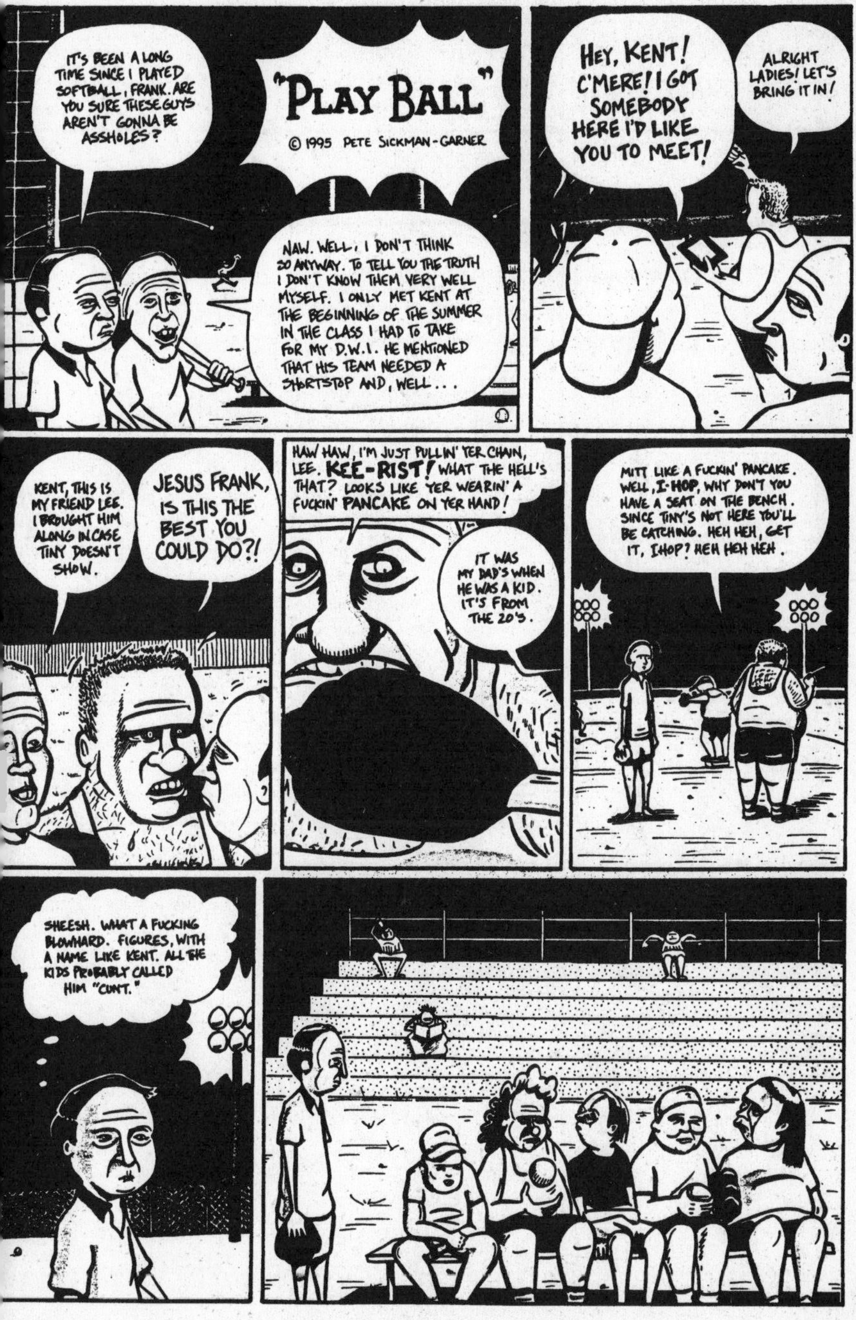
"PLAY BALL"
© 1995 PETE SICKMAN-GARNER
IT'S BEEN A LONG TIME SINCE I PLAYED SOFTBALL, FRANK. ARE YOU SURE THESE GUYS AREN'T GONNA BE ASSHOLES?
NAW. WELL, I DON'T THINK SO ANYWAY. TO TELL YOU THE TRUTH I DON'T KNOW THEM VERY WELL MYSELF. I ONLY MET KENT AT THE BEGINNING OF THE SUMMER IN THE CLASS I HAD TO TAKE FOR MY D.W.I. HE MENTIONED THAT HIS TEAM NEEDED A SHORTSTOP AND, WELL...
HEY, KENT! C'MERE! I GOT SOMEBODY HERE I'D LIKE YOU TO MEET!
ALRIGHT LADIES! LET'S BRING IT IN!
KENT, THIS IS MY FRIEND LEE. I BROUGHT HIM ALONG IN CASE TINY DOESN'T SHOW.
JESUS FRANK, IS THIS THE BEST YOU COULD DO?!
HAW HAW, I'M JUST PULLIN' YER CHAIN, LEE. KEE-RIST! WHAT THE HELL'S THAT? LOOKS LIKE YER WEARIN' A FUCKIN' PANCAKE ON YER HAND!
IT WAS MY DAD'S WHEN HE WAS A KID. IT'S FROM THE 20'S.
MITT LIKE A FUCKIN' PANCAKE. WELL, I-HOP, WHY DON'T YOU HAVE A SEAT ON THE BENCH. SINCE TINY'S NOT HERE YOU'LL BE CATCHING. HEH HEH, GET IT, IHOP? HEH HEH HEH.
SHEESH. WHAT A FUCKING BLOWHARD. FIGURES, WITH A NAME LIKE KENT. ALL THE KIDS PROBABLY CALLED HIM "CUNT."

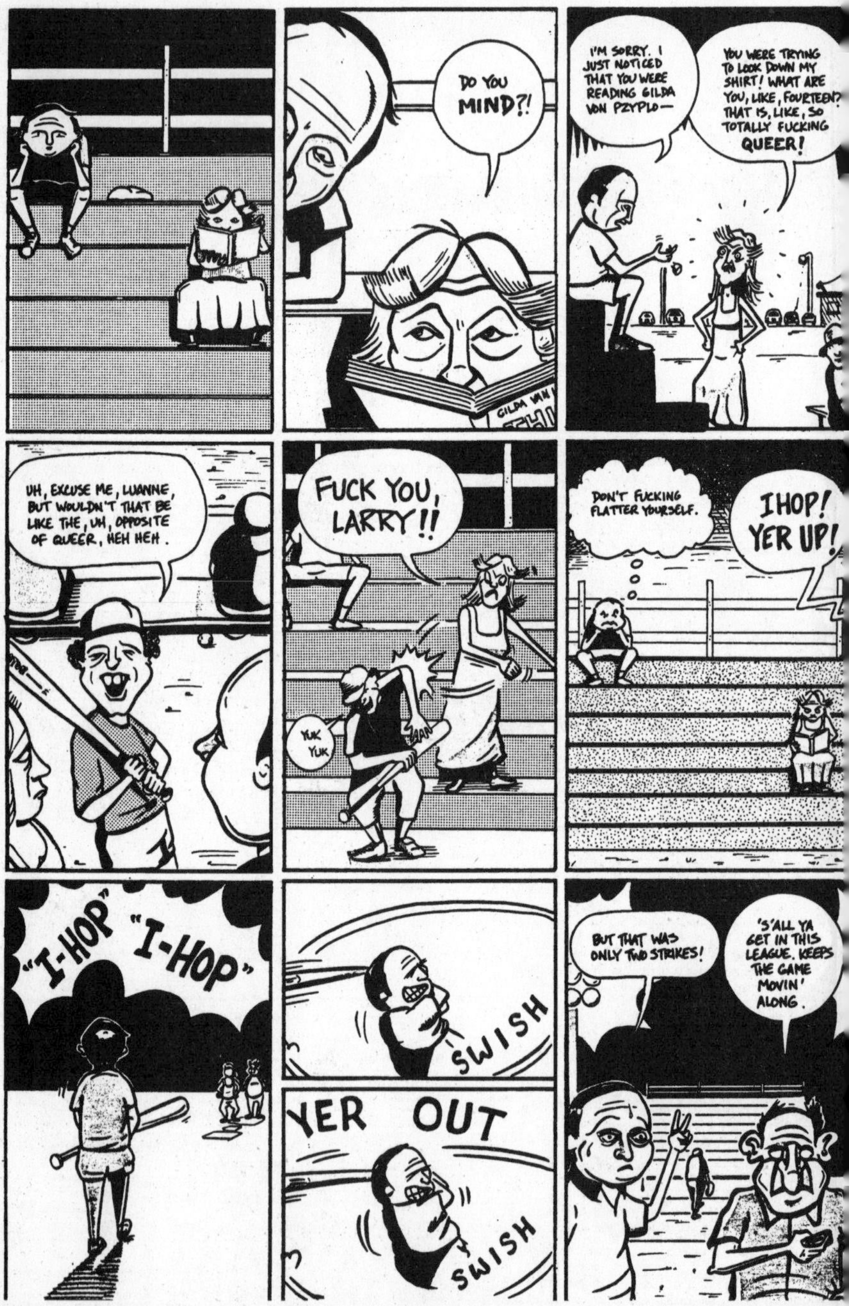
DO YOU MIND?!
I'M SORRY. I JUST NOTICED THAT YOU WERE READING GILDA VON PZYPLO—
YOU WERE TRYING TO LOOK DOWN MY SHIRT! WHAT ARE YOU, LIKE, FOURTEEN? THAT IS, LIKE, SO TOTALLY FUCKING QUEER!
UH, EXCUSE ME, LUANNE, BUT WOULDN'T THAT BE LIKE THE, UH, OPPOSITE OF QUEER, HEH HEH.
FUCK YOU, LARRY!!
YUK YUK
DON'T FUCKING FLATTER YOURSELF.
IHOP! YER UP!
"I-HOP" "I-HOP"
SWISH
YER OUT
SWISH
BUT THAT WAS ONLY TWO STRIKES!
'S'ALL YA GET IN THIS LEAGUE. KEEPS THE GAME MOVIN' ALONG.

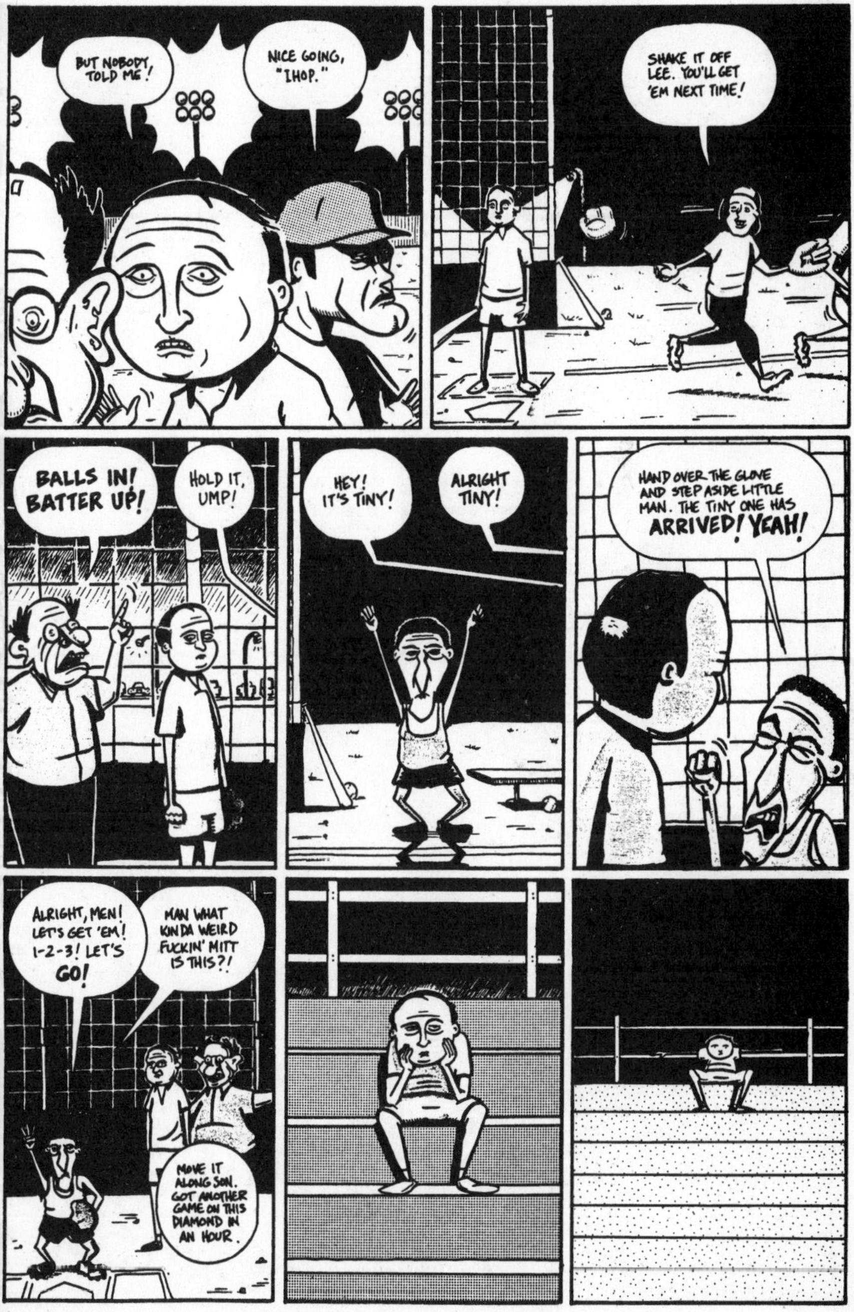
BUT NOBODY TOLD ME!
NICE GOING, "IHOP."
SHAKE IT OFF LEE. YOU'LL GET 'EM NEXT TIME!
BALLS IN! BATTER UP!
HOLD IT, UMP!
HEY! IT'S TINY!
ALRIGHT TINY!
HAND OVER THE GLOVE AND STEP ASIDE LITTLE MAN. THE TINY ONE HAS ARRIVED! YEAH!
ALRIGHT, MEN! LET'S GET 'EM! 1-2-3! LET'S GO!
MAN WHAT KINDA WEIRD FUCKIN' MITT IS THIS?!
MOVE IT ALONG SON. GOT ANOTHER GAME ON THIS DIAMOND IN AN HOUR.

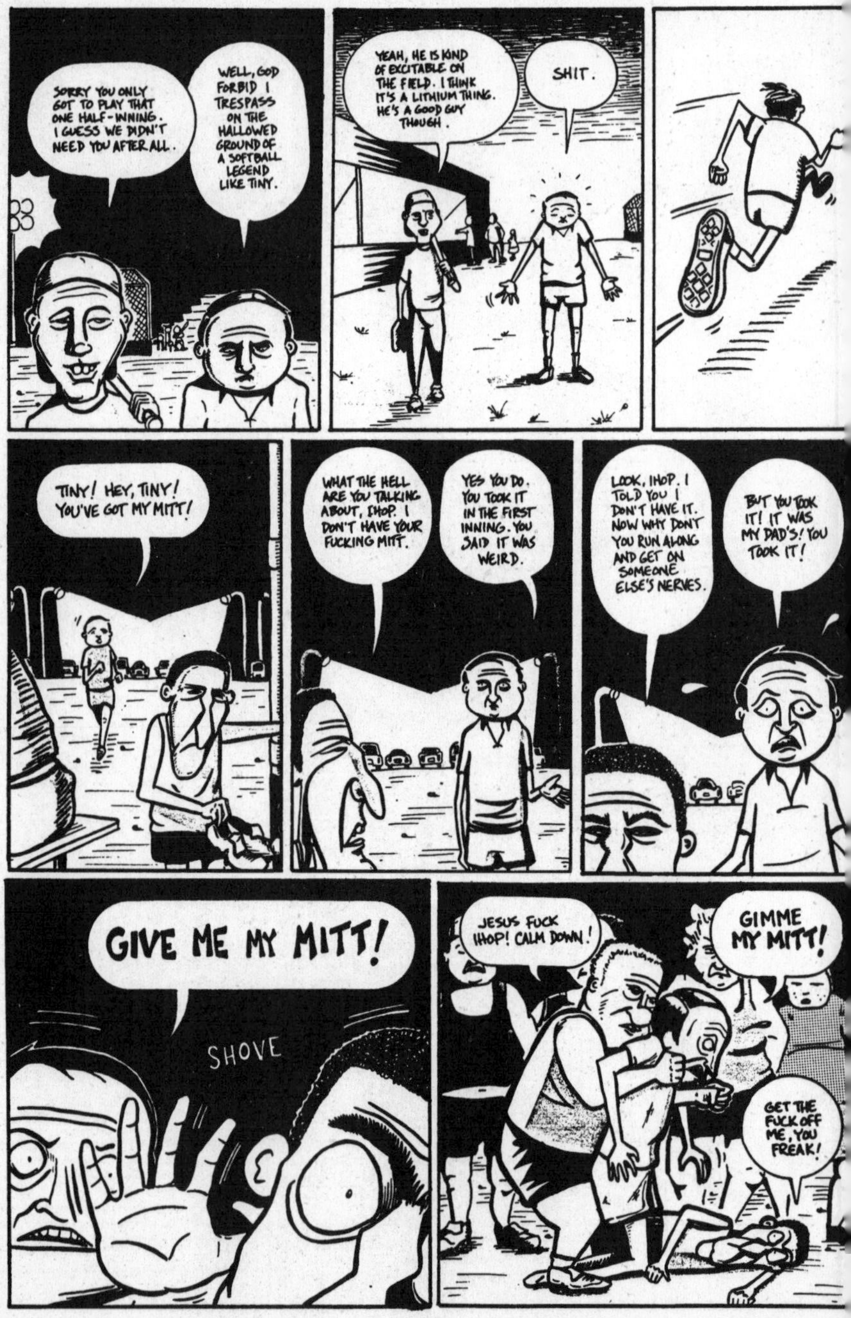

SORRY YOU ONLY GOT TO PLAY THAT ONE HALF-INNING. I GUESS WE DIDN'T NEED YOU AFTER ALL.
WELL, GOD FORBID I TRESPASS ON THE HALLOWED GROUND OF A SOFTBALL LEGEND LIKE TINY.
YEAH, HE IS KIND OF EXCITABLE ON THE FIELD. I THINK IT'S A LITHIUM THING. HE'S A GOOD GUY THOUGH.
SHIT.
TINY! HEY, TINY! YOU'VE GOT MY MITT!
WHAT THE HELL ARE YOU TALKING ABOUT, IHOP. I DON'T HAVE YOUR FUCKING MITT.
YES YOU DO. YOU TOOK IT IN THE FIRST INNING. YOU SAID IT WAS WEIRD.
LOOK, IHOP. I TOLD YOU I DON'T HAVE IT. NOW WHY DON'T YOU RUN ALONG AND GET ON SOMEONE ELSE'S NERVES.
BUT YOU TOOK IT! IT WAS MY DAD'S! YOU TOOK IT!
GIVE ME MY MITT!
SHOVE
JESUS FUCK IHOP! CALM DOWN!
GIMME MY MITT!
GET THE FUCK OFF ME, YOU FREAK!

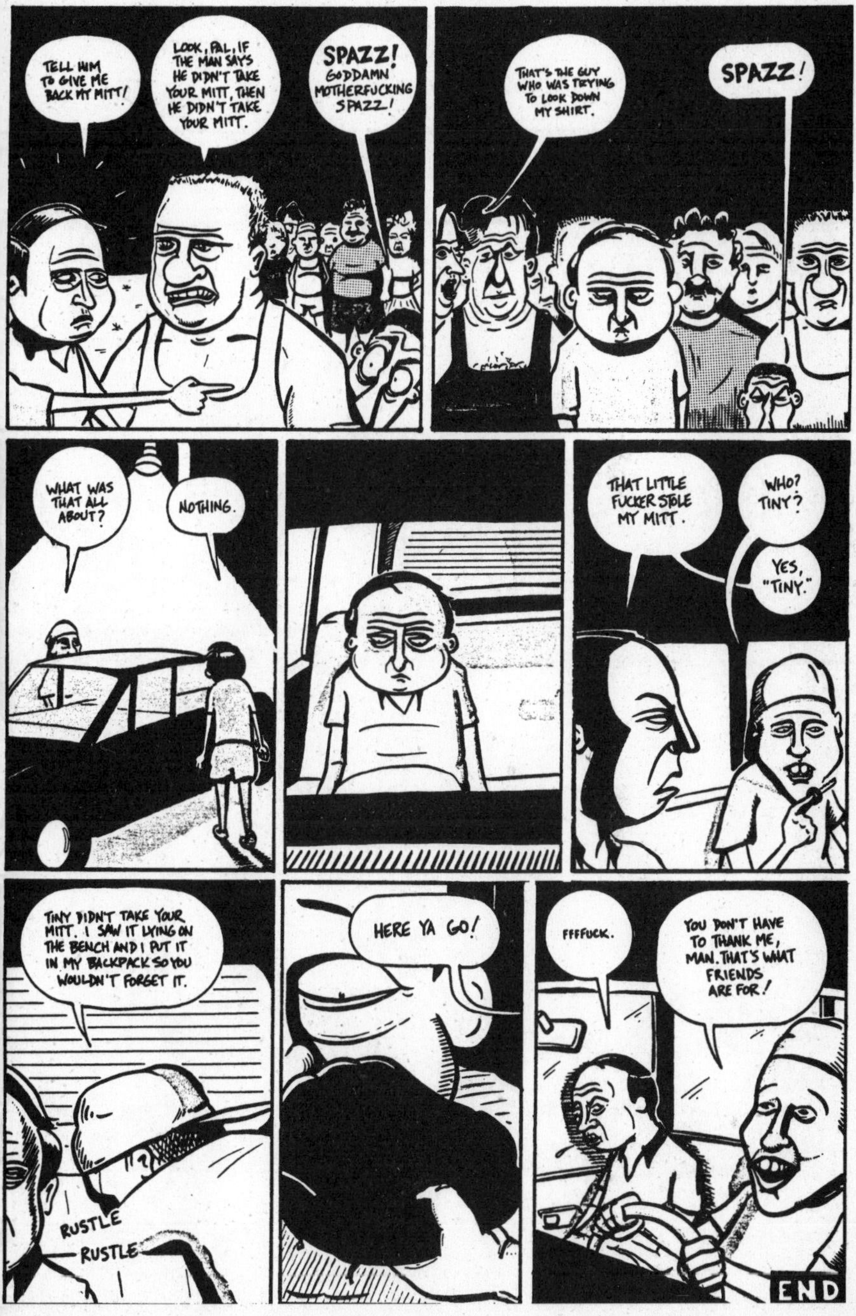
TELL HIM TO GIVE ME BACK MY MITT!
LOOK, PAL, IF THE MAN SAYS HE DIDN'T TAKE YOUR MITT, THEN HE DIDN'T TAKE YOUR MITT.
SPAZZ! GODDAMN MOTHERFUCKING SPAZZ!
THAT'S THE GUY WHO WAS TRYING TO LOOK DOWN MY SHIRT.
SPAZZ!
WHAT WAS THAT ALL ABOUT?
NOTHING.
THAT LITTLE FUCKER STOLE MY MITT.
WHO? TINY?
YES, "TINY."
TINY DIDN'T TAKE YOUR MITT. I SAW IT LYING ON THE BENCH AND I PUT IT IN MY BACKPACK SO YOU WOULDN'T FORGET IT.
RUSTLE
RUSTLE
HERE YA GO!
FFFFUCK.
YOU DON'T HAVE TO THANK ME, MAN. THAT'S WHAT FRIENDS ARE FOR!
END

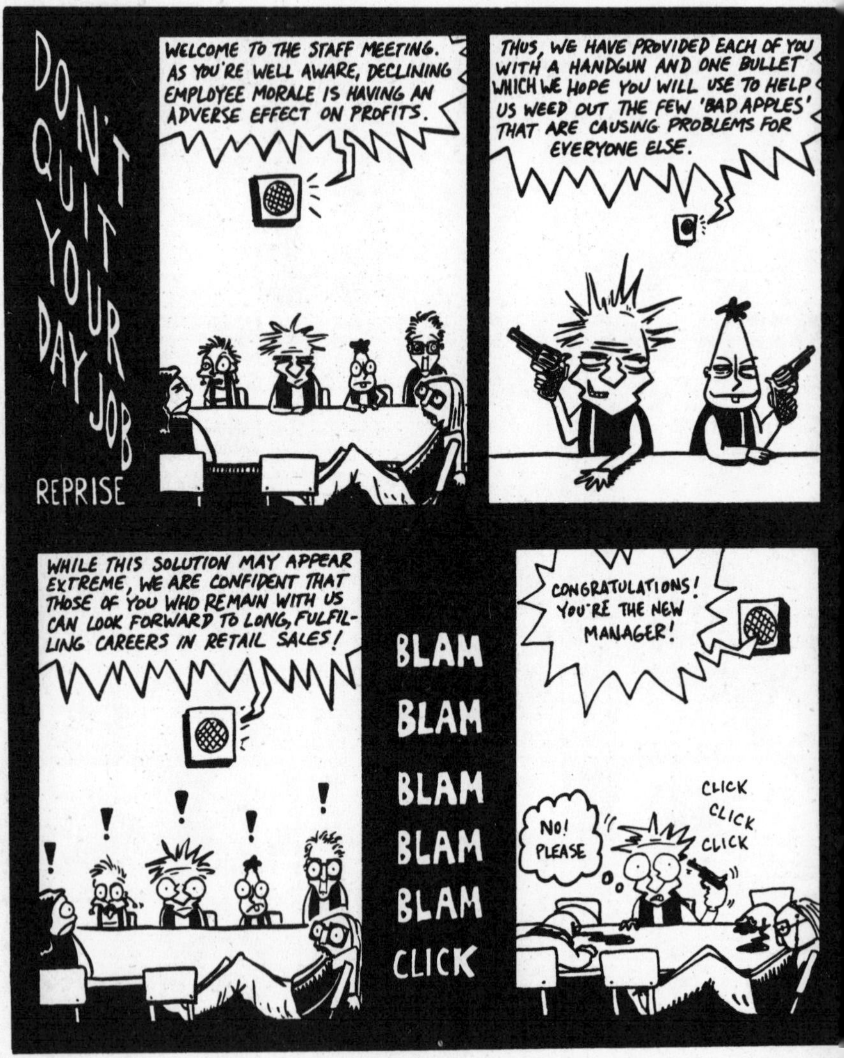
DON'T QUIT YOUR DAY JOB
REPRISE
WELCOME TO THE STAFF MEETING. AS YOU'RE WELL AWARE, DECLINING EMPLOYEE MORALE IS HAVING AN ADVERSE EFFECT ON PROFITS.
THUS, WE HAVE PROVIDED EACH OF YOU WITH A HANDGUN AND ONE BULLET WHICH WE HOPE YOU WILL USE TO HELP US WEED OUT THE FEW 'BAD APPLES' THAT ARE CAUSING PROBLEMS FOR EVERYONE ELSE.
WHILE THIS SOLUTION MAY APPEAR EXTREME, WE ARE CONFIDENT THAT THOSE OF YOU WHO REMAIN WITH US CAN LOOK FORWARD TO LONG, FULFIL-LING CAREERS IN RETAIL SALES!
!
!
!
!
!
BLAM
BLAM
BLAM
BLAM
BLAM
CLICK
CONGRATULATIONS! YOU'RE THE NEW MANAGER!
NO! PLEASE
CLICK
CLICK
CLICK

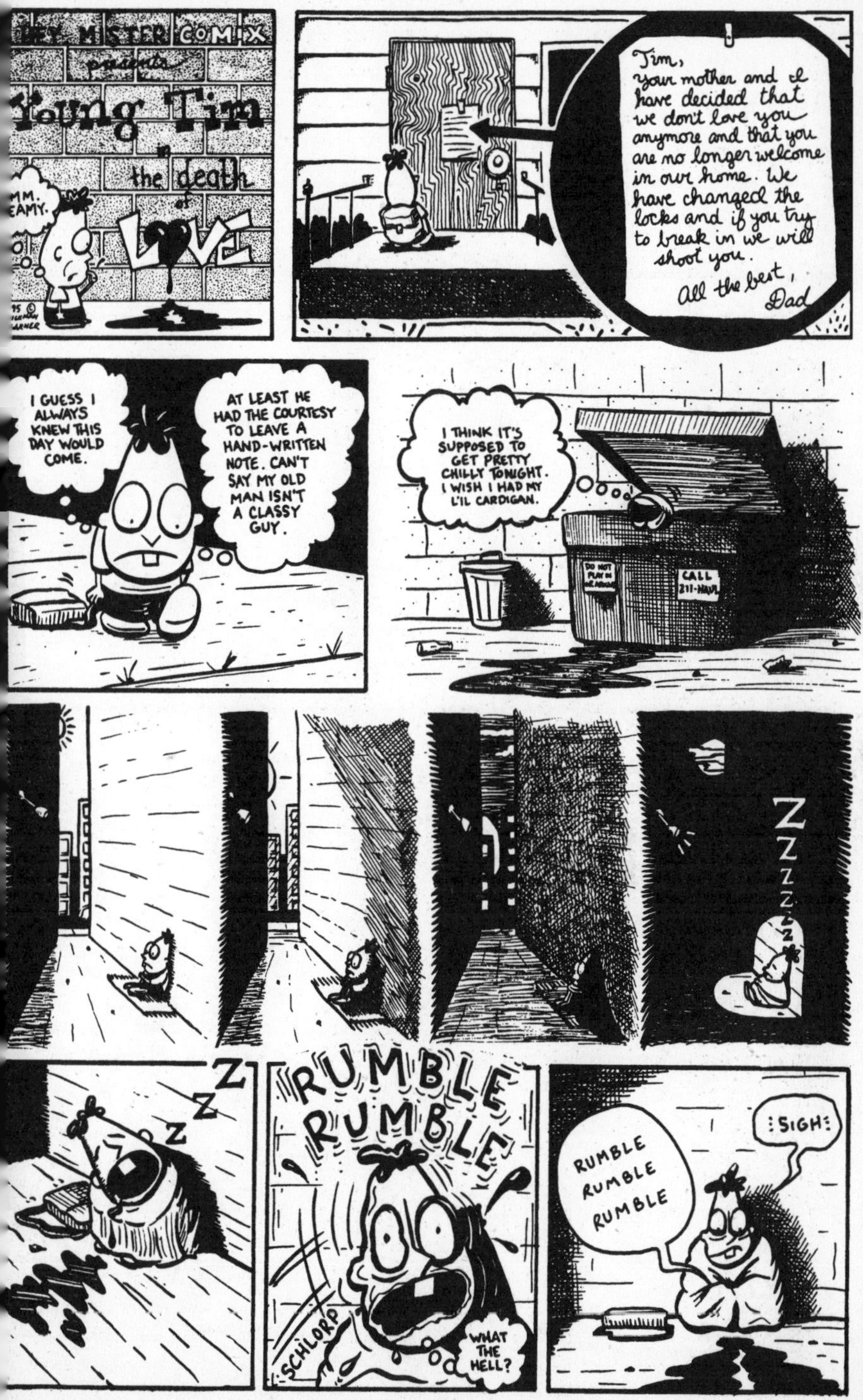
MISTER COMIX
Young Tim
the death
LOVE
Tim, your mother and I have decided that we don't love you anymore and that you are no longer welcome in our home. We have changed the locks and if you try to break in we will shoot you. All the best, Dad
I GUESS I ALWAYS KNEW THIS DAY WOULD COME.
AT LEAST HE HAD THE COURTESY TO LEAVE A HAND-WRITTEN NOTE. CAN'T SAY MY OLD MAN ISN'T A CLASSY GUY.
I THINK IT'S SUPPOSED TO GET PRETTY CHILLY TONIGHT. I WISH I HAD MY L'IL CARDIGAN.
CALL 311-HAUL
ZZZZZZZ
ZZZ
RUMBLE RUMBLE
SCHLORP
WHAT THE HELL?
RUMBLE RUMBLE RUMBLE
SIGH

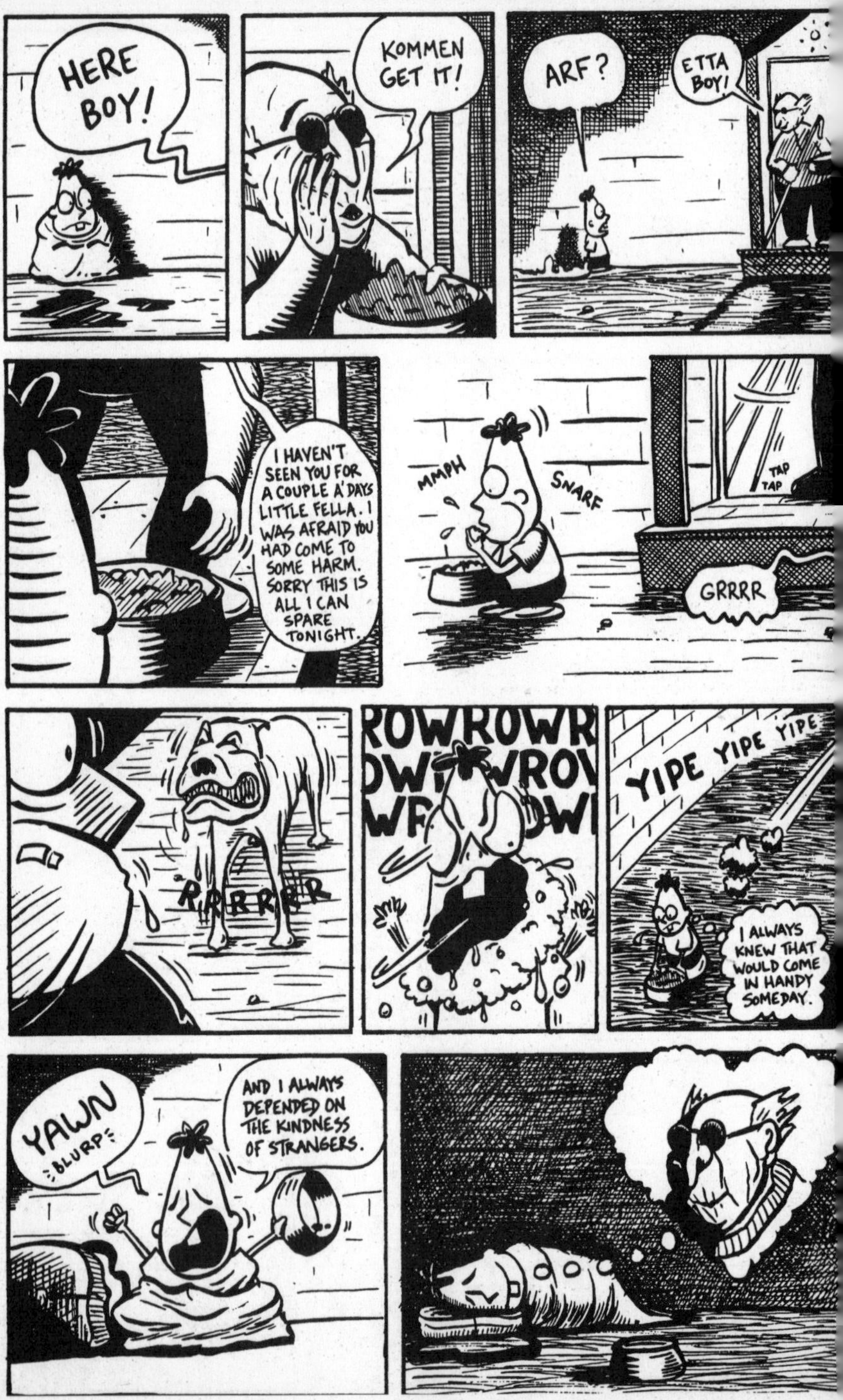
HERE BOY!
KOMMEN GET IT!
ARF?
ETTA BOY!
I HAVEN'T SEEN YOU FOR A COUPLE A' DAYS LITTLE FELLA. I WAS AFRAID YOU HAD COME TO SOME HARM. SORRY THIS IS ALL I CAN SPARE TONIGHT.
MMPH
SNARF
TAP TAP
GRRRR
RRRRRR
ROWROWR
YIPE YIPE YIPE YIPE
I ALWAYS KNEW THAT WOULD COME IN HANDY SOMEDAY.
YAWN
BLURP
AND I ALWAYS DEPENDED ON THE KINDNESS OF STRANGERS.

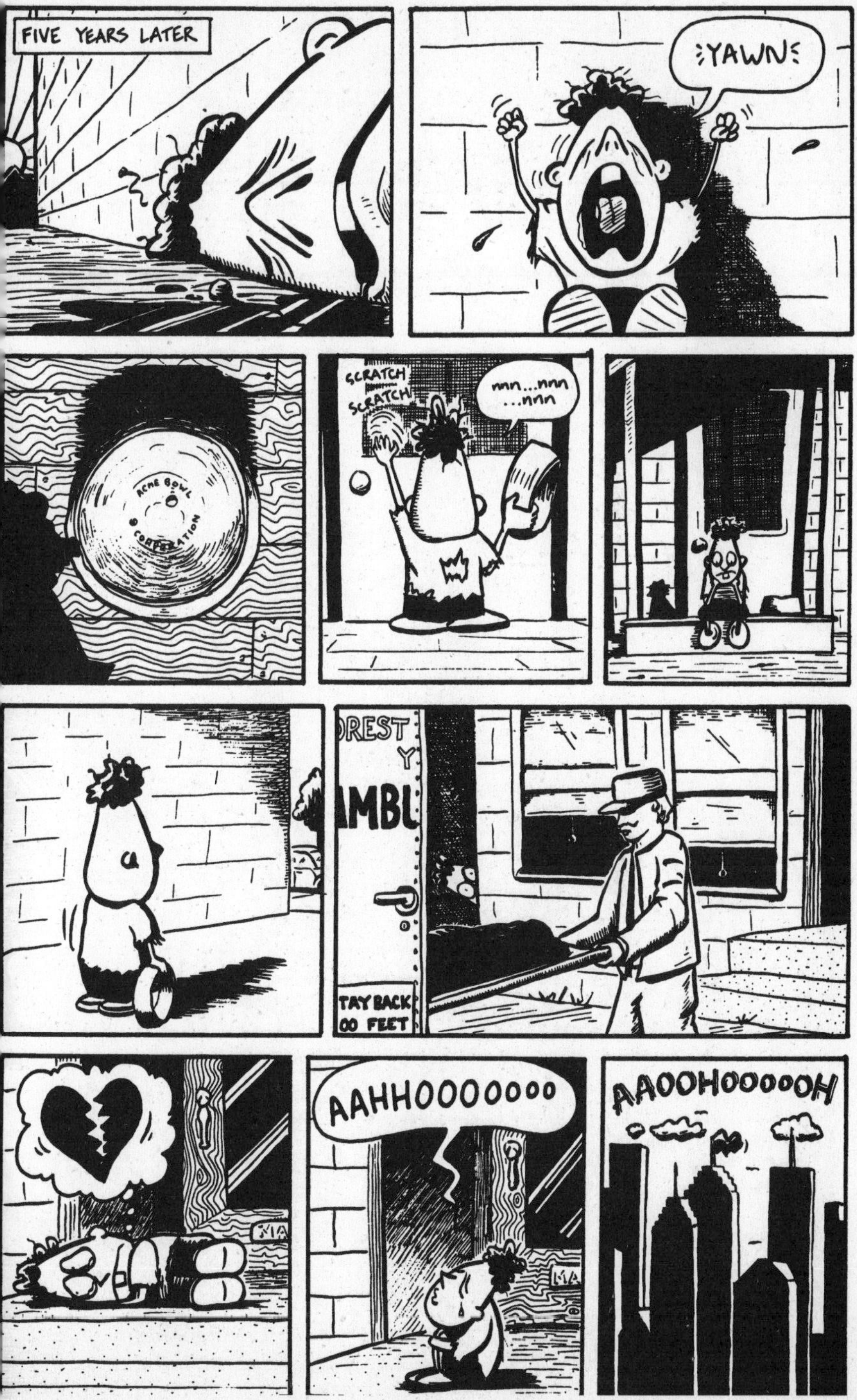
FIVE YEARS LATER
YAWN
ACME BOWL CORPORATION
SCRATCH SCRATCH
nnn...nnn ...nnn
TAY BACK
00 FEET
AAHHOOOOOOO
AAOOHOOOOOH

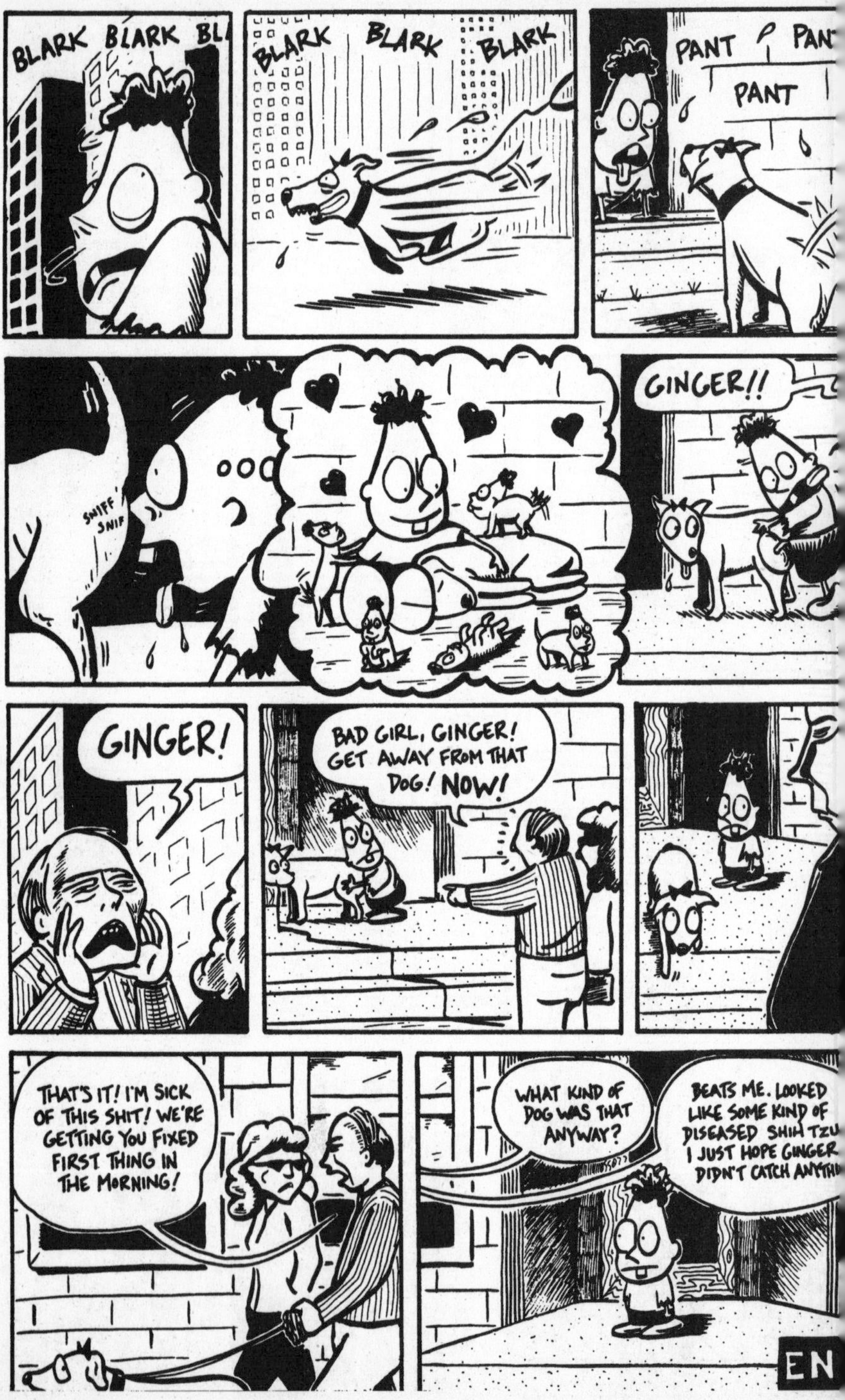
BLARK BLARK
BLARK BLARK BLARK
PANT PANT
PANT
SNIFF SNIF
GINGER!!
GINGER!
BAD GIRL, GINGER! GET AWAY FROM THAT DOG! NOW!
THAT'S IT! I'M SICK OF THIS SHIT! WE'RE GETTING YOU FIXED FIRST THING IN THE MORNING!
WHAT KIND OF DOG WAS THAT ANYWAY?
BEATS ME. LOOKED LIKE SOME KIND OF DISEASED SHIH
I JUST HOPE GINGER DIDN'T CATCH

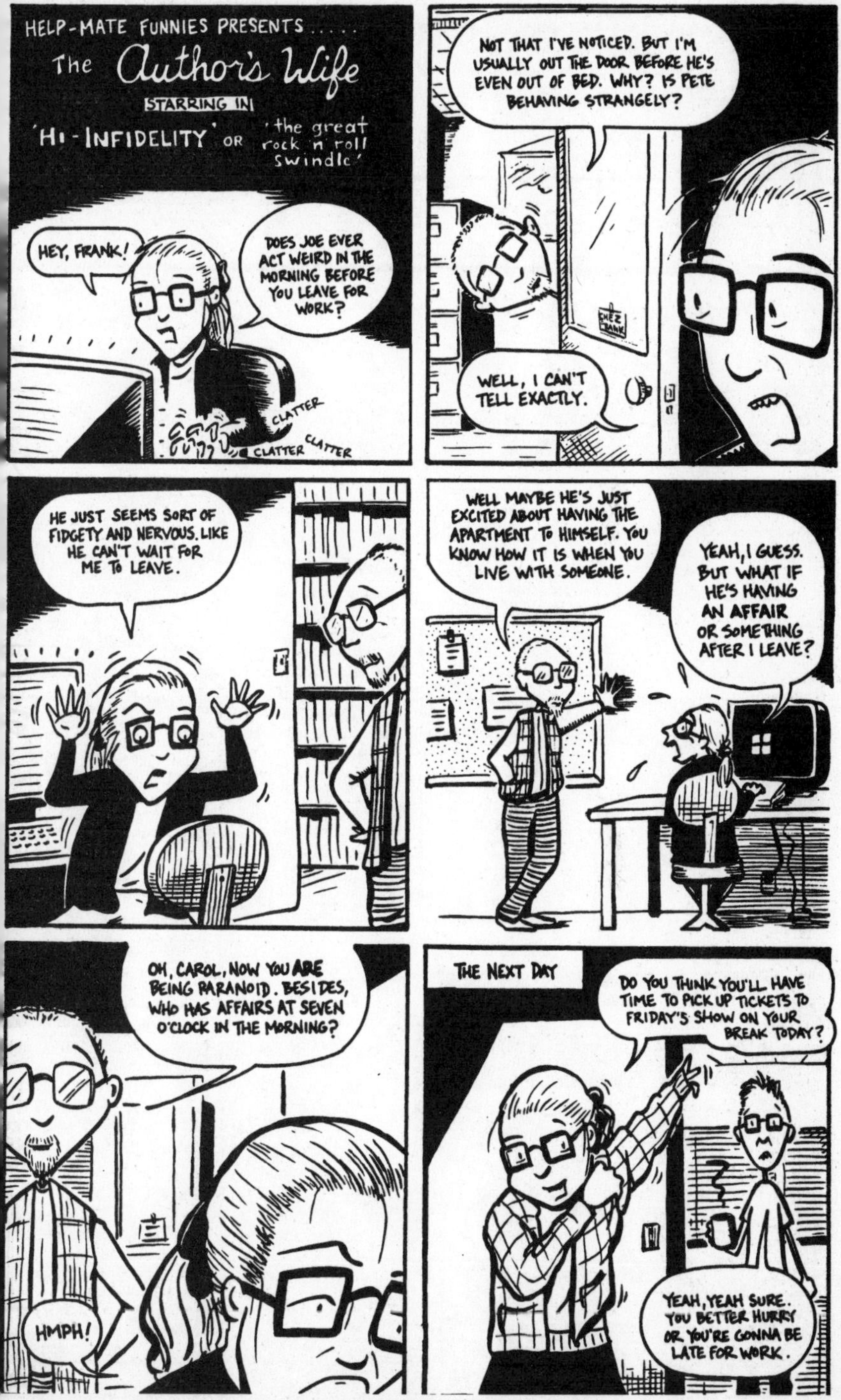
HELP-MATE FUNNIES PRESENTS.....
The Author's Wife
STARRING IN
'HI-INFIDELITY' OR 'the great rock 'n' roll swindle'
HEY, FRANK!
DOES JOE EVER ACT WEIRD IN THE MORNING BEFORE YOU LEAVE FOR WORK?
CLATTER
CLATTER
CLATTER
NOT THAT I'VE NOTICED. BUT I'M USUALLY OUT THE DOOR BEFORE HE'S EVEN OUT OF BED. WHY? IS PETE BEHAVING STRANGELY?
WELL, I CAN'T TELL EXACTLY.
HE JUST SEEMS SORT OF FIDGETY AND NERVOUS. LIKE HE CAN'T WAIT FOR ME TO LEAVE.
WELL MAYBE HE'S JUST EXCITED ABOUT HAVING THE APARTMENT TO HIMSELF. YOU KNOW HOW IT IS WHEN YOU LIVE WITH SOMEONE.
YEAH, I GUESS. BUT WHAT IF HE'S HAVING AN AFFAIR OR SOMETHING AFTER I LEAVE?
OH, CAROL, NOW YOU ARE BEING PARANOID. BESIDES, WHO HAS AFFAIRS AT SEVEN O'CLOCK IN THE MORNING?
HMPH!
THE NEXT DAY
DO YOU THINK YOU'LL HAVE TIME TO PICK UP TICKETS TO FRIDAY'S SHOW ON YOUR BREAK TODAY?
YEAH, YEAH SURE. YOU BETTER HURRY OR YOU'RE GONNA BE LATE FOR WORK.

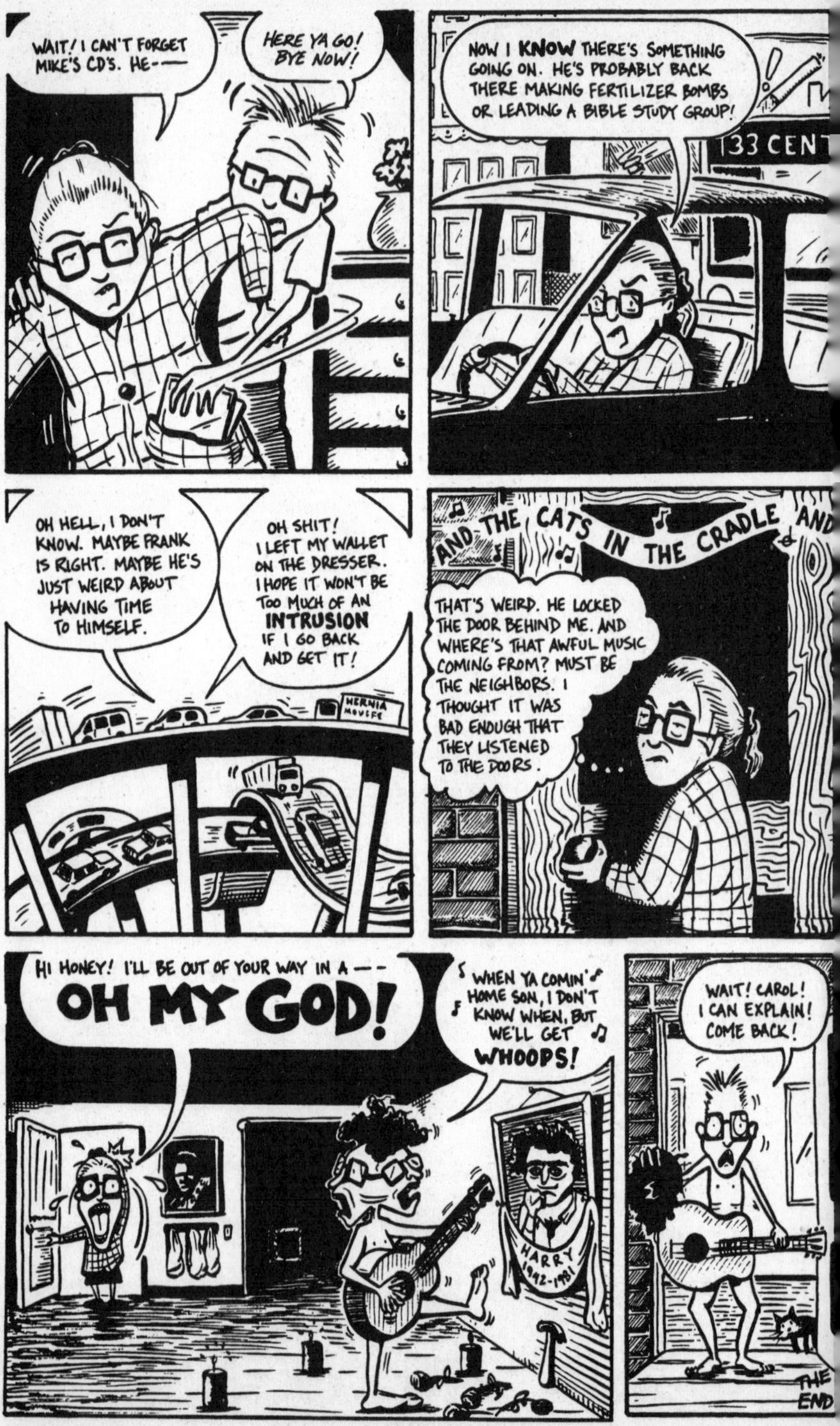

WAIT! I CAN'T FORGET MIKE'S CD'S. HE-—
HERE YA GO! BYE NOW!
NOW I KNOW THERE'S SOMETHING GOING ON. HE'S PROBABLY BACK THERE MAKING FERTILIZER BOMBS OR LEADING A BIBLE STUDY GROUP!
133 CENT
OH HELL, I DON'T KNOW. MAYBE FRANK IS RIGHT. MAYBE HE'S JUST WEIRD ABOUT HAVING TIME TO HIMSELF.
OH SHIT! I LEFT MY WALLET ON THE DRESSER. I HOPE IT WON'T BE TOO MUCH OF AN INTRUSION IF I GO BACK AND GET IT!
HERNIA MOUSSE
AND THE CATS IN THE CRADLE AND
THAT'S WEIRD. HE LOCKED THE DOOR BEHIND ME. AND WHERE'S THAT AWFUL MUSIC COMING FROM? MUST BE THE NEIGHBORS. I THOUGHT IT WAS BAD ENOUGH THAT THEY LISTENED TO THE DOORS.
HI HONEY! I'LL BE OUT OF YOUR WAY IN A ——
OH MY GOD!
WHEN YA COMIN' HOME SON, I DON'T KNOW WHEN, BUT WE'LL GET
WHOOPS!
HARRY 1942-1981
WAIT! CAROL! I CAN EXPLAIN! COME BACK!
THE END

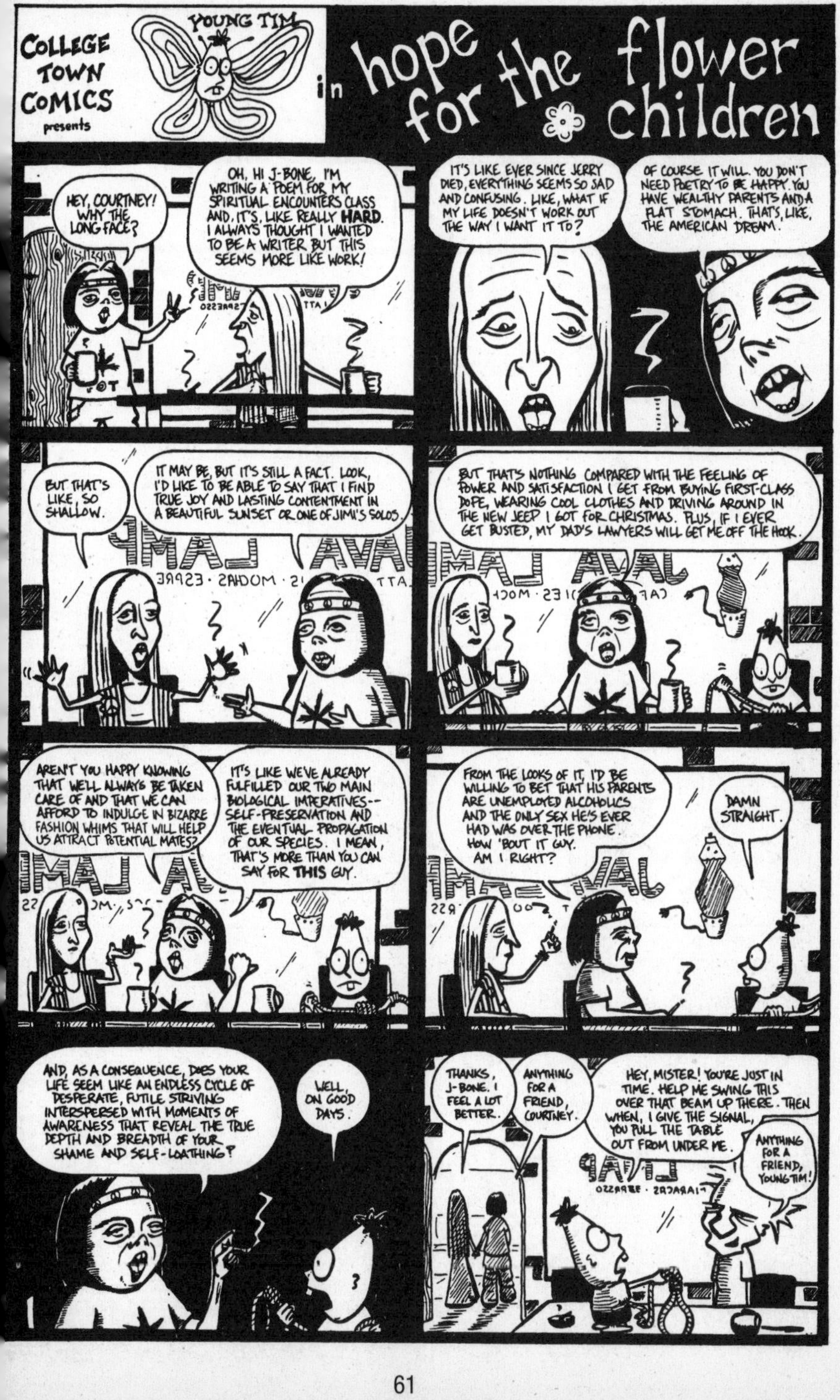
COLLEGE TOWN COMICS presents
YOUNG TIM
in hope for the flower children
HEY, COURTNEY! WHY THE LONG FACE?
OH, HI J-BONE, I'M WRITING A POEM FOR MY SPIRITUAL ENCOUNTERS CLASS AND, IT'S, LIKE REALLY HARD. I ALWAYS THOUGHT I WANTED TO BE A WRITER BUT THIS SEEMS MORE LIKE WORK!
IT'S LIKE EVER SINCE JERRY DIED, EVERYTHING SEEMS SO SAD AND CONFUSING. LIKE, WHAT IF MY LIFE DOESN'T WORK OUT THE WAY I WANT IT TO?
OF COURSE IT WILL. YOU DON'T NEED POETRY TO BE HAPPY. YOU HAVE WEALTHY PARENTS AND A FLAT STOMACH. THAT'S, LIKE, THE AMERICAN DREAM.
BUT THAT'S LIKE, SO SHALLOW.
IT MAY BE, BUT IT'S STILL A FACT. LOOK, I'D LIKE TO BE ABLE TO SAY THAT I FIND TRUE JOY AND LASTING CONTENTMENT IN A BEAUTIFUL SUNSET OR ONE OF JIMI'S SOLOS.
BUT THAT'S NOTHING COMPARED WITH THE FEELING OF POWER AND SATISFACTION I GET FROM BUYING FIRST-CLASS DOPE, WEARING COOL CLOTHES AND DRIVING AROUND IN THE NEW JEEP I GOT FOR CHRISTMAS. PLUS, IF I EVER GET BUSTED, MY DAD'S LAWYERS WILL GET ME OFF THE HOOK.
AREN'T YOU HAPPY KNOWING THAT WE'LL ALWAYS BE TAKEN CARE OF AND THAT WE CAN AFFORD TO INDULGE IN BIZARRE FASHION WHIMS THAT WILL HELP US ATTRACT POTENTIAL MATES?
IT'S LIKE WE'VE ALREADY FULFILLED OUR TWO MAIN BIOLOGICAL IMPERATIVES-- SELF-PRESERVATION AND THE EVENTUAL PROPAGATION OF OUR SPECIES. I MEAN, THAT'S MORE THAN YOU CAN SAY FOR THIS GUY.
FROM THE LOOKS OF IT, I'D BE WILLING TO BET THAT HIS PARENTS ARE UNEMPLOYED ALCOHOLICS AND THE ONLY SEX HE'S EVER HAD WAS OVER THE PHONE. HOW 'BOUT IT GUY. AM I RIGHT?
DAMN STRAIGHT.
AND, AS A CONSEQUENCE, DOES YOUR LIFE SEEM LIKE AN ENDLESS CYCLE OF DESPERATE, FUTILE STRIVING INTERSPERSED WITH MOMENTS OF AWARENESS THAT REVEAL THE TRUE DEPTH AND BREADTH OF YOUR SHAME AND SELF-LOATHING?
WELL, ON GOOD DAYS.
THANKS, J-BONE. I FEEL A LOT BETTER.
ANYTHING FOR A FRIEND, COURTNEY.
HEY, MISTER! YOU'RE JUST IN TIME. HELP ME SWING THIS OVER THAT BEAM UP THERE. THEN WHEN, I GIVE THE SIGNAL, YOU PULL THE TABLE OUT FROM UNDER ME.
ANYTHING FOR A FRIEND, YOUNG TIM!

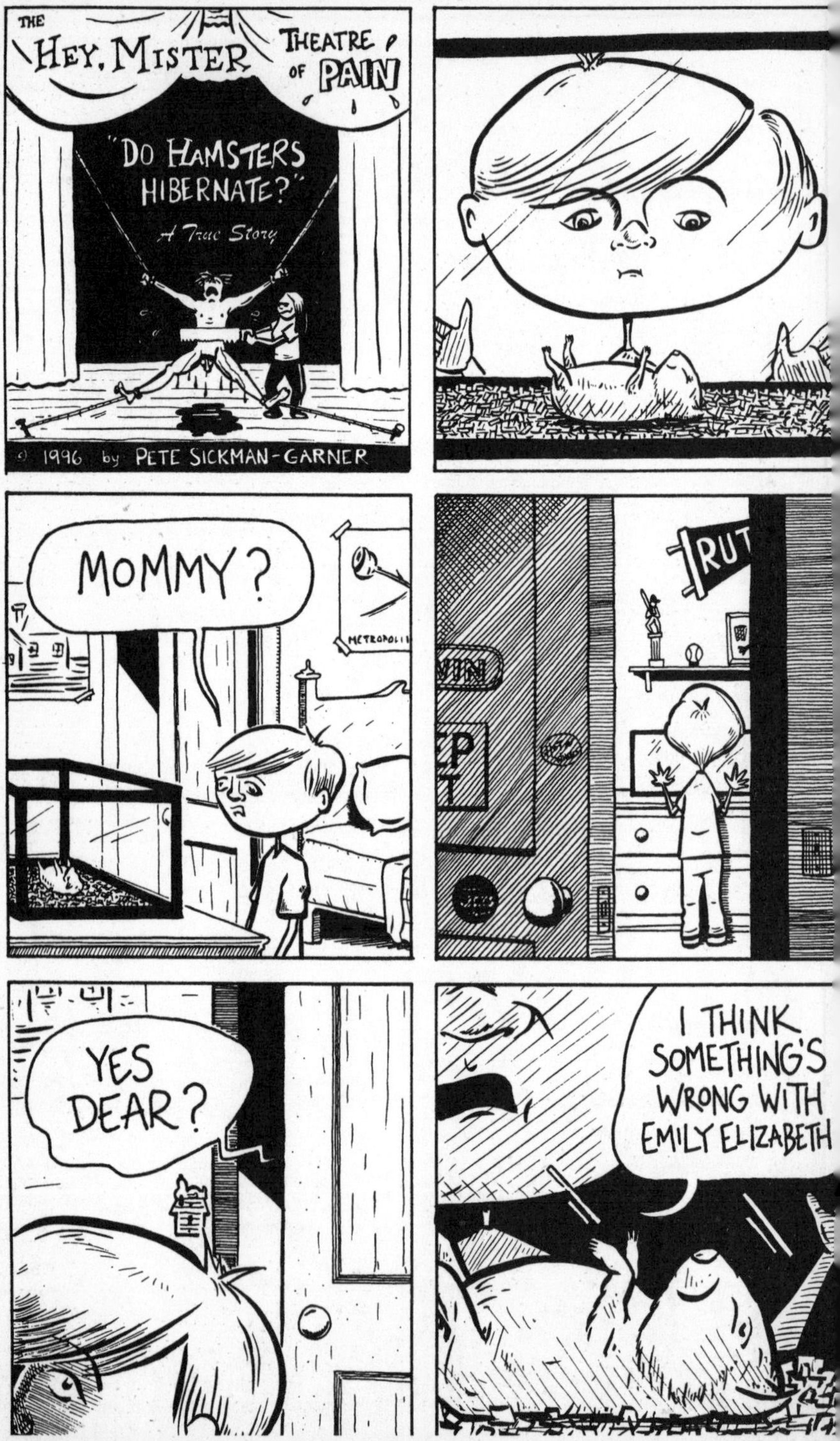
THE HEY, MISTER THEATRE OF PAIN
"DO HAMSTERS HIBERNATE?"
A True Story
© 1996 by PETE SICKMAN-GARNER
MOMMY?
YES DEAR?
I THINK SOMETHING'S WRONG WITH EMILY ELIZABETH

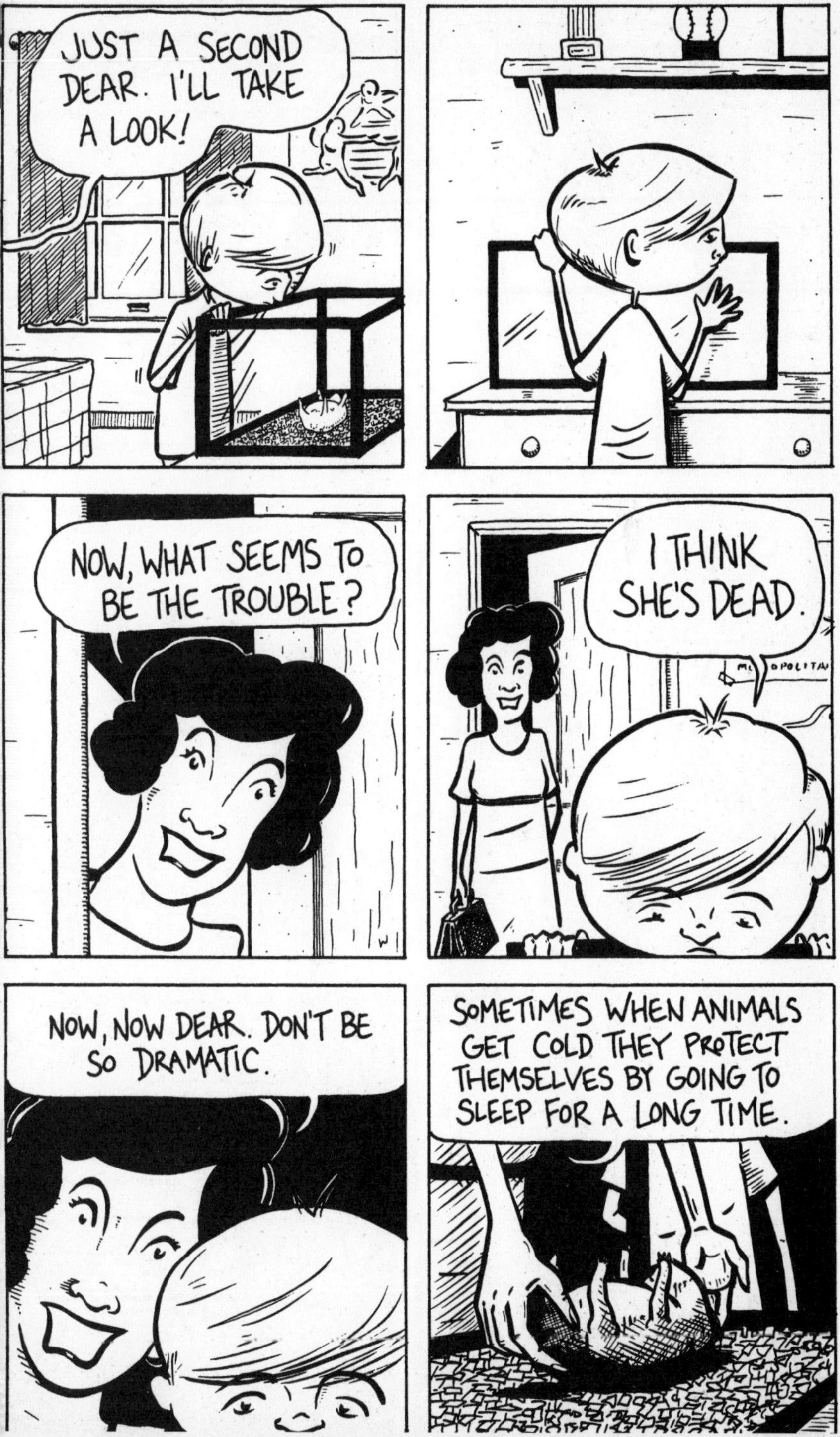
JUST A SECOND DEAR. I'LL TAKE A LOOK!
NOW, WHAT SEEMS TO BE THE TROUBLE?
I THINK SHE'S DEAD.
NOW, NOW DEAR. DON'T BE SO DRAMATIC.
SOMETIMES WHEN ANIMALS GET COLD THEY PROTECT THEMSELVES BY GOING TO SLEEP FOR A LONG TIME.

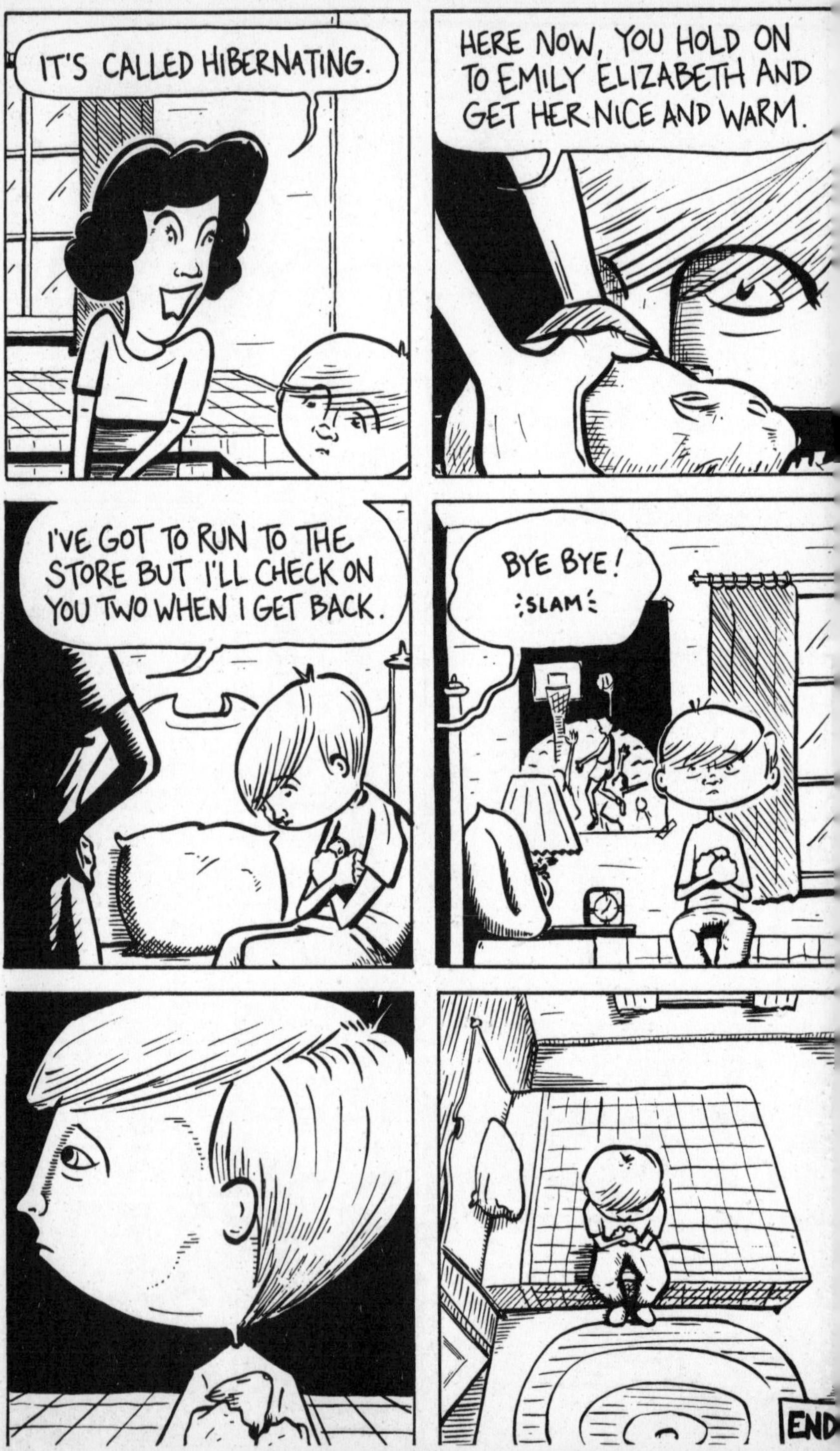
IT'S CALLED HIBERNATING.
HERE NOW, YOU HOLD ON TO EMILY ELIZABETH AND GET HER NICE AND WARM.
I'VE GOT TO RUN TO THE STORE BUT I'LL CHECK ON YOU TWO WHEN I GET BACK.
BYE BYE!
SLAM
END

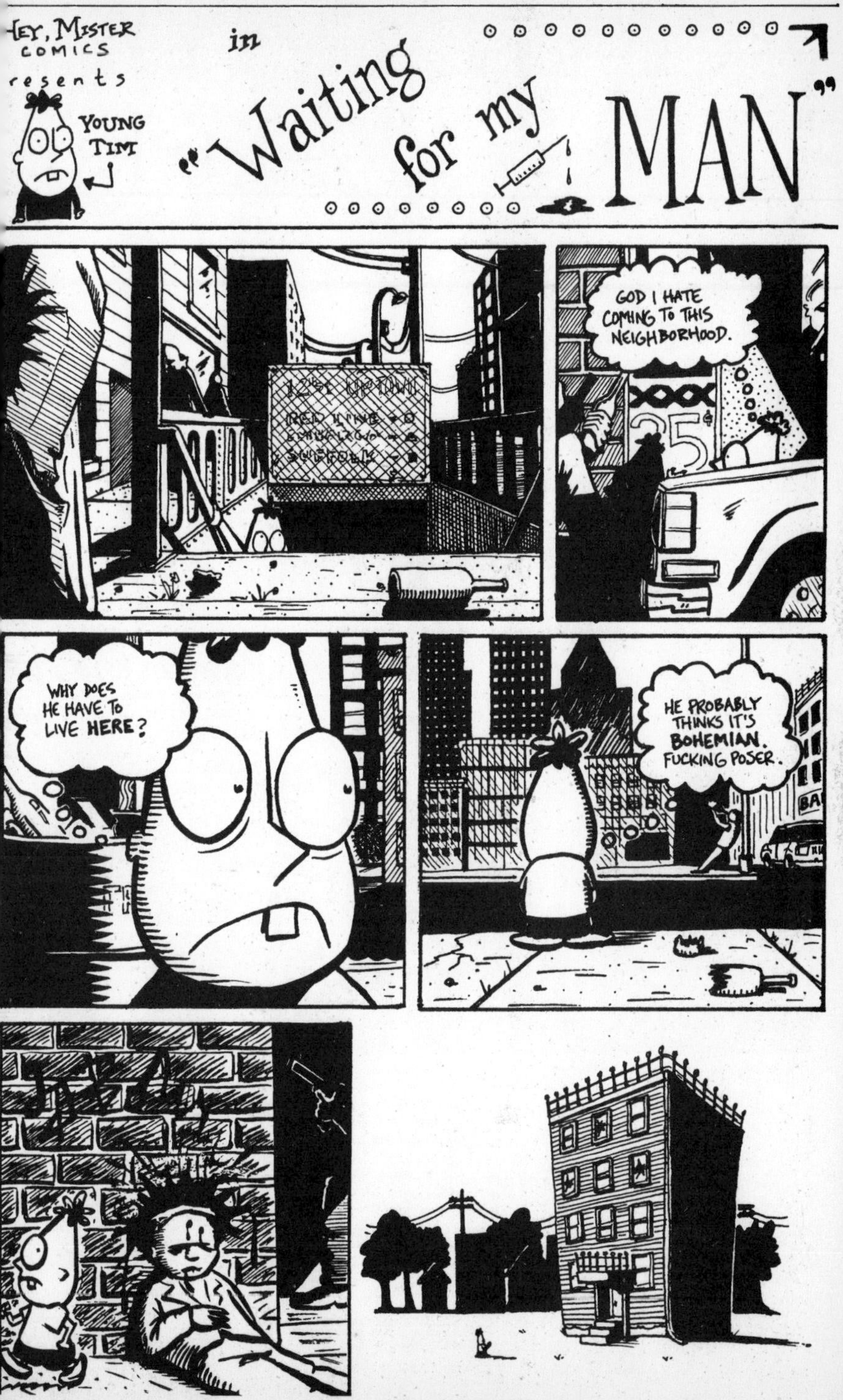

HEY, MISTER COMICS
presents
YOUNG TIM
in
"Waiting for my MAN"
GOD I HATE COMING TO THIS NEIGHBORHOOD.
35¢
WHY DOES HE HAVE TO LIVE HERE?
HE PROBABLY THINKS IT'S BOHEMIAN. FUCKING POSER.

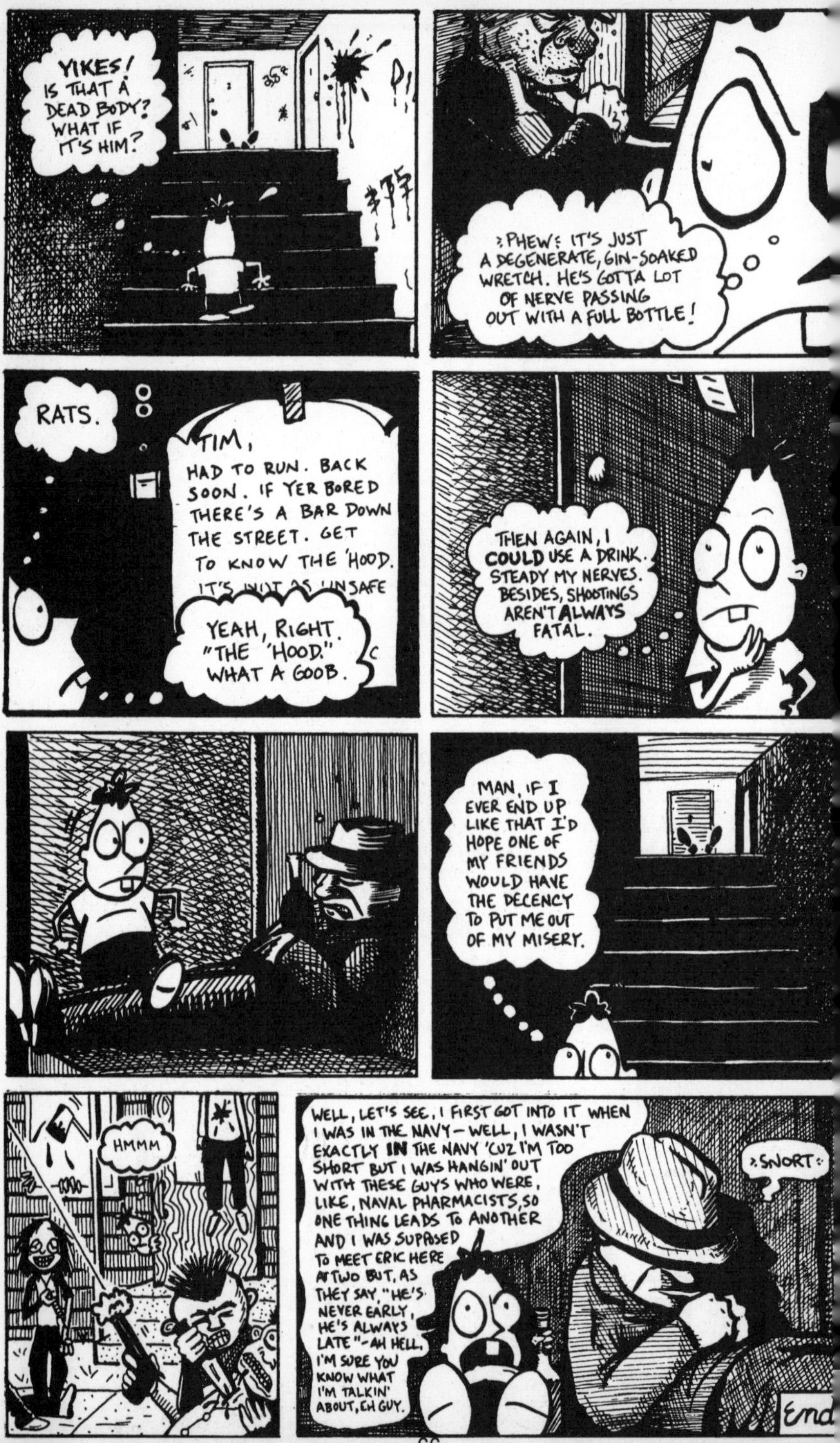
YIKES! IS THAT A DEAD BODY? WHAT IF IT'S HIM?
:PHEW: IT'S JUST A DEGENERATE, GIN-SOAKED WRETCH. HE'S GOTTA LOT OF NERVE PASSING OUT WITH A FULL BOTTLE!
RATS.
TIM, HAD TO RUN. BACK SOON. IF YER BORED THERE'S A BAR DOWN THE STREET. GET TO KNOW THE 'HOOD. IT'S NOT AS UNSAFE
YEAH, RIGHT. "THE 'HOOD." WHAT A GOOB.
THEN AGAIN, I COULD USE A DRINK. STEADY MY NERVES. BESIDES, SHOOTINGS AREN'T ALWAYS FATAL.
MAN, IF I EVER END UP LIKE THAT I'D HOPE ONE OF MY FRIENDS WOULD HAVE THE DECENCY TO PUT ME OUT OF MY MISERY.
HMMM
WELL, LET'S SEE, I FIRST GOT INTO IT WHEN I WAS IN THE NAVY—WELL, I WASN'T EXACTLY IN THE NAVY 'CUZ I'M TOO SHORT BUT I WAS HANGIN' OUT WITH THESE GUYS WHO WERE, LIKE, NAVAL PHARMACISTS, SO ONE THING LEADS TO ANOTHER AND I WAS SUPPOSED TO MEET ERIC HERE AT TWO BUT, AS THEY SAY, "HE'S NEVER EARLY, HE'S ALWAYS LATE"—AH HELL, I'M SURE YOU KNOW WHAT I'M TALKIN' ABOUT, EH GUY.
:SNORT:
End

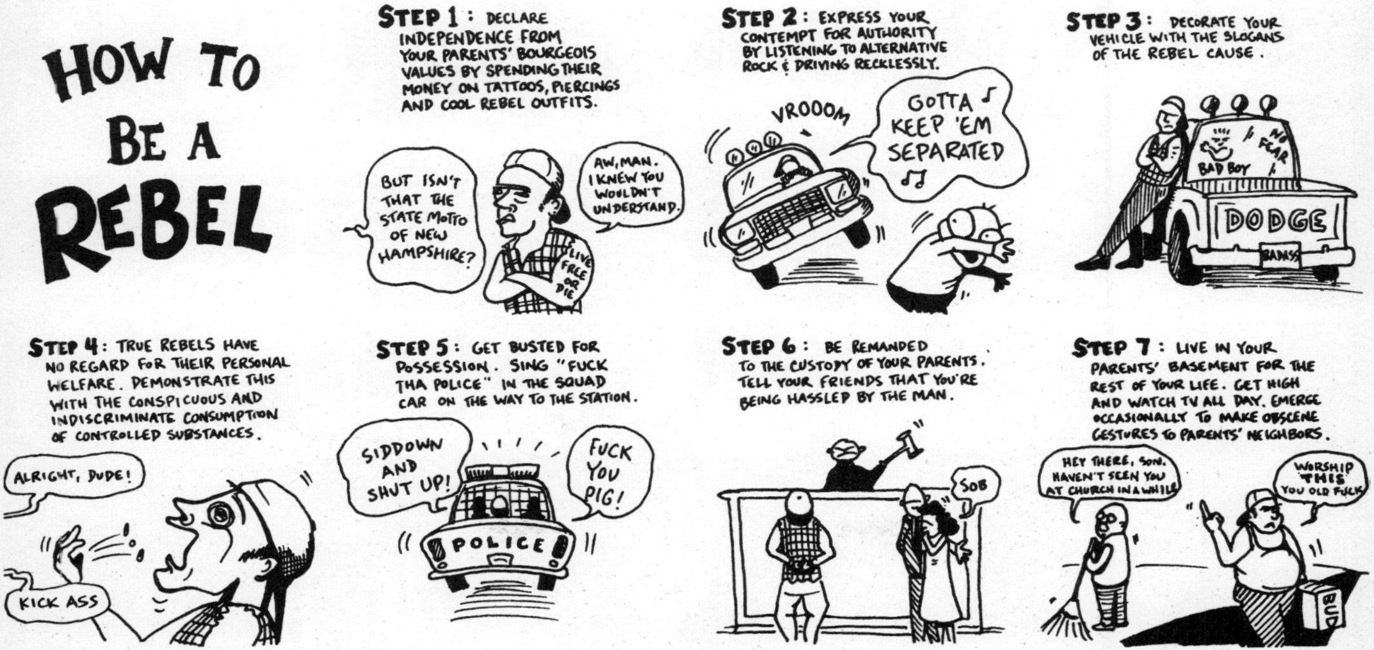
HOW TO BE A REBEL
STEP 1: DECLARE INDEPENDENCE FROM YOUR PARENTS' BOURGEOIS VALUES BY SPENDING THEIR MONEY ON TATTOOS, PIERCINGS AND COOL REBEL OUTFITS.
BUT ISN'T THAT THE STATE MOTTO OF NEW HAMPSHIRE?
AW, MAN. I KNEW YOU WOULDN'T UNDERSTAND.
LIVE FREE OR DIE
STEP 2: EXPRESS YOUR CONTEMPT FOR AUTHORITY BY LISTENING TO ALTERNATIVE ROCK & DRIVING RECKLESSLY.
VROOOM
GOTTA KEEP 'EM SEPARATED
STEP 3: DECORATE YOUR VEHICLE WITH THE SLOGANS OF THE REBEL CAUSE.
BAD BOY
NO FEAR
DODGE
STEP 4: TRUE REBELS HAVE NO REGARD FOR THEIR PERSONAL WELFARE. DEMONSTRATE THIS WITH THE CONSPICUOUS AND INDISCRIMINATE CONSUMPTION OF CONTROLLED SUBSTANCES.
ALRIGHT, DUDE!
KICK ASS
STEP 5: GET BUSTED FOR POSSESSION. SING "FUCK THA POLICE" IN THE SQUAD CAR ON THE WAY TO THE STATION.
SIDDOWN AND SHUT UP!
FUCK YOU PIG!
POLICE
STEP 6: BE REMANDED TO THE CUSTODY OF YOUR PARENTS. TELL YOUR FRIENDS THAT YOU'RE BEING HASSLED BY THE MAN.
SOB
STEP 7: LIVE IN YOUR PARENTS' BASEMENT FOR THE REST OF YOUR LIFE. GET HIGH AND WATCH TV ALL DAY. EMERGE OCCASIONALLY TO MAKE OBSCENE GESTURES TO PARENTS' NEIGHBORS.
HEY THERE, SON. HAVEN'T SEEN YOU AT CHURCH IN A WHILE
WORSHIP THIS YOU OLD FUCK
BUD

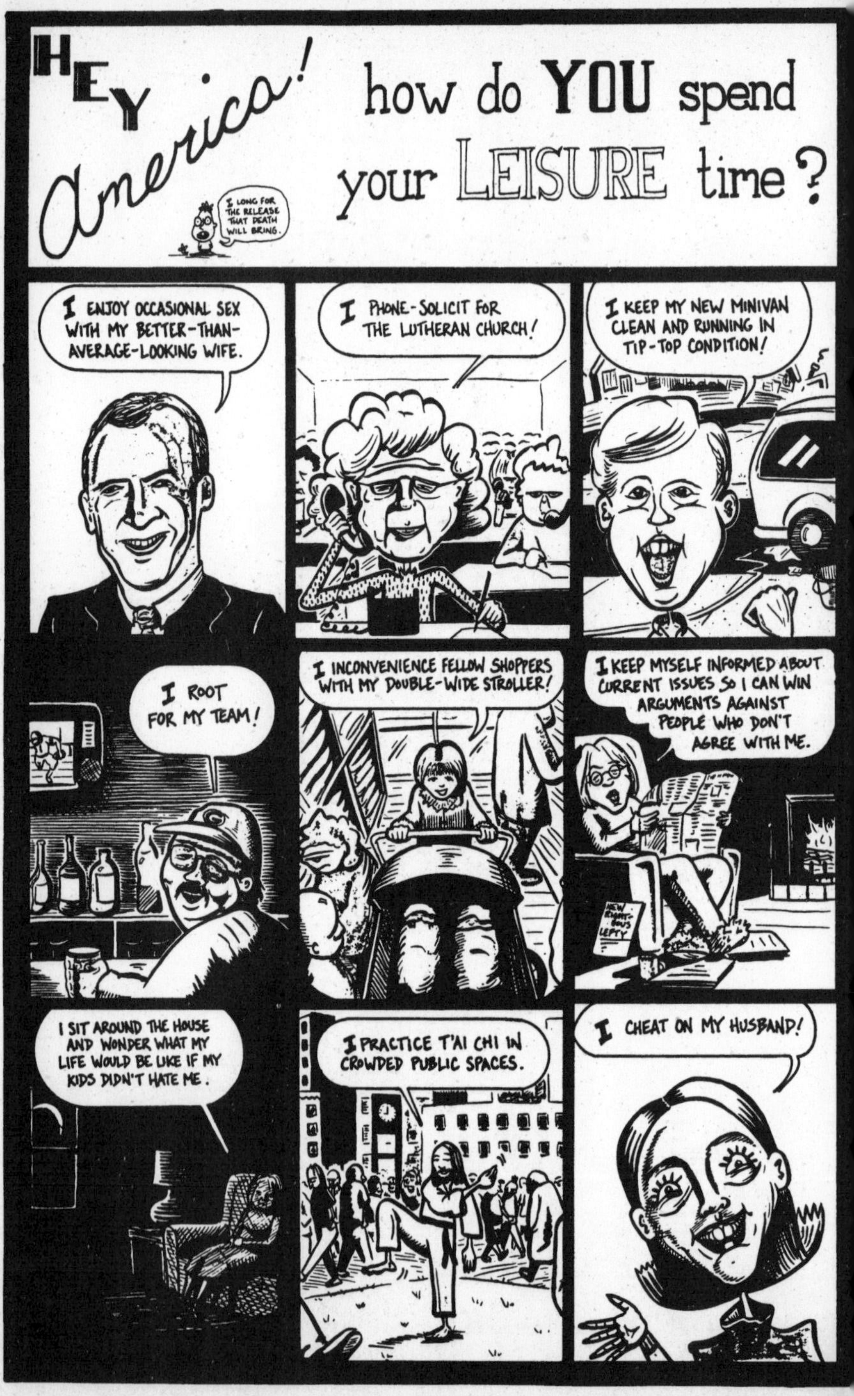
HEY America!
how do YOU spend your LEISURE time?
I LONG FOR THE RELEASE THAT DEATH WILL BRING.
I ENJOY OCCASIONAL SEX WITH MY BETTER-THAN-AVERAGE-LOOKING WIFE.
I PHONE-SOLICIT FOR THE LUTHERAN CHURCH!
I KEEP MY NEW MINIVAN CLEAN AND RUNNING IN TIP-TOP CONDITION!
I ROOT FOR MY TEAM!
I INCONVENIENCE FELLOW SHOPPERS WITH MY DOUBLE-WIDE STROLLER!
I KEEP MYSELF INFORMED ABOUT CURRENT ISSUES SO I CAN WIN ARGUMENTS AGAINST PEOPLE WHO DON'T AGREE WITH ME.
I SIT AROUND THE HOUSE AND WONDER WHAT MY LIFE WOULD BE LIKE IF MY KIDS DIDN'T HATE ME.
I PRACTICE T'AI CHI IN CROWDED PUBLIC SPACES.
I CHEAT ON MY HUSBAND!

# I HATE YOU AND I WISH YOU WERE DEAD

HEY, MISTER!

WHAT?

THAT WAS AUNT MARY. SHE SAID TO MEET HER AT THE BRICKHOUSE AT SIX!

I GUESS SOMETHING REALLY WEIRD HAPPENED AT WORK TODAY.

OK. WHATEVER.

SHE SAID TO — — OH FER CRYIN' OUT LOUD!! YOU'RE NOT WATCHING "VAGINA TOWN" AGAIN ARE YOU?

WHAT'S YER POINT?

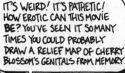

IT'S WEIRD! IT'S PATHETIC! HOW EROTIC CAN THIS MOVIE BE? YOU'VE SEEN IT SO MANY TIMES YOU COULD PROBABLY DRAW A RELIEF MAP OF CHERRY BLOSSOM'S GENITALS FROM MEMORY.

HEY, YOUNG TIM, WHY DON'T YOU GO FUCK YOURSELF?

OH, YEAH? WELL SPEAKING OF FUCKING YOURSELF, TELL ME WHAT'S THE POINT OF WATCHING PORN IF YOU'RE NOT GONNA WHACK OFF?

WHAT MAKES YOU THINK I'M NOT GONNA WHACK OFF?

WELL MAKE IT SNAPPY. AUNT MARY WANTS US TO BE AT THE BAR WHEN SHE GETS THERE.

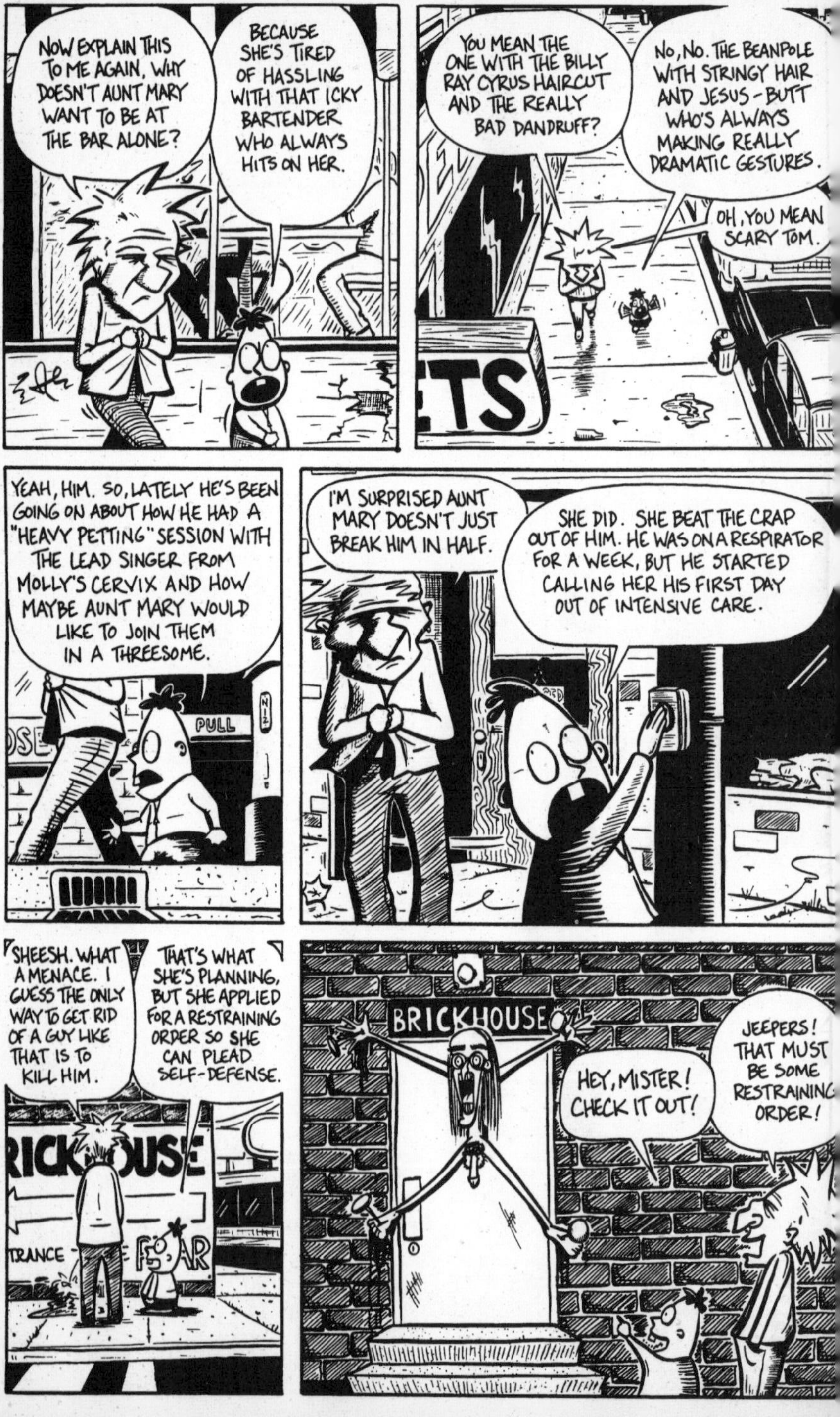
NOW EXPLAIN THIS TO ME AGAIN. WHY DOESN'T AUNT MARY WANT TO BE AT THE BAR ALONE?
BECAUSE SHE'S TIRED OF HASSLING WITH THAT ICKY BARTENDER WHO ALWAYS HITS ON HER.
YOU MEAN THE ONE WITH THE BILLY RAY CYRUS HAIRCUT AND THE REALLY BAD DANDRUFF?
NO, NO. THE BEANPOLE WITH STRINGY HAIR AND JESUS-BUTT WHO'S ALWAYS MAKING REALLY DRAMATIC GESTURES.
OH, YOU MEAN SCARY TOM.
YEAH, HIM. SO, LATELY HE'S BEEN GOING ON ABOUT HOW HE HAD A "HEAVY PETTING" SESSION WITH THE LEAD SINGER FROM MOLLY'S CERVIX AND HOW MAYBE AUNT MARY WOULD LIKE TO JOIN THEM IN A THREESOME.
PULL
I'M SURPRISED AUNT MARY DOESN'T JUST BREAK HIM IN HALF.
SHE DID. SHE BEAT THE CRAP OUT OF HIM. HE WAS ON A RESPIRATOR FOR A WEEK, BUT HE STARTED CALLING HER HIS FIRST DAY OUT OF INTENSIVE CARE.
SHEESH. WHAT A MENACE. I GUESS THE ONLY WAY TO GET RID OF A GUY LIKE THAT IS TO KILL HIM.
THAT'S WHAT SHE'S PLANNING, BUT SHE APPLIED FOR A RESTRAINING ORDER SO SHE CAN PLEAD SELF-DEFENSE.
BRICKHOUSE
HEY, MISTER! CHECK IT OUT!
JEEPERS! THAT MUST BE SOME RESTRAINING ORDER!

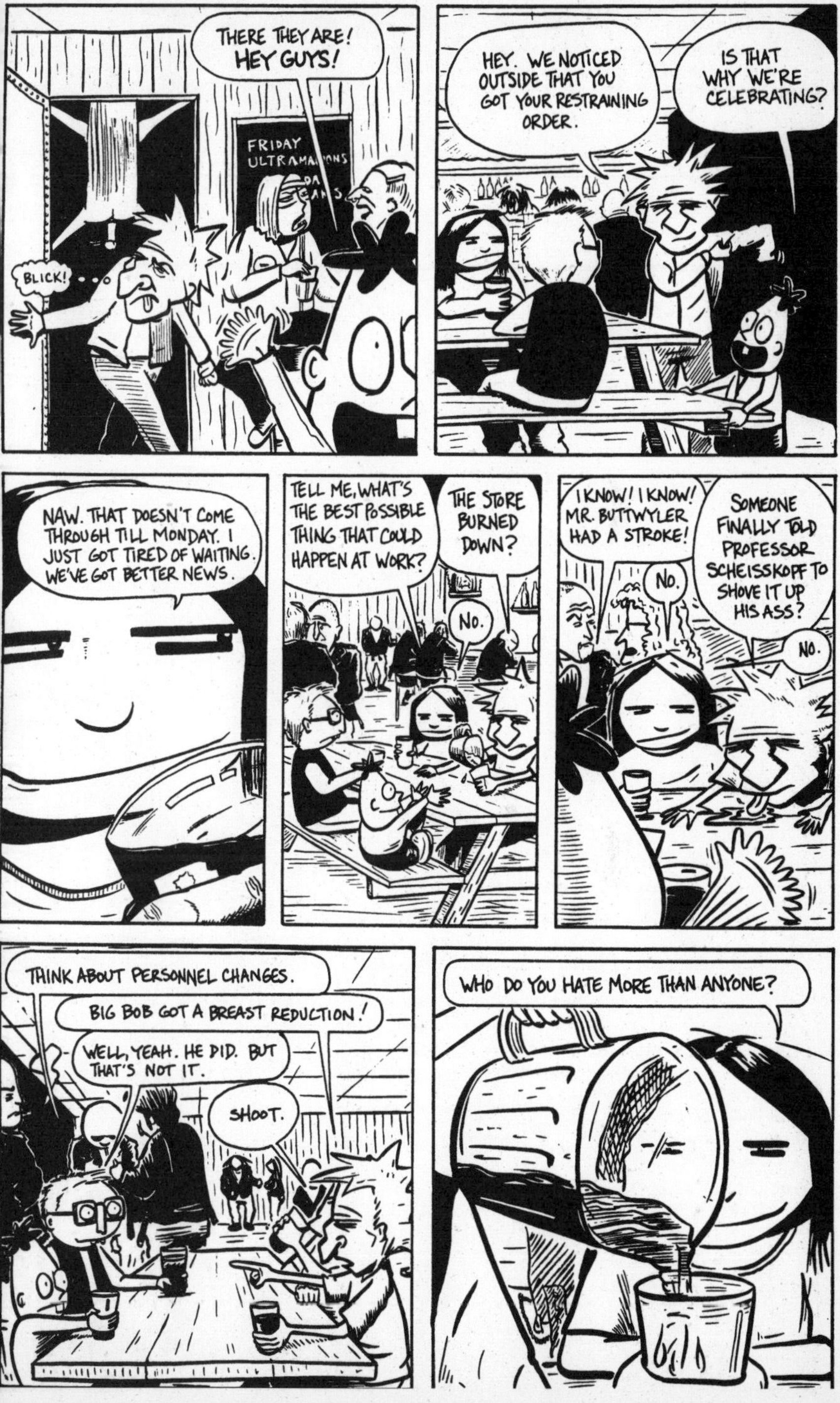
THERE THEY ARE! HEY GUYS!
FRIDAY ULTRAMA
BLICK!
HEY. WE NOTICED OUTSIDE THAT YOU GOT YOUR RESTRAINING ORDER.
IS THAT WHY WE'RE CELEBRATING?
NAW. THAT DOESN'T COME THROUGH TILL MONDAY. I JUST GOT TIRED OF WAITING. WE'VE GOT BETTER NEWS.
TELL ME, WHAT'S THE BEST POSSIBLE THING THAT COULD HAPPEN AT WORK?
THE STORE BURNED DOWN?
NO.
I KNOW! I KNOW! MR. BUTTWYLER HAD A STROKE!
NO.
SOMEONE FINALLY TOLD PROFESSOR SCHEISSKOPF TO SHOVE IT UP HIS ASS?
NO.
THINK ABOUT PERSONNEL CHANGES.
BIG BOB GOT A BREAST REDUCTION!
WELL, YEAH. HE DID. BUT THAT'S NOT IT.
SHOOT.
WHO DO YOU HATE MORE THAN ANYONE?

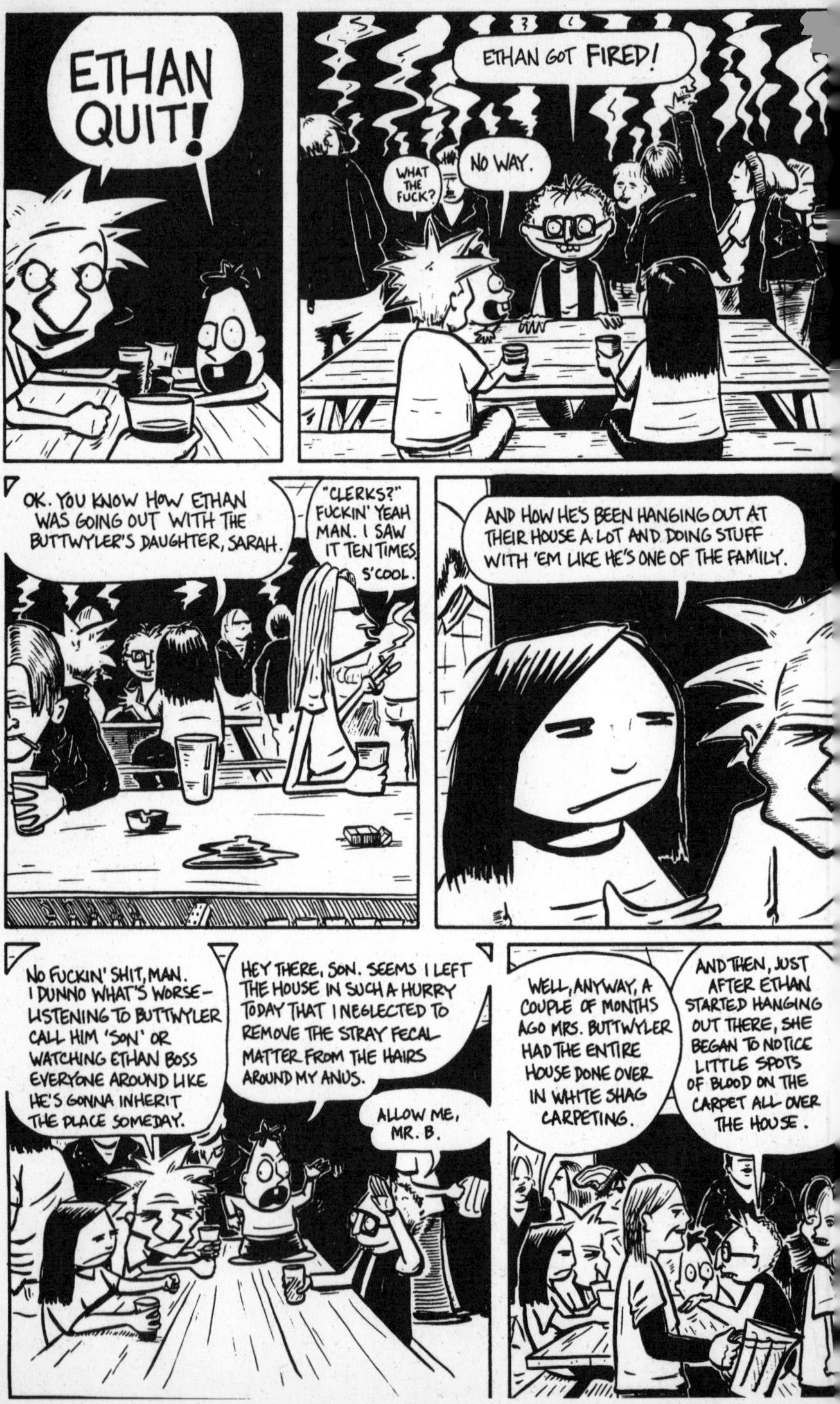

ETHAN QUIT!
ETHAN GOT FIRED!
WHAT THE FUCK?
NO WAY.
OK. YOU KNOW HOW ETHAN WAS GOING OUT WITH THE BUTTWYLER'S DAUGHTER, SARAH.
"CLERKS?" FUCKIN' YEAH MAN. I SAW IT TEN TIMES. S'COOL.
AND HOW HE'S BEEN HANGING OUT AT THEIR HOUSE A LOT AND DOING STUFF WITH 'EM LIKE HE'S ONE OF THE FAMILY.
NO FUCKIN' SHIT, MAN. I DUNNO WHAT'S WORSE- LISTENING TO BUTTWYLER CALL HIM 'SON' OR WATCHING ETHAN BOSS EVERYONE AROUND LIKE HE'S GONNA INHERIT THE PLACE SOMEDAY.
HEY THERE, SON. SEEMS I LEFT THE HOUSE IN SUCH A HURRY TODAY THAT I NEGLECTED TO REMOVE THE STRAY FECAL MATTER FROM THE HAIRS AROUND MY ANUS.
ALLOW ME, MR. B.
WELL, ANYWAY, A COUPLE OF MONTHS AGO MRS. BUTTWYLER HAD THE ENTIRE HOUSE DONE OVER IN WHITE SHAG CARPETING.
AND THEN, JUST AFTER ETHAN STARTED HANGING OUT THERE, SHE BEGAN TO NOTICE LITTLE SPOTS OF BLOOD ON THE CARPET ALL OVER THE HOUSE.

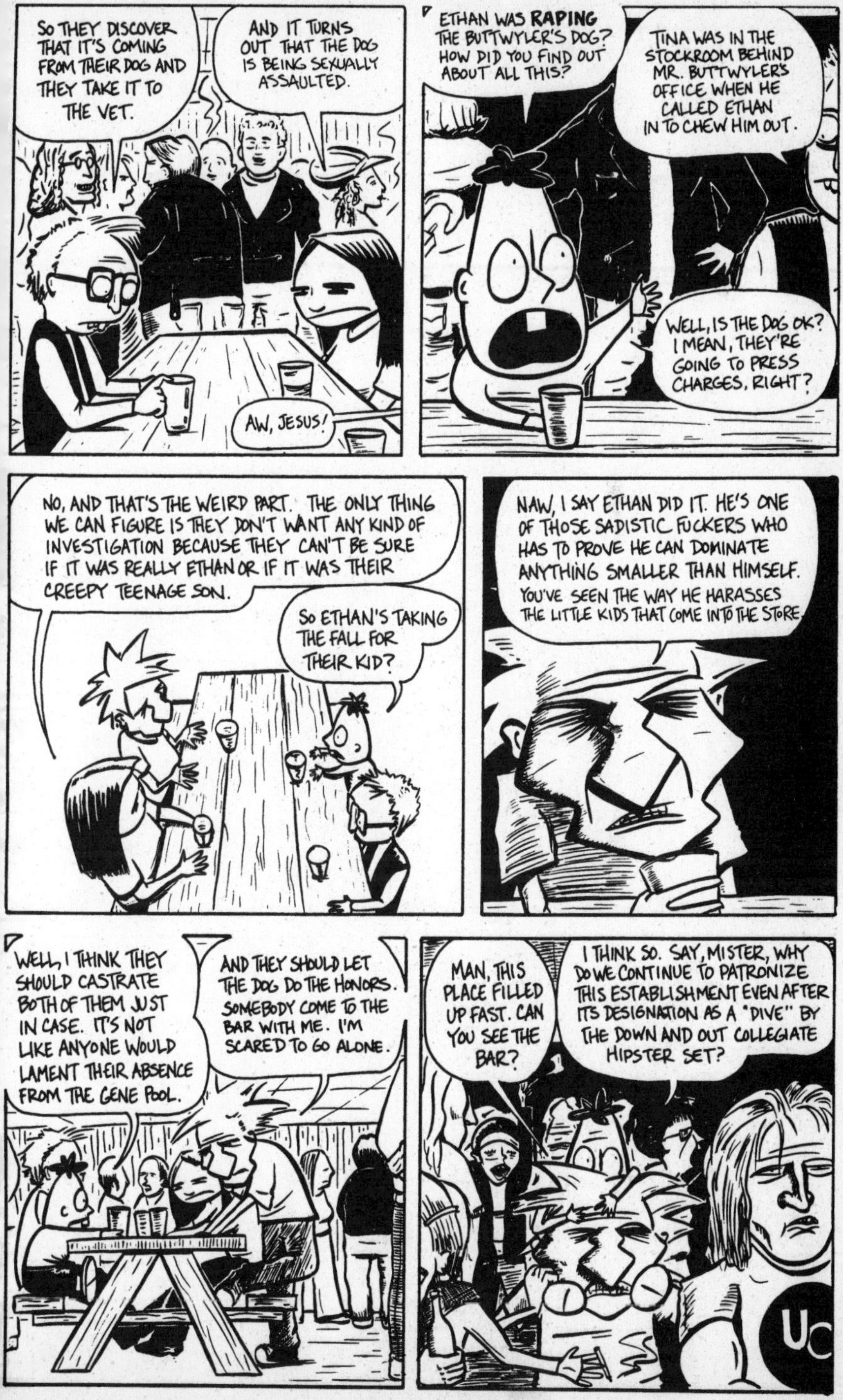
SO THEY DISCOVER THAT IT'S COMING FROM THEIR DOG AND THEY TAKE IT TO THE VET.
AND IT TURNS OUT THAT THE DOG IS BEING SEXUALLY ASSAULTED.
AW, JESUS!
ETHAN WAS **RAPING** THE BUTTWYLER'S DOG? HOW DID YOU FIND OUT ABOUT ALL THIS?
TINA WAS IN THE STOCKROOM BEHIND MR. BUTTWYLER'S OFFICE WHEN HE CALLED ETHAN IN TO CHEW HIM OUT.
WELL, IS THE DOG OK? I MEAN, THEY'RE GOING TO PRESS CHARGES, RIGHT?
NO, AND THAT'S THE WEIRD PART. THE ONLY THING WE CAN FIGURE IS THEY DON'T WANT ANY KIND OF INVESTIGATION BECAUSE THEY CAN'T BE SURE IF IT WAS REALLY ETHAN OR IF IT WAS THEIR CREEPY TEENAGE SON.
SO ETHAN'S TAKING THE FALL FOR THEIR KID?
NAW, I SAY ETHAN DID IT. HE'S ONE OF THOSE SADISTIC FUCKERS WHO HAS TO PROVE HE CAN DOMINATE ANYTHING SMALLER THAN HIMSELF. YOU'VE SEEN THE WAY HE HARASSES THE LITTLE KIDS THAT COME INTO THE STORE.
WELL, I THINK THEY SHOULD CASTRATE BOTH OF THEM JUST IN CASE. IT'S NOT LIKE ANYONE WOULD LAMENT THEIR ABSENCE FROM THE GENE POOL.
AND THEY SHOULD LET THE DOG DO THE HONORS. SOMEBODY COME TO THE BAR WITH ME. I'M SCARED TO GO ALONE.
MAN, THIS PLACE FILLED UP FAST. CAN YOU SEE THE BAR?
I THINK SO. SAY, MISTER, WHY DO WE CONTINUE TO PATRONIZE THIS ESTABLISHMENT EVEN AFTER ITS DESIGNATION AS A "DIVE" BY THE DOWN AND OUT COLLEGIATE HIPSTER SET?
UC

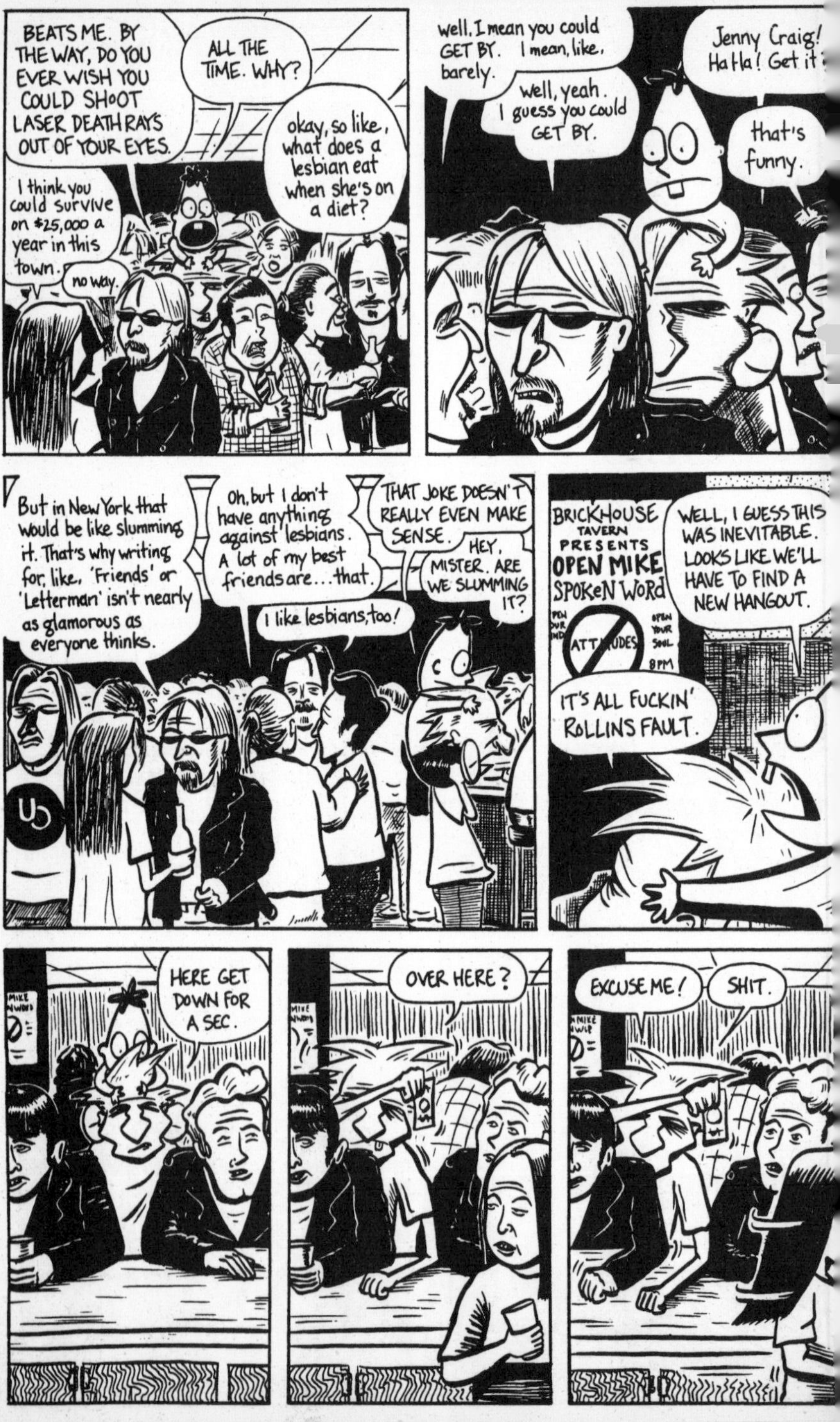
BEATS ME. BY THE WAY, DO YOU EVER WISH YOU COULD SHOOT LASER DEATH RAYS OUT OF YOUR EYES.
ALL THE TIME. WHY?
okay, so like, what does a lesbian eat when she's on a diet?
I think you could survive on $25,000 a year in this town.
no way.
Well, I mean you could GET BY. I mean, like, barely.
Well, yeah. I guess you could GET BY.
Jenny Craig! Ha Ha! Get it?
that's funny.
But in New York that would be like slumming it. That's why writing for, like, 'Friends' or 'Letterman' isn't nearly as glamorous as everyone thinks.
Oh, but I don't have anything against lesbians. A lot of my best friends are...that.
THAT JOKE DOESN'T REALLY EVEN MAKE SENSE.
HEY, MISTER. ARE WE SLUMMING IT?
I like lesbians, too!
BRICKHOUSE TAVERN PRESENTS OPEN MIKE SPOKeN WORd
ATTITUDES
OPEN YOUR SOUL
8PM
WELL, I GUESS THIS WAS INEVITABLE. LOOKS LIKE WE'LL HAVE TO FIND A NEW HANGOUT.
IT'S ALL FUCKIN' ROLLINS FAULT.
HERE GET DOWN FOR A SEC.
OVER HERE?
EXCUSE ME!
SHIT.

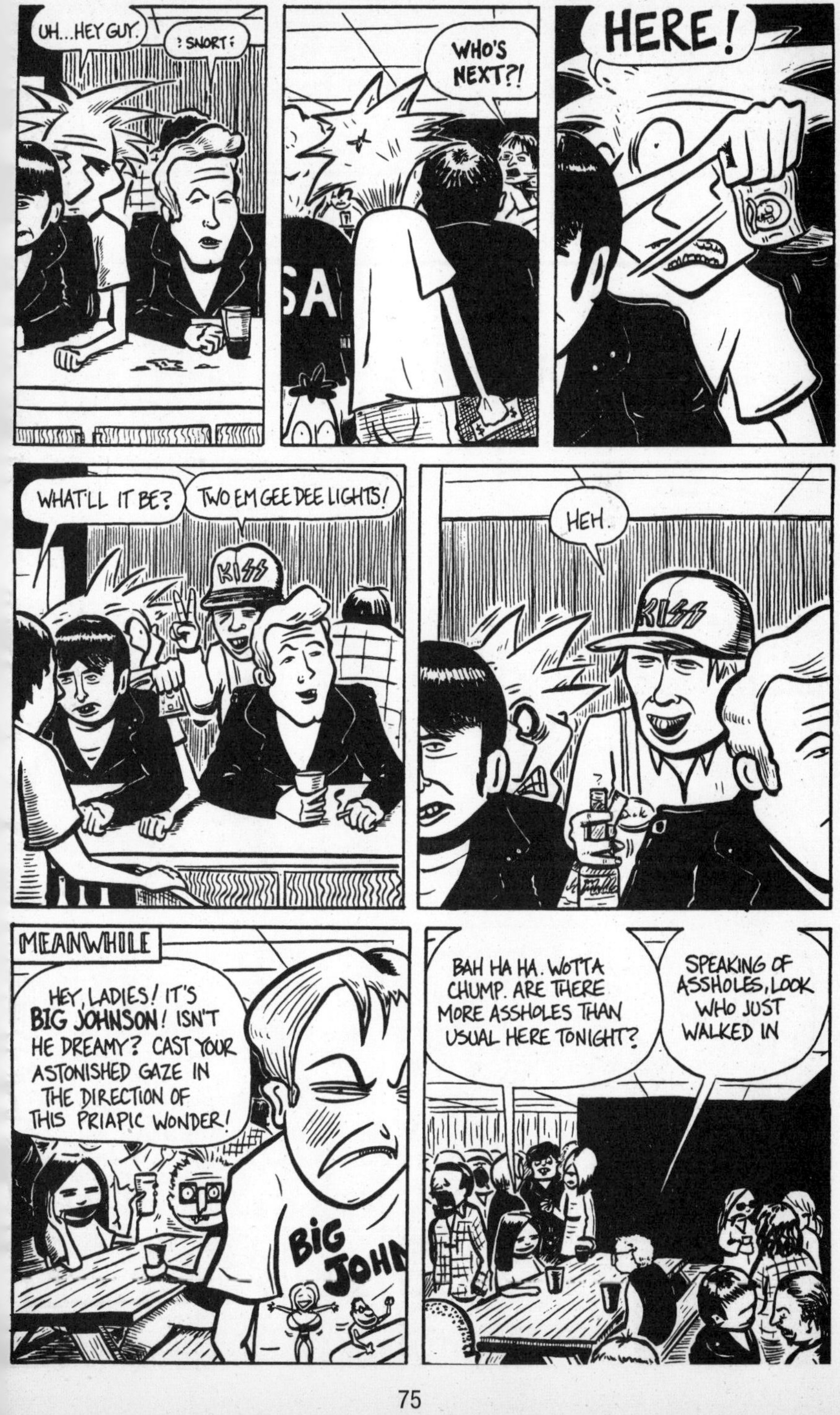
UH...HEY GUY.
? SNORT ?
WHO'S NEXT?!
SA
HERE!
WHAT'LL IT BE?
TWO EM GEE DEE LIGHTS!
KISS
HEH.
KISS
MEANWHILE
HEY, LADIES! IT'S BIG JOHNSON! ISN'T HE DREAMY? CAST YOUR ASTONISHED GAZE IN THE DIRECTION OF THIS PRIAPIC WONDER!
BIG JOHN
BAH HA HA. WOTTA CHUMP. ARE THERE MORE ASSHOLES THAN USUAL HERE TONIGHT?
SPEAKING OF ASSHOLES, LOOK WHO JUST WALKED IN

HOLY SHIT! IT'S ETHAN! **HEY ETHAN!** FWEET ♪ OVER HERE!

ARE YOU OUTTA YER MIND

HEH HEH. I WOULDN'T MISS THIS OPPORTUNITY FOR ALL THE BEER IN WISCONSIN.

HEY GUYS.

HANGIN' OUT, I SEE. HAVIN' A COUPLE A BEERS AFTER WORK. THAT'S COOL.

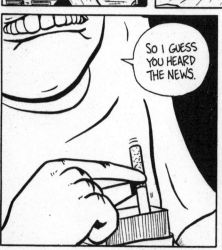

SO I GUESS YOU HEARD THE NEWS.

UH...YEAH?

NO ETHAN! PRAY, TELL MAN WHAT CHEER?

I'M QUITTIN' THE BOOKSTORE MAAN. I GOT A JOB WORKIN' FOR A BOOKIE.

IT'S GONNA BE TOTALLY COOL, MAN. MAKIN' DROP OFFS AND SHIT. NO MORE KISSIN' PROFESSOR WEISSKOPF'S BIG, HAIRY BUTT.

REALLY? I HEARD YOU GOT FIRED BECAUSE YOU COULDN'T KEEP YOUR PECKER OUT OF A DOG'S BIG HAIRY BUTT.

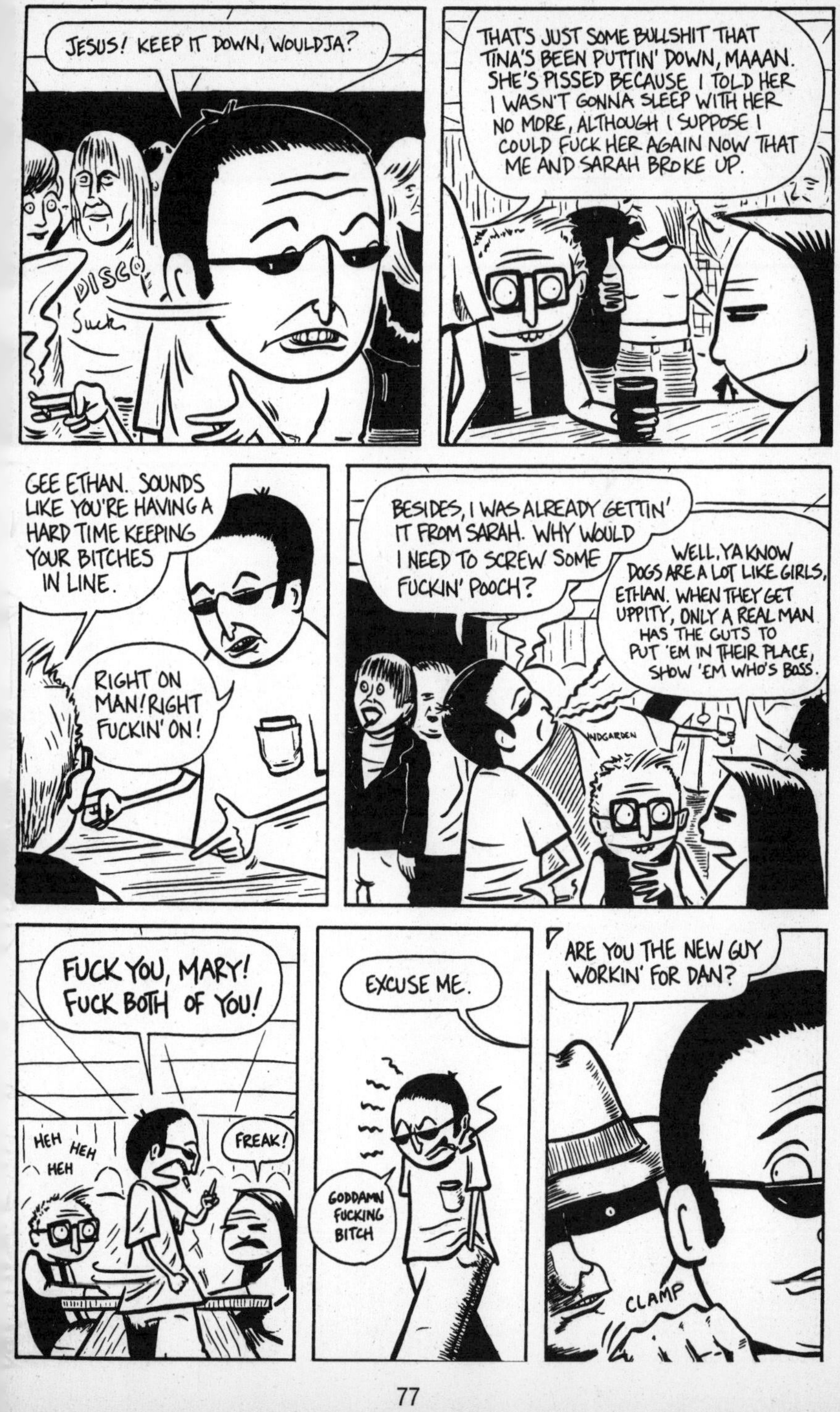

JESUS! KEEP IT DOWN, WOULDJA?
DISCO Sucks
THAT'S JUST SOME BULLSHIT THAT TINA'S BEEN PUTTIN' DOWN, MAAAN. SHE'S PISSED BECAUSE I TOLD HER I WASN'T GONNA SLEEP WITH HER NO MORE, ALTHOUGH I SUPPOSE I COULD FUCK HER AGAIN NOW THAT ME AND SARAH BROKE UP.
GEE ETHAN. SOUNDS LIKE YOU'RE HAVING A HARD TIME KEEPING YOUR BITCHES IN LINE.
RIGHT ON MAN! RIGHT FUCKIN' ON!
BESIDES, I WAS ALREADY GETTIN' IT FROM SARAH. WHY WOULD I NEED TO SCREW SOME FUCKIN' POOCH?
WELL, YA KNOW DOGS ARE A LOT LIKE GIRLS, ETHAN. WHEN THEY GET UPPITY, ONLY A REAL MAN HAS THE GUTS TO PUT 'EM IN THEIR PLACE, SHOW 'EM WHO'S BOSS.
FUCK YOU, MARY! FUCK BOTH OF YOU!
HEH HEH HEH
FREAK!
EXCUSE ME.
GODDAMN FUCKING BITCH
ARE YOU THE NEW GUY WORKIN' FOR DAN?
CLAMP

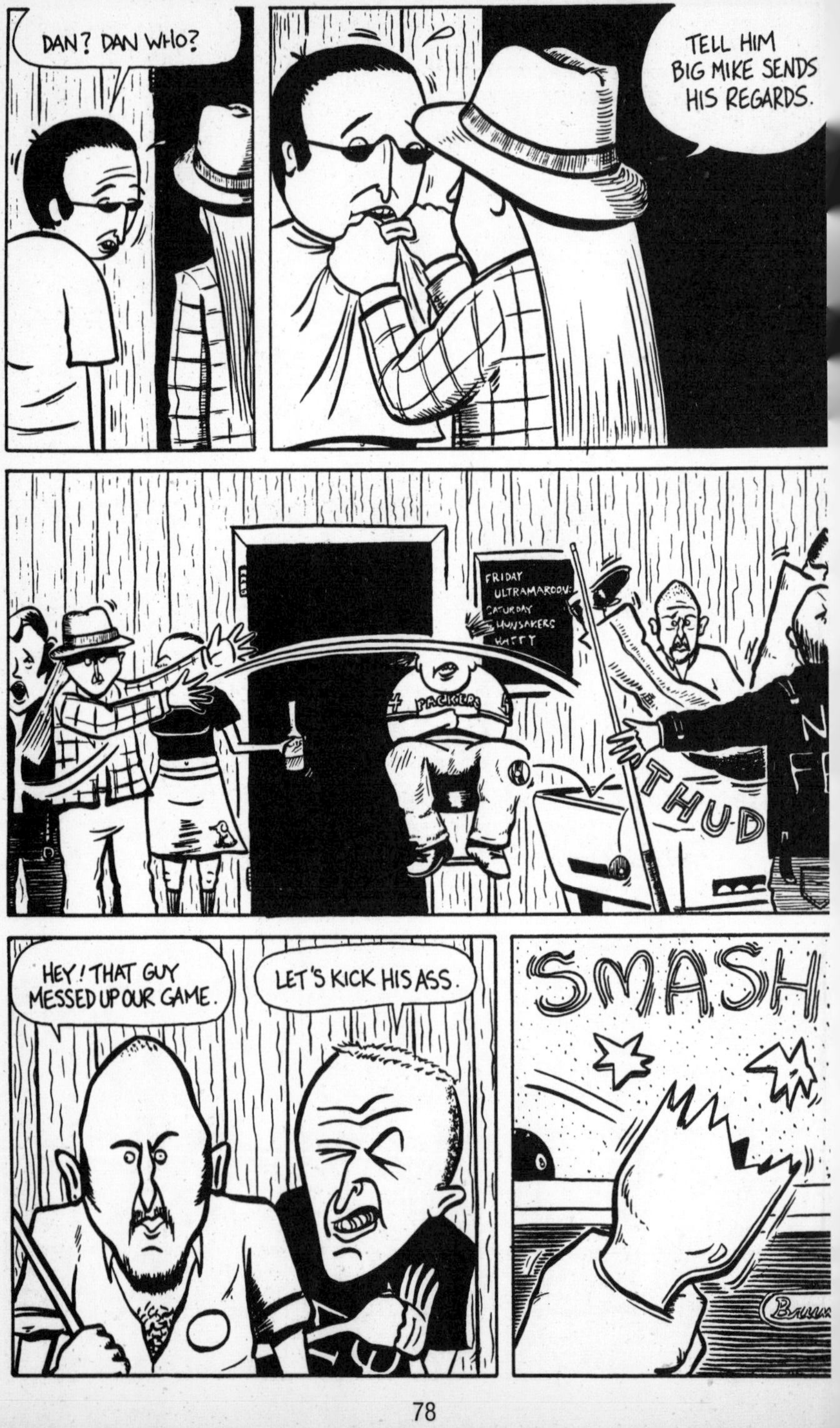
DAN? DAN WHO?
TELL HIM BIG MIKE SENDS HIS REGARDS.
FRIDAY
ULTRAMAROON:
SATURDAY
HUNSAKERS
PACKERS
THUD
HEY! THAT GUY MESSED UP OUR GAME.
LET'S KICK HIS ASS.
SMASH

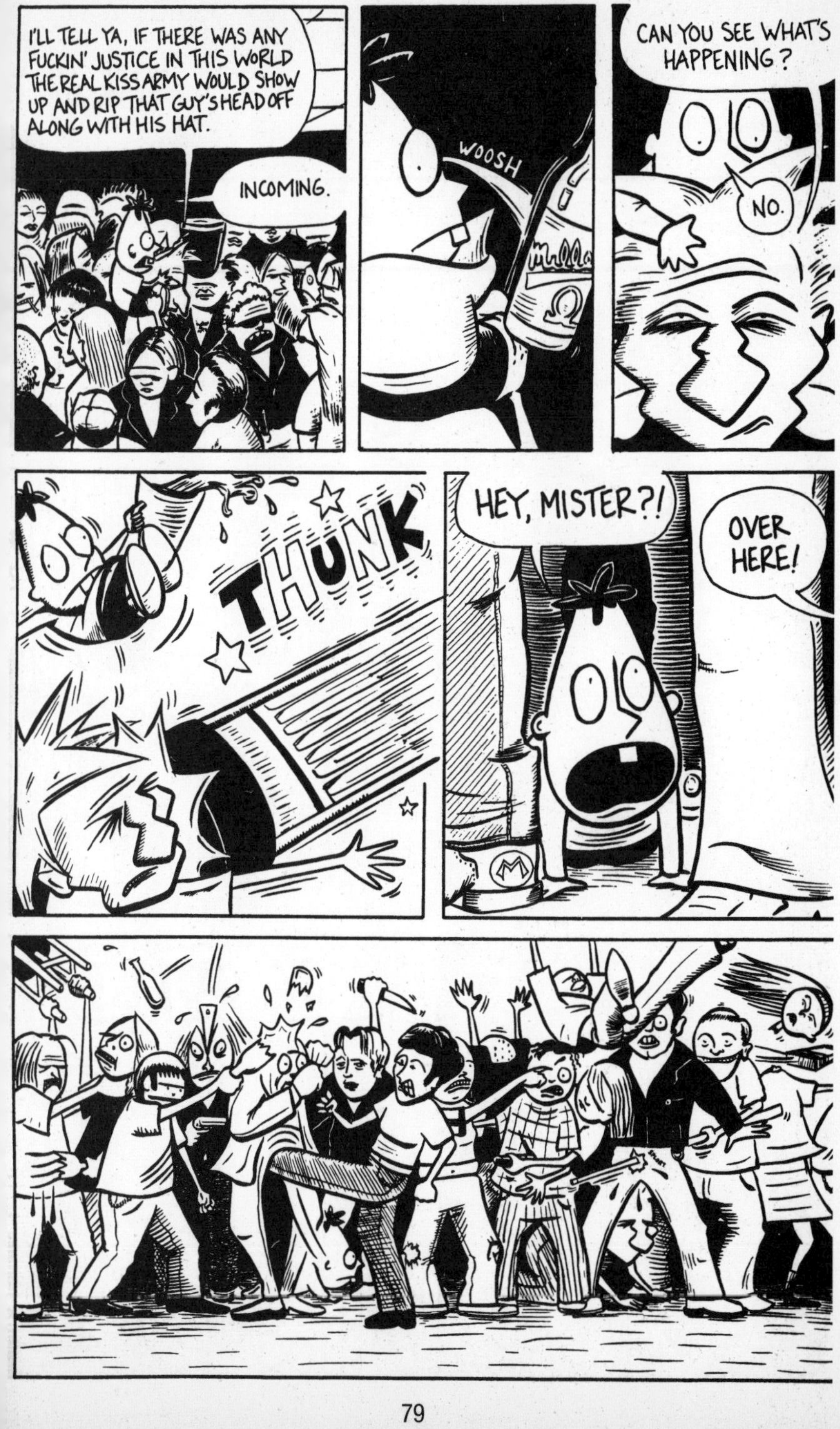

I'LL TELL YA, IF THERE WAS ANY FUCKIN' JUSTICE IN THIS WORLD THE REAL KISS ARMY WOULD SHOW UP AND RIP THAT GUY'S HEAD OFF ALONG WITH HIS HAT.
INCOMING.
WOOSH
CAN YOU SEE WHAT'S HAPPENING?
NO.
THUNK
HEY, MISTER?!
OVER HERE!

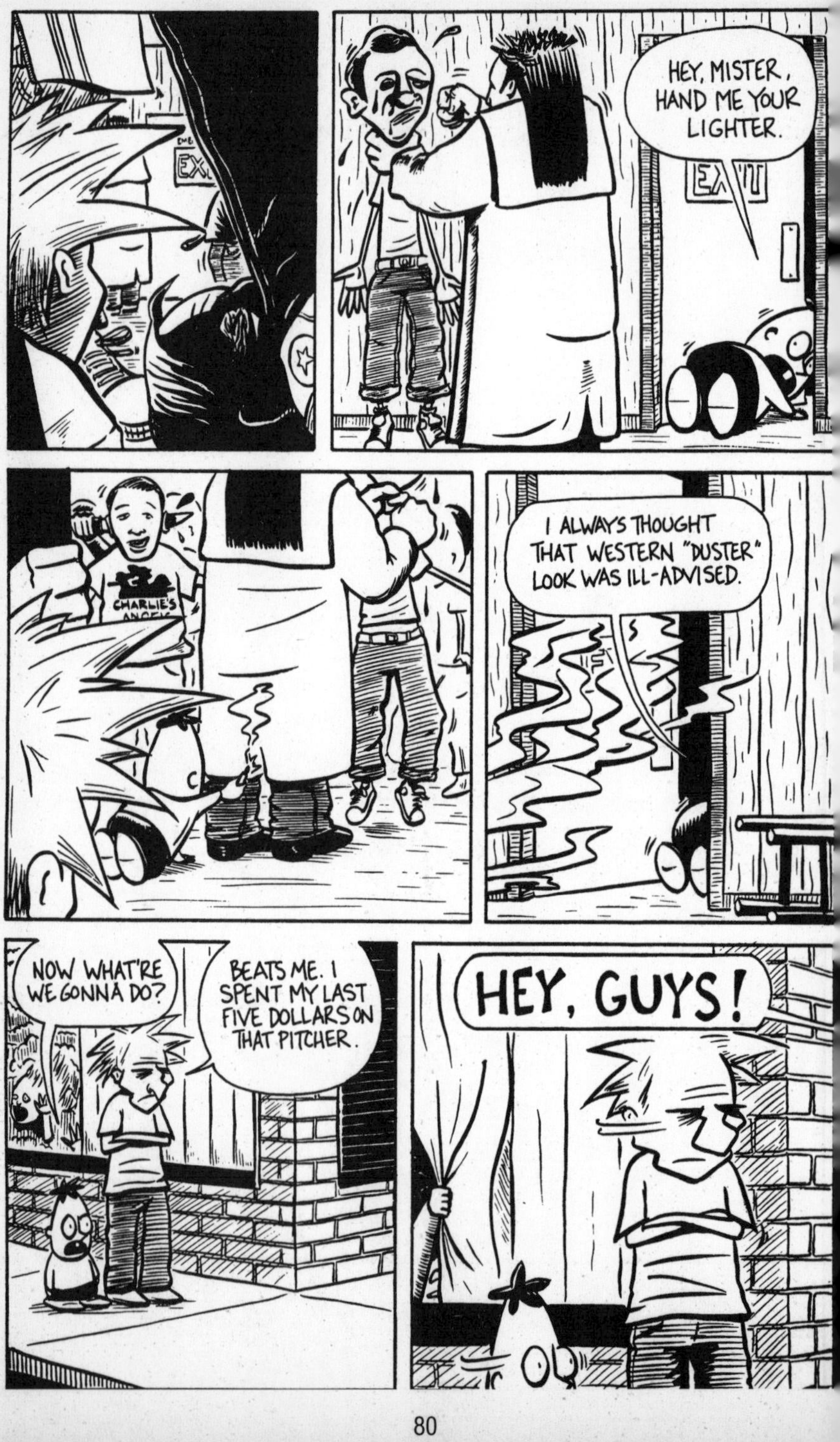
EXIT
HEY, MISTER, HAND ME YOUR LIGHTER.
EXIT
CHARLIE'S
I ALWAYS THOUGHT THAT WESTERN "DUSTER" LOOK WAS ILL-ADVISED.
NOW WHAT'RE WE GONNA DO?
BEATS ME. I SPENT MY LAST FIVE DOLLARS ON THAT PITCHER.
HEY, GUYS!

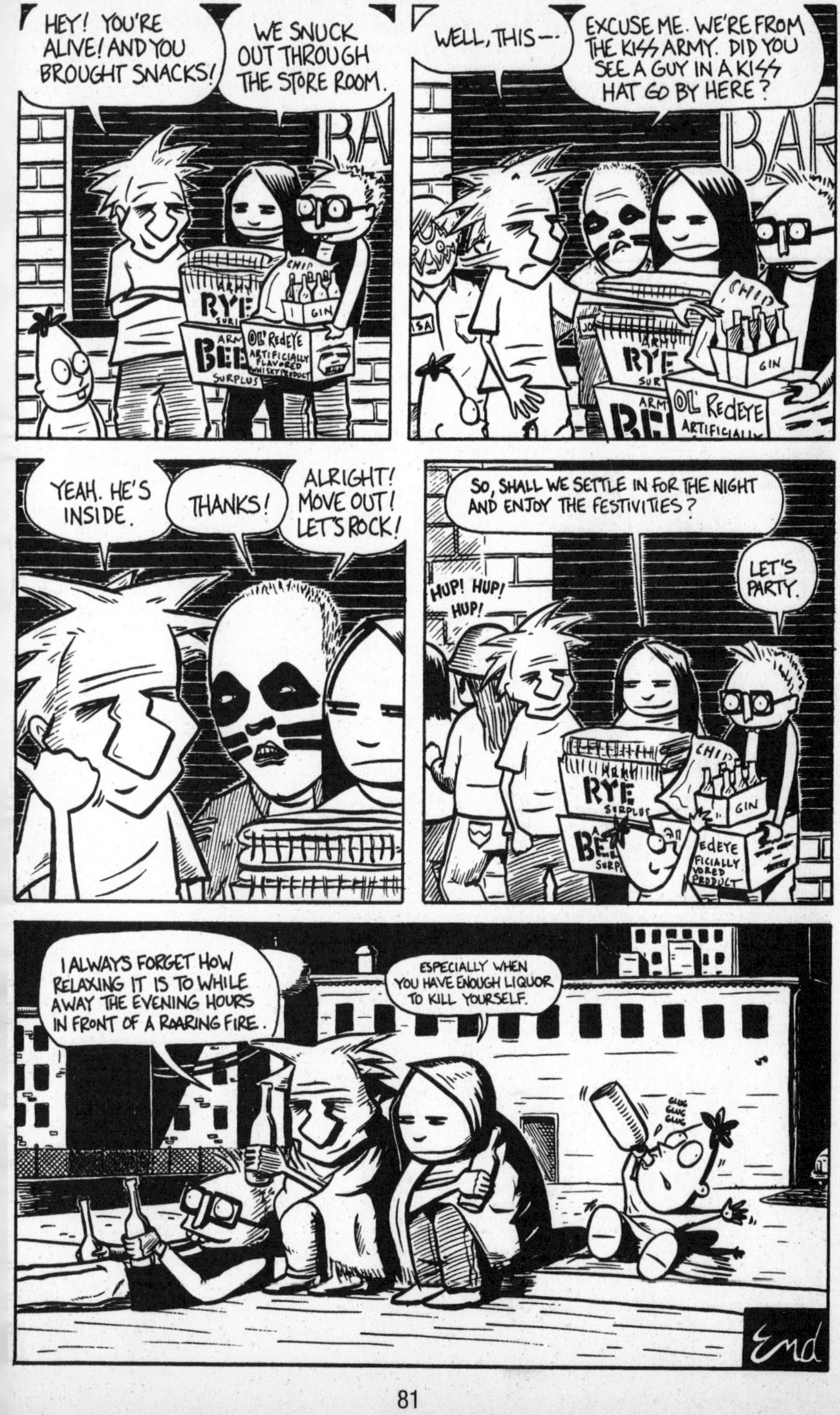
HEY! YOU'RE ALIVE! AND YOU BROUGHT SNACKS!
WE SNUCK OUT THROUGH THE STORE ROOM.
WELL, THIS--
EXCUSE ME. WE'RE FROM THE KISS ARMY. DID YOU SEE A GUY IN A KISS HAT GO BY HERE?
YEAH. HE'S INSIDE.
THANKS!
ALRIGHT! MOVE OUT! LET'S ROCK!
SO, SHALL WE SETTLE IN FOR THE NIGHT AND ENJOY THE FESTIVITIES?
HUP! HUP! HUP!
LET'S PARTY.
I ALWAYS FORGET HOW RELAXING IT IS TO WHILE AWAY THE EVENING HOURS IN FRONT OF A ROARING FIRE.
ESPECIALLY WHEN YOU HAVE ENOUGH LIQUOR TO KILL YOURSELF.
GLUG GLUG GLUG
End

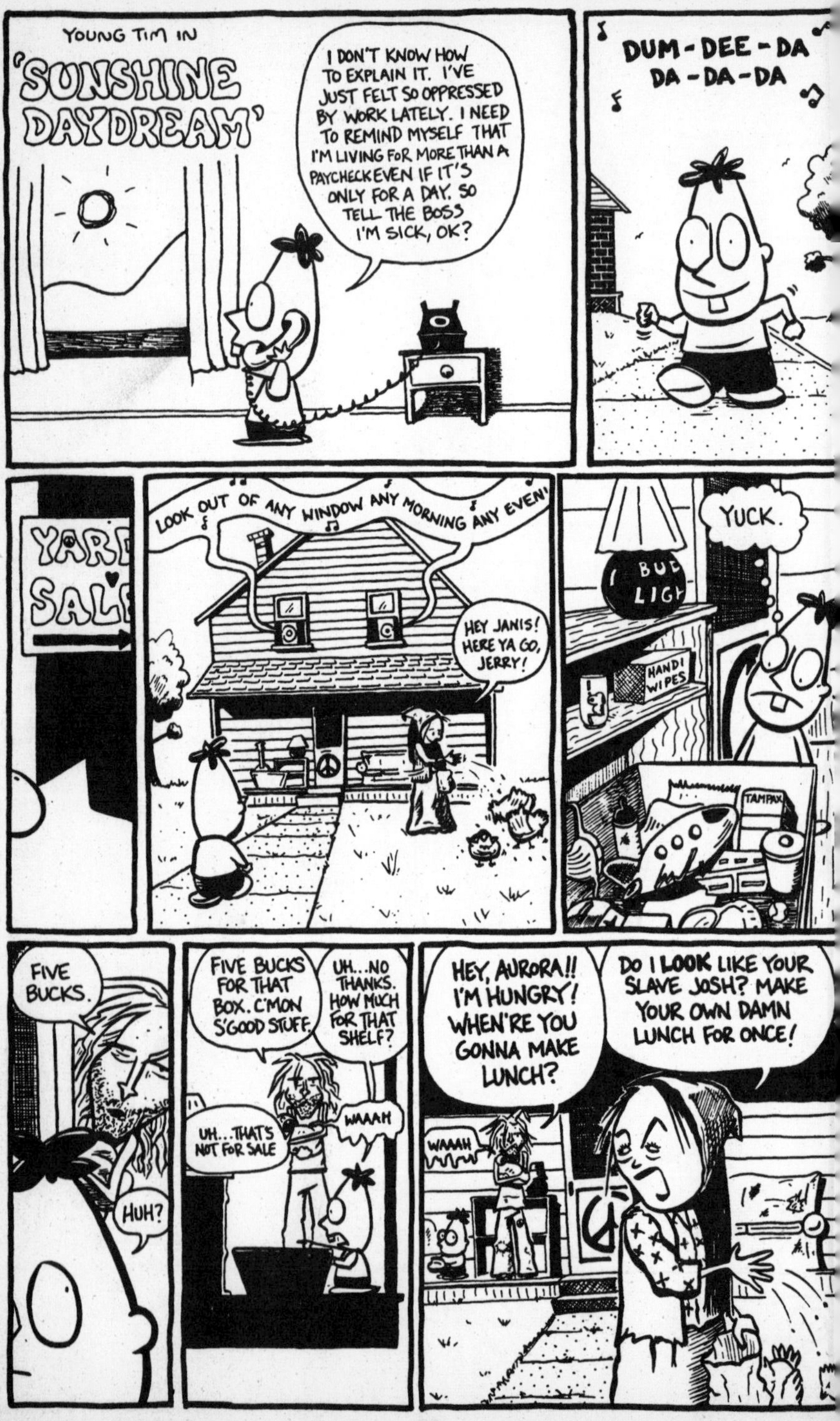
YOUNG TIM IN
'SUNSHINE DAYDREAM'
I DON'T KNOW HOW TO EXPLAIN IT. I'VE JUST FELT SO OPPRESSED BY WORK LATELY. I NEED TO REMIND MYSELF THAT I'M LIVING FOR MORE THAN A PAYCHECK EVEN IF IT'S ONLY FOR A DAY. SO TELL THE BOSS I'M SICK, OK?
DUM-DEE-DA DA-DA-DA
YARD SALE
LOOK OUT OF ANY WINDOW ANY MORNING ANY EVEN'
HEY JANIS! HERE YA GO, JERRY!
YUCK.
BUD LIGHT
HANDI WIPES
TAMPAX
FIVE BUCKS.
HUH?
FIVE BUCKS FOR THAT BOX. C'MON S'GOOD STUFF.
UH...NO THANKS. HOW MUCH FOR THAT SHELF?
UH...THAT'S NOT FOR SALE
WAAAH
WAAAH
HEY, AURORA!! I'M HUNGRY! WHEN'RE YOU GONNA MAKE LUNCH?
DO I LOOK LIKE YOUR SLAVE JOSH? MAKE YOUR OWN DAMN LUNCH FOR ONCE!

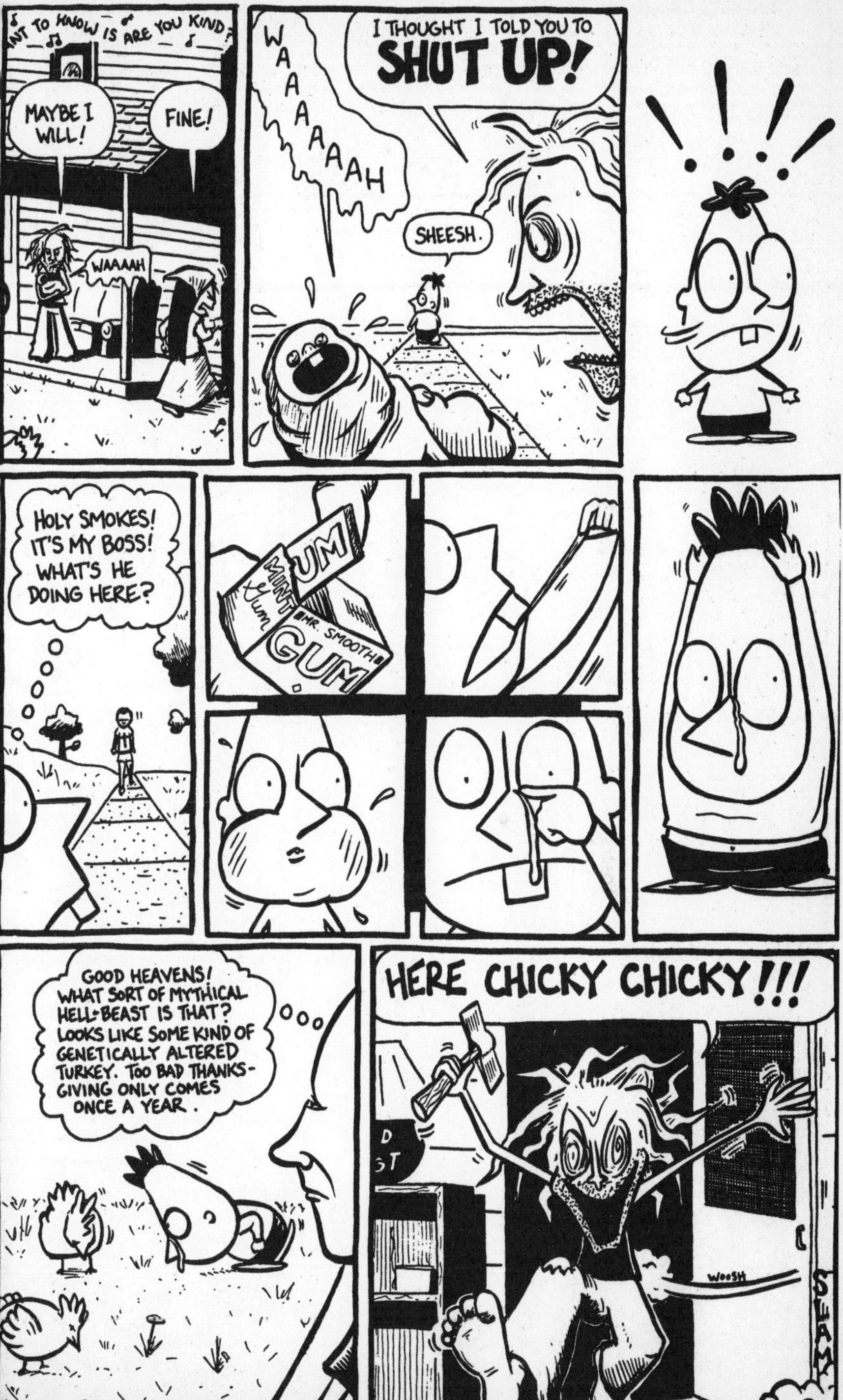

NT TO KNOW IS ARE YOU KIND
MAYBE I WILL!
FINE!
WAAAAH
WAAAAAAAAH
I THOUGHT I TOLD YOU TO SHUT UP!
SHEESH.
! ! ! !
HOLY SMOKES! IT'S MY BOSS! WHAT'S HE DOING HERE?
UM
MINT Gum
MR. SMOOTH
GUM
GOOD HEAVENS! WHAT SORT OF MYTHICAL HELL-BEAST IS THAT? LOOKS LIKE SOME KIND OF GENETICALLY ALTERED TURKEY. TOO BAD THANKS-GIVING ONLY COMES ONCE A YEAR.
HERE CHICKY CHICKY!!!
WOOSH
SLAM

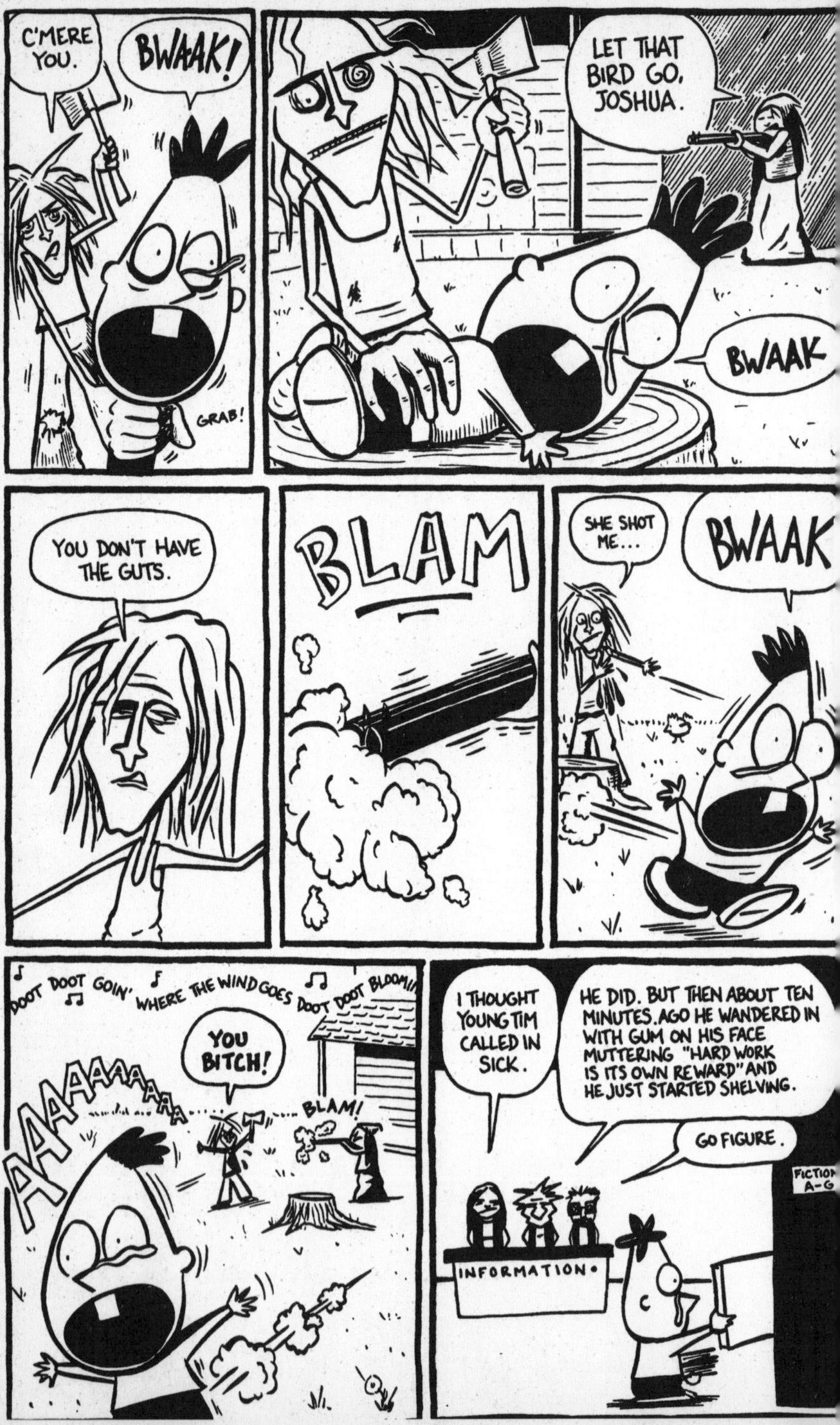

C'MERE YOU.
BWAAK!
GRAB!
LET THAT BIRD GO, JOSHUA.
BWAAK
YOU DON'T HAVE THE GUTS.
BLAM
SHE SHOT ME...
BWAAK
DOOT DOOT GOIN' WHERE THE WIND GOES DOOT DOOT BLOOM
YOU BITCH!
AAAAAAAAAAA
BLAM!
I THOUGHT YOUNG TIM CALLED IN SICK.
HE DID. BUT THEN ABOUT TEN MINUTES AGO HE WANDERED IN WITH GUM ON HIS FACE MUTTERING "HARD WORK IS ITS OWN REWARD" AND HE JUST STARTED SHELVING.
GO FIGURE.
FICTION A-G
INFORMATION

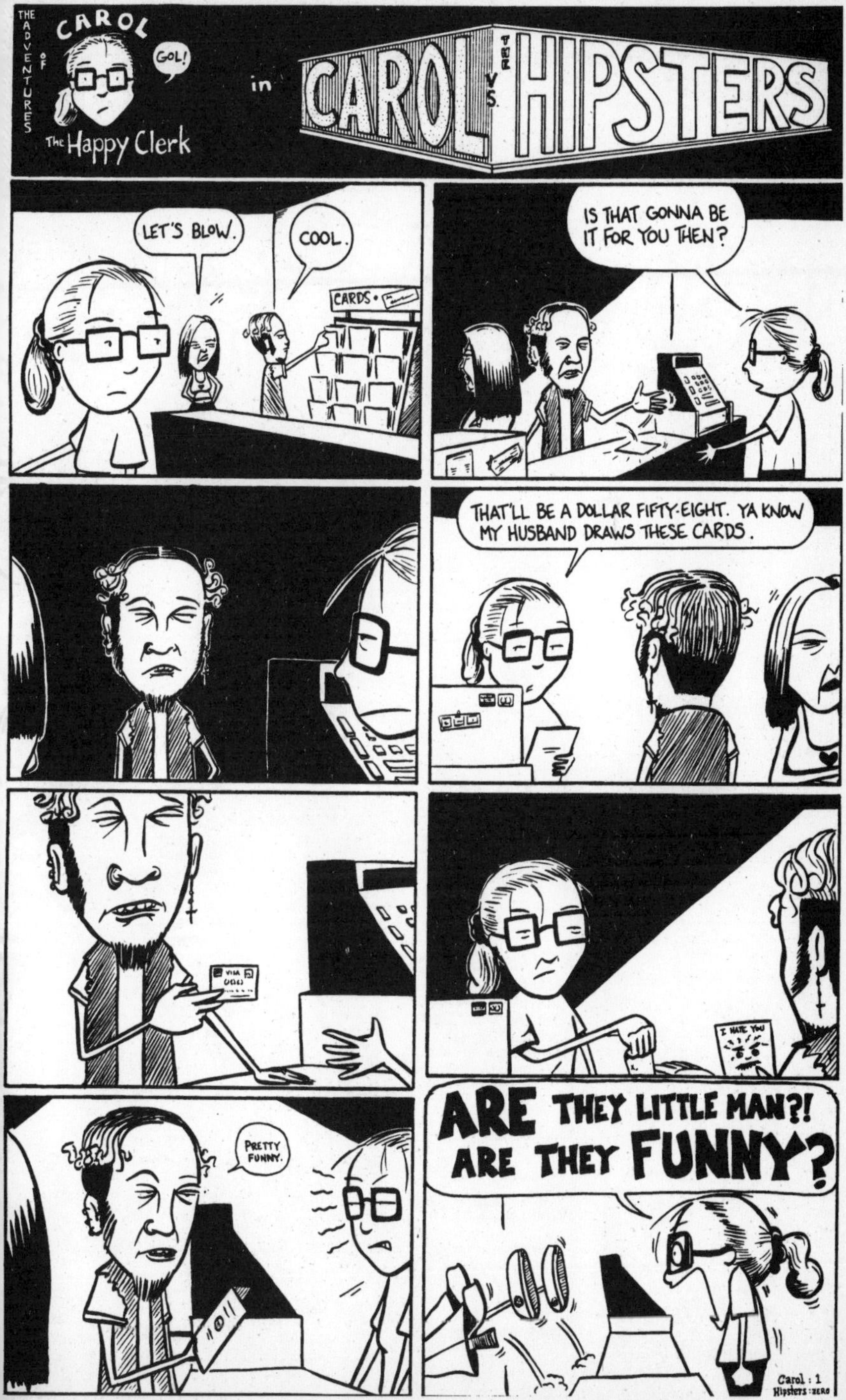
THE ADVENTURES OF CAROL
GOL!
The Happy Clerk
in
CAROL VS. THE HIPSTERS
LET'S BLOW.
COOL.
CARDS
IS THAT GONNA BE IT FOR YOU THEN?
THAT'LL BE A DOLLAR FIFTY-EIGHT. YA KNOW MY HUSBAND DRAWS THESE CARDS.
VISA
I HATE YOU
PRETTY FUNNY.
ARE THEY LITTLE MAN?! ARE THEY FUNNY?
Carol : 1
Hipsters : ZERO

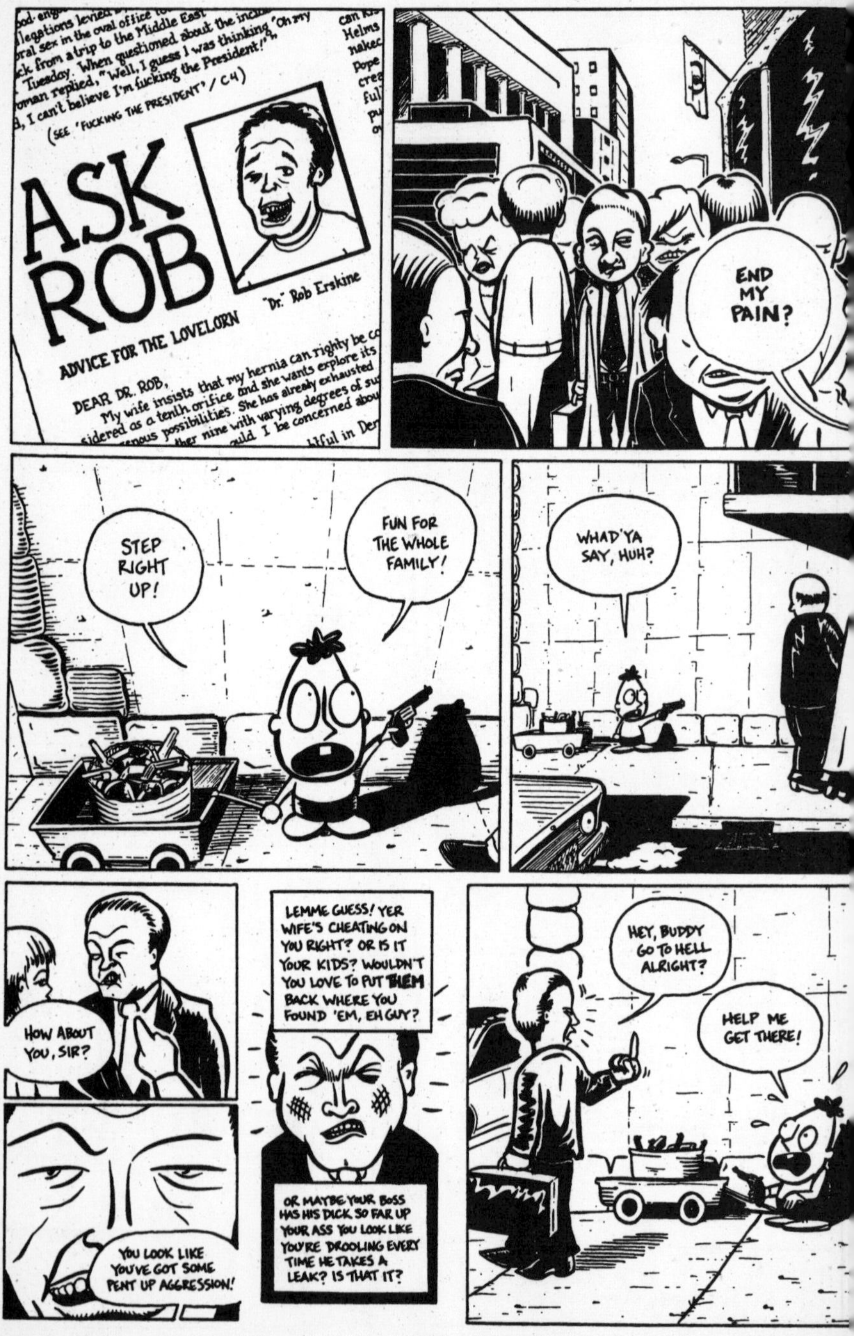
llegations levied
oral sex in the oval office
ck from a trip to the Middle East
Tuesday. When questioned about the incid
oman replied, "Well, I guess I was thinking 'Oh my
d, I can't believe I'm fucking the President'!"
(SEE 'FUCKING THE PRESIDENT' / C4)
ASK ROB
"Dr." Rob Erskine
ADVICE FOR THE LOVELORN
DEAR DR. ROB,
My wife insists that my hernia can rightly be co
sidered as a tenth orifice and she wants explore its
She has already exhausted
with varying degrees of su
I be concerned abou
END MY PAIN?
STEP RIGHT UP!
FUN FOR THE WHOLE FAMILY!
WHAD'YA SAY, HUH?
HOW ABOUT YOU, SIR?
YOU LOOK LIKE YOU'VE GOT SOME PENT UP AGGRESSION!
LEMME GUESS! YER WIFE'S CHEATING ON YOU RIGHT? OR IS IT YOUR KIDS? WOULDN'T YOU LOVE TO PUT THEM BACK WHERE YOU FOUND 'EM, EH GUY?
OR MAYBE YOUR BOSS HAS HIS DICK SO FAR UP YOUR ASS YOU LOOK LIKE YOU'RE DROOLING EVERY TIME HE TAKES A LEAK? IS THAT IT?
HEY, BUDDY GO TO HELL ALRIGHT?
HELP ME GET THERE!

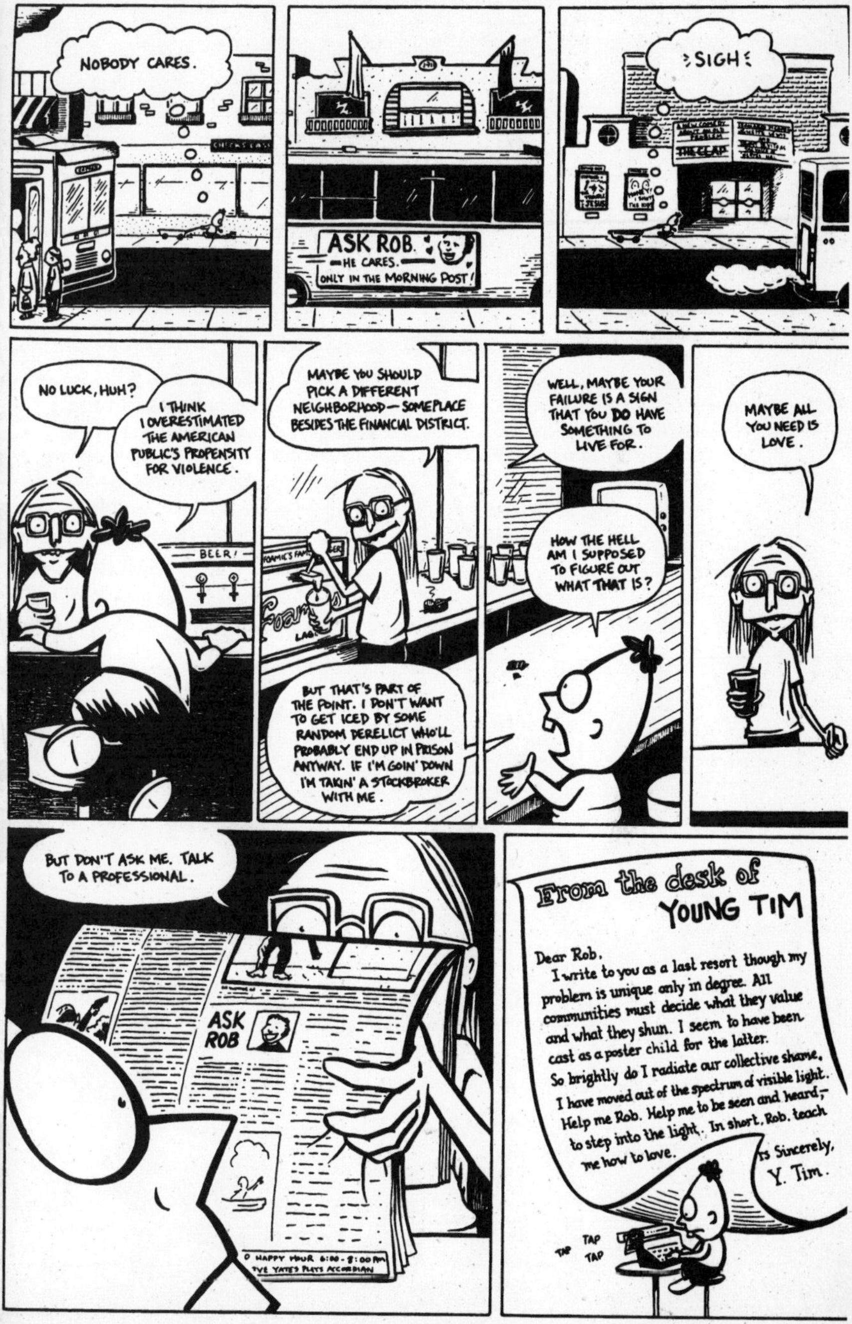
NOBODY CARES.
ASK ROB. HE CARES. ONLY IN THE MORNING POST!
SIGH
NO LUCK, HUH?
I THINK I OVERESTIMATED THE AMERICAN PUBLIC'S PROPENSITY FOR VIOLENCE.
BEER!
MAYBE YOU SHOULD PICK A DIFFERENT NEIGHBORHOOD—SOMEPLACE BESIDES THE FINANCIAL DISTRICT.
BUT THAT'S PART OF THE POINT. I DON'T WANT TO GET ICED BY SOME RANDOM DERELICT WHO'LL PROBABLY END UP IN PRISON ANYWAY. IF I'M GOIN' DOWN I'M TAKIN' A STOCKBROKER WITH ME.
WELL, MAYBE YOUR FAILURE IS A SIGN THAT YOU DO HAVE SOMETHING TO LIVE FOR.
HOW THE HELL AM I SUPPOSED TO FIGURE OUT WHAT THAT IS?
MAYBE ALL YOU NEED IS LOVE.
BUT DON'T ASK ME. TALK TO A PROFESSIONAL.
ASK ROB
HAPPY HOUR 6:00-8:00 PM
From the desk of YOUNG TIM
Dear Rob,
I write to you as a last resort though my problem is unique only in degree. All communities must decide what they value and what they shun. I seem to have been cast as a poster child for the latter. So brightly do I radiate our collective shame, I have moved out of the spectrum of visible light. Help me Rob. Help me to be seen and heard,– to step into the light. In short, Rob, teach me how to love.
rs Sincerely,
Y. Tim.
TAP TAP TAP

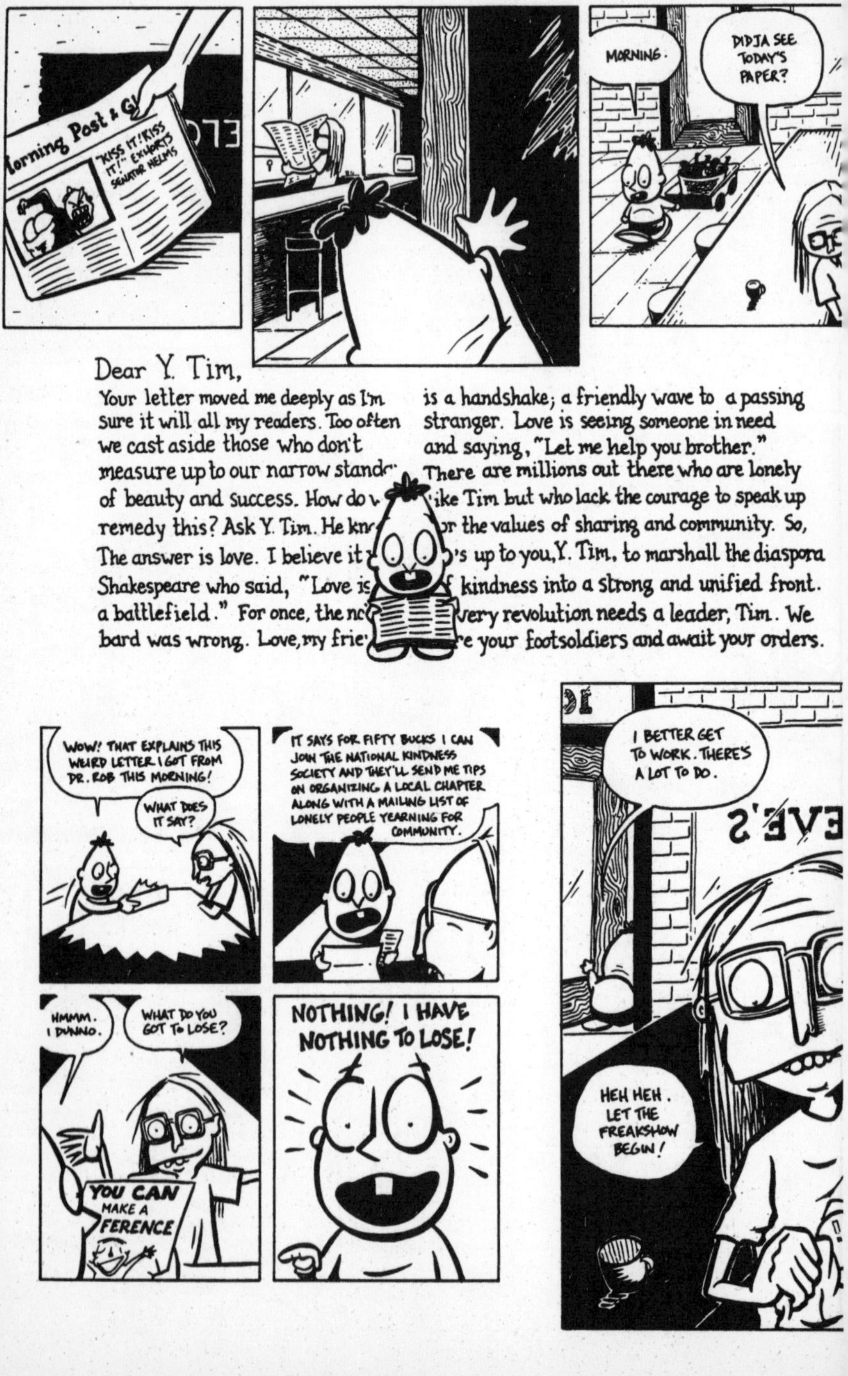
Morning Post & G
"KISS IT! KISS IT!" EXHORTS SENATOR HELMS
MORNING.
DIDJA SEE TODAY'S PAPER?
Dear Y. Tim,
Your letter moved me deeply as I'm
sure it will all my readers. Too often
we cast aside those who don't
measure up to our narrow stand
of beauty and success. How do
remedy this? Ask Y. Tim. He kn
The answer is love. I believe it
Shakespeare who said, "Love is
a battlefield." For once, the
bard was wrong. Love, my frie
is a handshake; a friendly wave to a passing
stranger. Love is seeing someone in need
and saying, "Let me help you brother."
There are millions out there who are lonely
ike Tim but who lack the courage to speak up
r the values of sharing and community. So,
's up to you, Y. Tim, to marshall the diaspora
kindness into a strong and unified front.
very revolution needs a leader, Tim. We
e your footsoldiers and await your orders.
WOW! THAT EXPLAINS THIS WEIRD LETTER I GOT FROM DR. ROB THIS MORNING!
WHAT DOES IT SAY?
IT SAYS FOR FIFTY BUCKS I CAN JOIN THE NATIONAL KINDNESS SOCIETY AND THEY'LL SEND ME TIPS ON ORGANIZING A LOCAL CHAPTER ALONG WITH A MAILING LIST OF LONELY PEOPLE YEARNING FOR COMMUNITY.
HMMM. I DUNNO.
WHAT DO YOU GOT TO LOSE?
YOU CAN MAKE A FERENCE
NOTHING! I HAVE NOTHING TO LOSE!
I BETTER GET TO WORK. THERE'S A LOT TO DO.
HEH HEH. LET THE FREAKSHOW BEGIN!

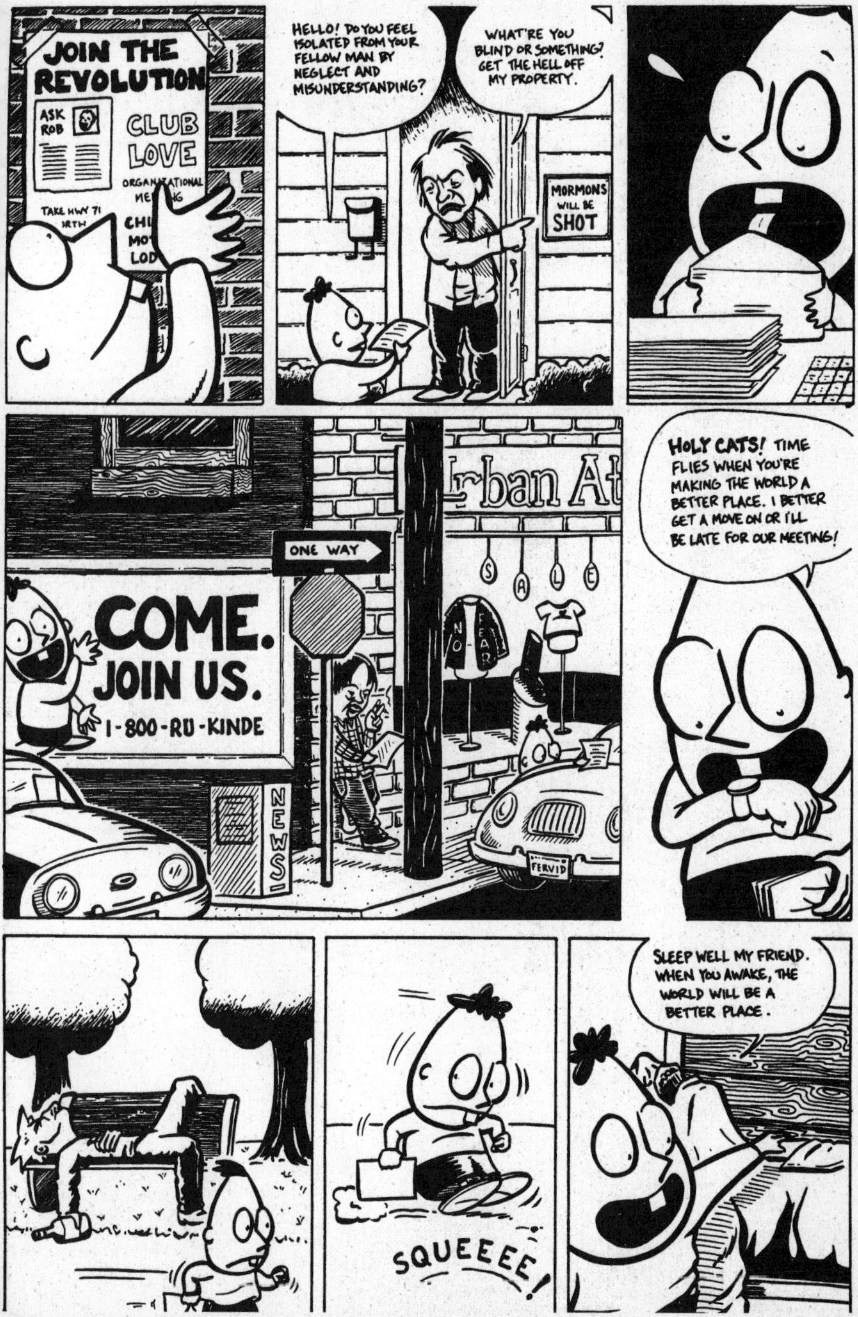
JOIN THE REVOLUTION
ASK ROB
CLUB LOVE
HELLO! DO YOU FEEL ISOLATED FROM YOUR FELLOW MAN BY NEGLECT AND MISUNDERSTANDING?
WHAT'RE YOU BLIND OR SOMETHING? GET THE HELL OFF MY PROPERTY.
MORMONS WILL BE SHOT
ONE WAY
Urban At
S A L E
COME. JOIN US. 1-800-RU-KINDE
NEWS
FERVID
HOLY CATS! TIME FLIES WHEN YOU'RE MAKING THE WORLD A BETTER PLACE. I BETTER GET A MOVE ON OR I'LL BE LATE FOR OUR MEETING!
SQUEEEE!
SLEEP WELL MY FRIEND. WHEN YOU AWAKE, THE WORLD WILL BE A BETTER PLACE.

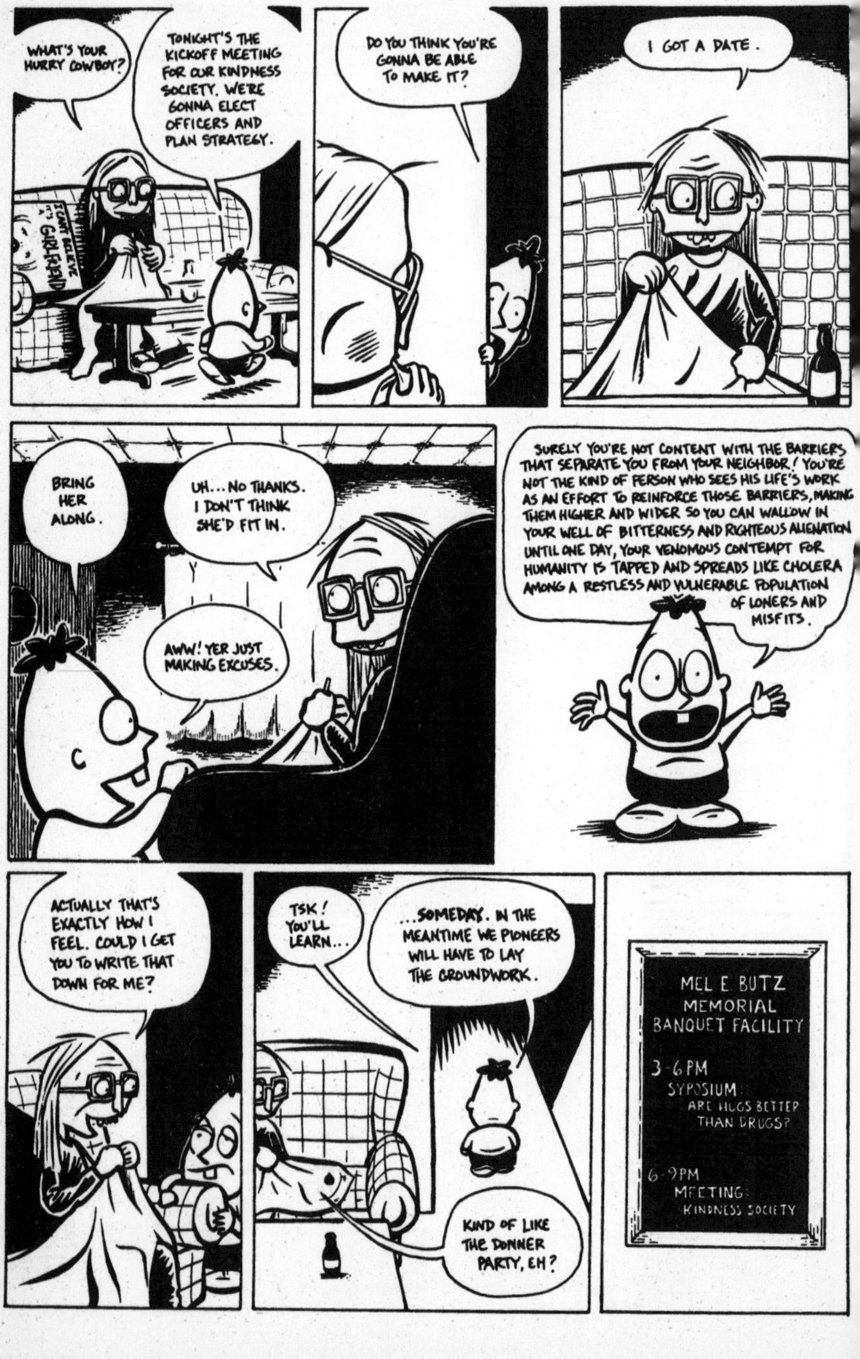
WHAT'S YOUR HURRY COWBOY?
TONIGHT'S THE KICKOFF MEETING FOR OUR KINDNESS SOCIETY. WE'RE GONNA ELECT OFFICERS AND PLAN STRATEGY.
I CAN'T BELIEVE IT'S A GIRLFRIEND
DO YOU THINK YOU'RE GONNA BE ABLE TO MAKE IT?
I GOT A DATE.
BRING HER ALONG.
UH... NO THANKS. I DON'T THINK SHE'D FIT IN.
AWW! YER JUST MAKING EXCUSES.
SURELY YOU'RE NOT CONTENT WITH THE BARRIERS THAT SEPARATE YOU FROM YOUR NEIGHBOR! YOU'RE NOT THE KIND OF PERSON WHO SEES HIS LIFE'S WORK AS AN EFFORT TO REINFORCE THOSE BARRIERS, MAKING THEM HIGHER AND WIDER SO YOU CAN WALLOW IN YOUR WELL OF BITTERNESS AND RIGHTEOUS ALIENATION UNTIL ONE DAY, YOUR VENOMOUS CONTEMPT FOR HUMANITY IS TAPPED AND SPREADS LIKE CHOLERA AMONG A RESTLESS AND VULNERABLE POPULATION OF LONERS AND MISFITS.
ACTUALLY THAT'S EXACTLY HOW I FEEL. COULD I GET YOU TO WRITE THAT DOWN FOR ME?
TSK! YOU'LL LEARN...
...SOMEDAY. IN THE MEANTIME WE PIONEERS WILL HAVE TO LAY THE GROUNDWORK.
KIND OF LIKE THE DONNER PARTY, EH?
MEL E. BUTZ MEMORIAL BANQUET FACILITY
3-6 PM SYPOSIUM: ARE HUGS BETTER THAN DRUGS?
6-9 PM MEETING: KINDNESS SOCIETY

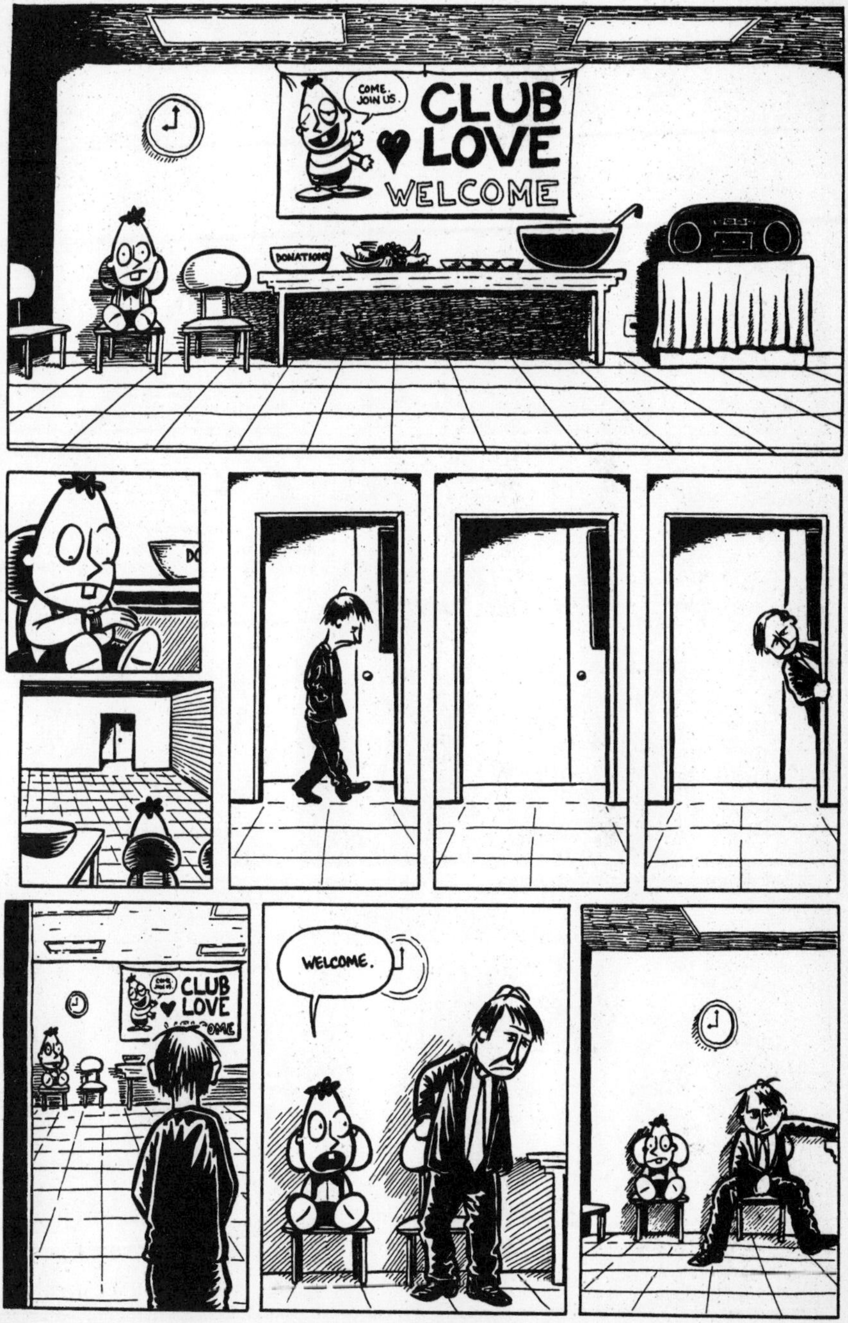
COME. JOIN US.
CLUB
LOVE
WELCOME
DONATIONS
WELCOME.

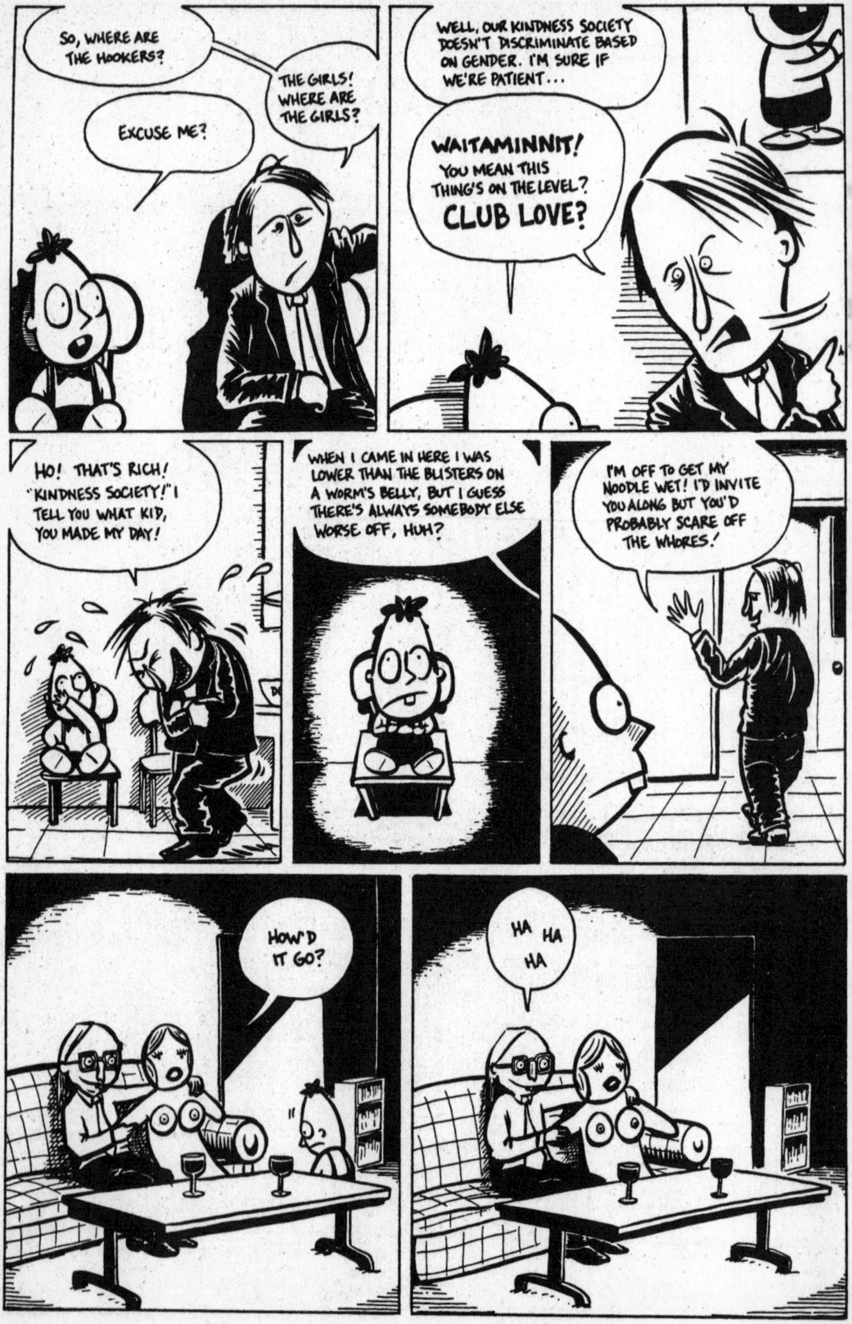

SO, WHERE ARE THE HOOKERS?
EXCUSE ME?
THE GIRLS! WHERE ARE THE GIRLS?
WELL, OUR KINDNESS SOCIETY DOESN'T DISCRIMINATE BASED ON GENDER. I'M SURE IF WE'RE PATIENT...
WAITAMINNIT! YOU MEAN THIS THING'S ON THE LEVEL? CLUB LOVE?
HO! THAT'S RICH! "KINDNESS SOCIETY!" I TELL YOU WHAT KID, YOU MADE MY DAY!
WHEN I CAME IN HERE I WAS LOWER THAN THE BLISTERS ON A WORM'S BELLY, BUT I GUESS THERE'S ALWAYS SOMEBODY ELSE WORSE OFF, HUH?
I'M OFF TO GET MY NOODLE WET! I'D INVITE YOU ALONG BUT YOU'D PROBABLY SCARE OFF THE WHORES!
HOW'D IT GO?
HA HA HA

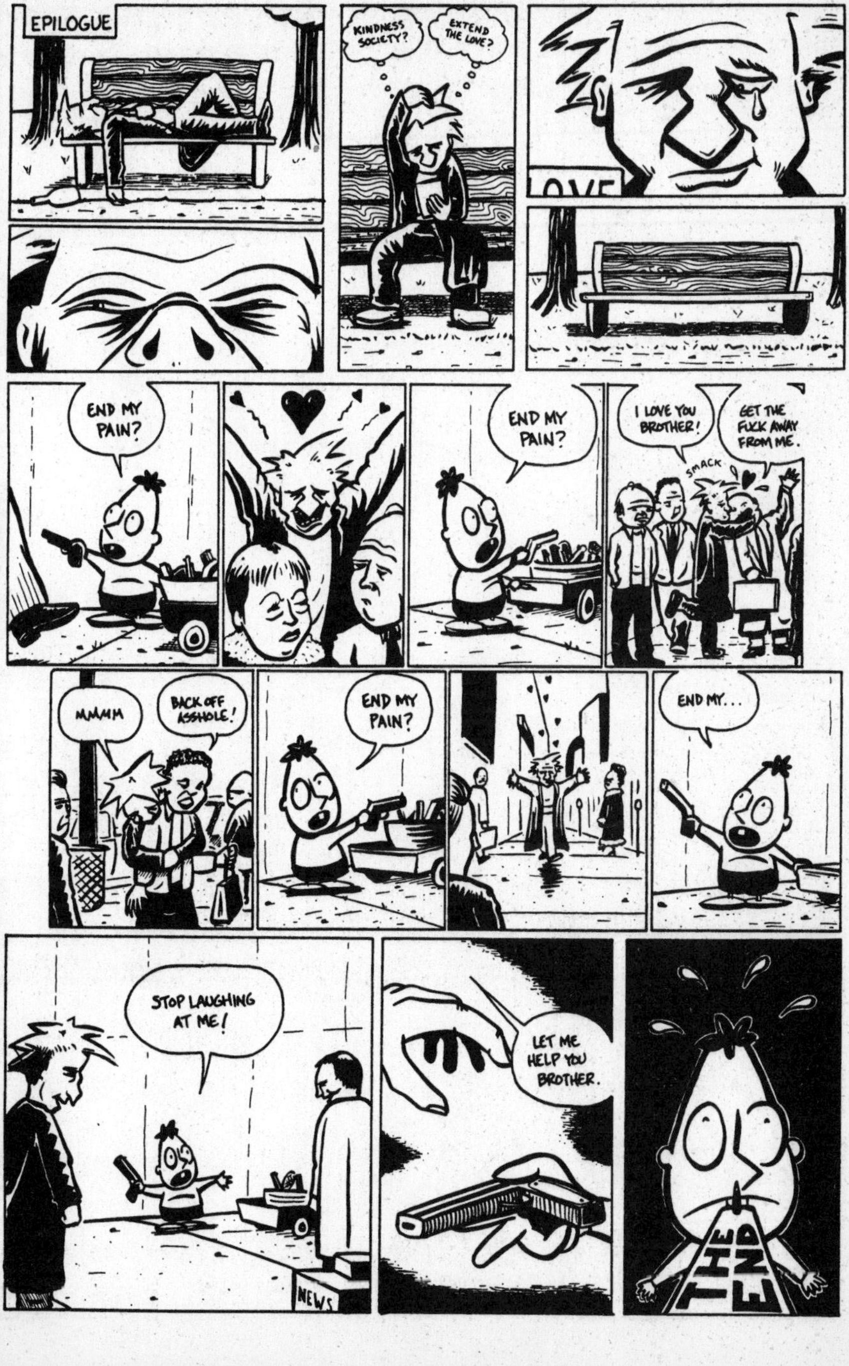
EPILOGUE
KINDNESS SOCIETY?
EXTEND THE LOVE?
LOVE
END MY PAIN?
END MY PAIN?
I LOVE YOU BROTHER!
GET THE FUCK AWAY FROM ME.
SMACK
MMMM
BACK OFF ASSHOLE!
END MY PAIN?
END MY...
STOP LAUGHING AT ME!
NEWS
LET ME HELP YOU BROTHER.
THE END

# aunt mary meets her maker

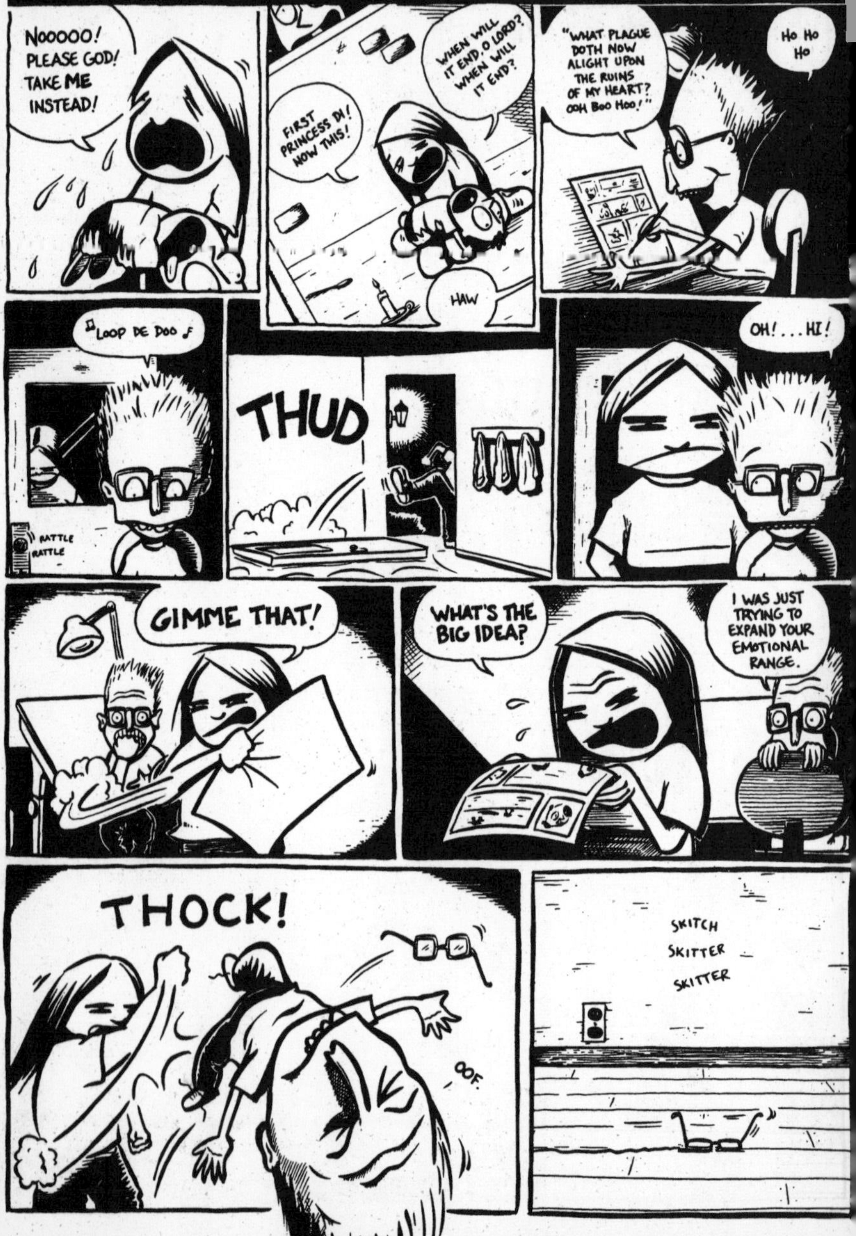
NOOOOO! PLEASE GOD! TAKE ME INSTEAD!
FIRST PRINCESS DI! NOW THIS!
WHEN WILL IT END, O LORD? WHEN WILL IT END?
HAW
"WHAT PLAGUE DOTH NOW ALIGHT UPON THE RUINS OF MY HEART? OOH BOO HOO!"
HO HO HO
LOOP DE DOO
RATTLE RATTLE
THUD
OH! ... HI!
GIMME THAT!
WHAT'S THE BIG IDEA?
I WAS JUST TRYING TO EXPAND YOUR EMOTIONAL RANGE.
THOCK!
OOF.
SKITCH
SKITTER
SKITTER

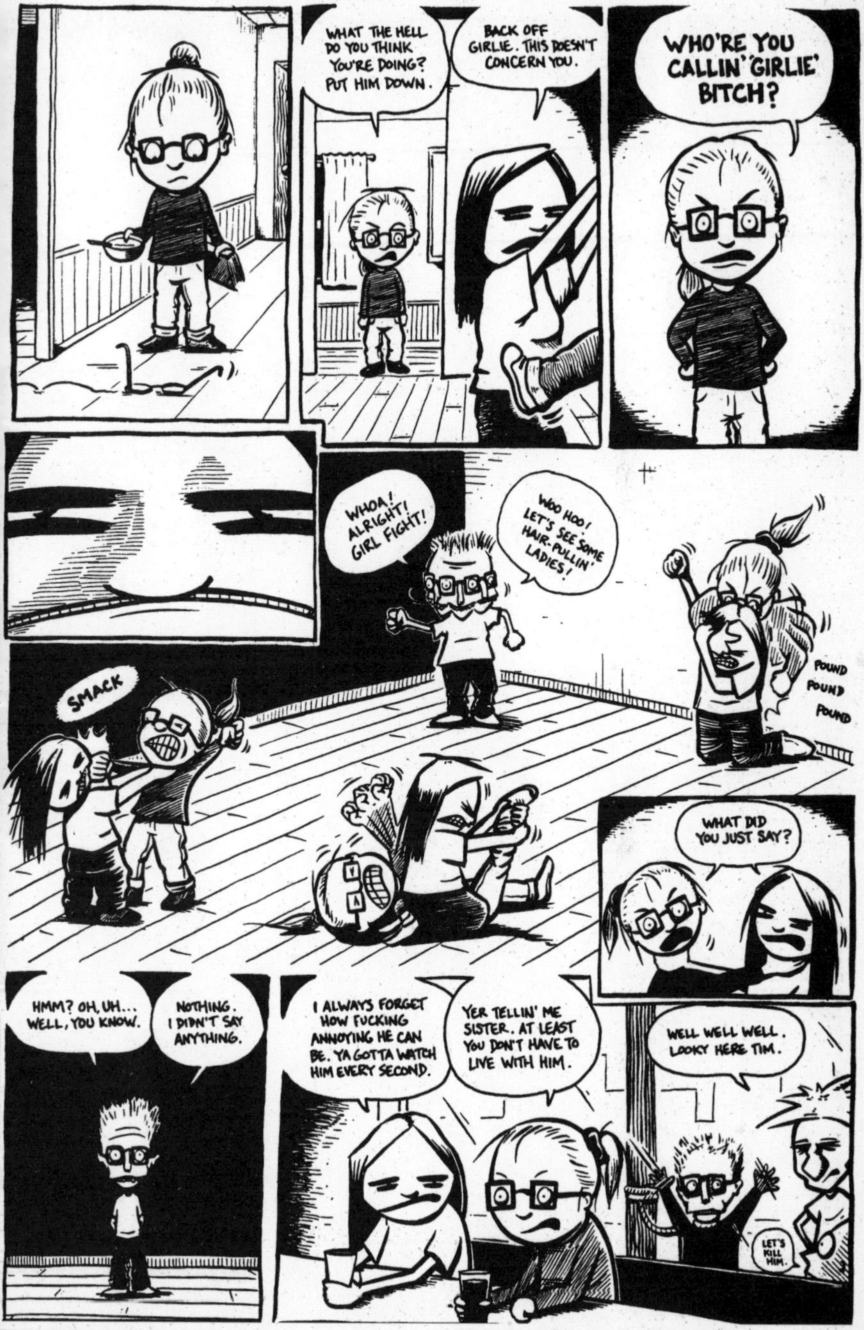
WHAT THE HELL DO YOU THINK YOU'RE DOING? PUT HIM DOWN.
BACK OFF GIRLIE. THIS DOESN'T CONCERN YOU.
WHO'RE YOU CALLIN' 'GIRLIE' BITCH?
WHOA! ALRIGHT! GIRL FIGHT!
WOO HOO! LET'S SEE SOME HAIR-PULLIN' LADIES!
POUND
POUND
POUND
SMACK
WHAT DID YOU JUST SAY?
HMM? OH, UH... WELL, YOU KNOW.
NOTHING. I DIDN'T SAY ANYTHING.
I ALWAYS FORGET HOW FUCKING ANNOYING HE CAN BE. YA GOTTA WATCH HIM EVERY SECOND.
YER TELLIN' ME SISTER. AT LEAST YOU DON'T HAVE TO LIVE WITH HIM.
WELL WELL WELL. LOOKY HERE TIM.
LET'S KILL HIM.

! P.O. Box 8326
Ann Arbor, MI 48107
pgarner@umich.edu